LIVING A DREAM

LIVING A DREAM

BY

SUZANNE GIESEMANN

Aventine Press

Published by Aventine Press
1023 4th Ave #204
Chula Vista, CA 91914, USA

www.aventinepress.com

ISBN: 1-59330-220-7
Printed in the United States of America

For Ty,

who continues to make my dreams come true

and

For Frank and Dee,

for showing us the way

CONTENTS

PROLOGUE

August, 2003; The North Atlantic Ocean, off the coast of Newfoundland

Forty-six feet is a lot of boat, but seventy feet is a lot of whale.

I sat on the narrow seat at the bow, gripping the rail. My feet dangled over the water like two pieces of bait. Moments earlier, the enormous creature had played submarine, diving beneath the surface to evade detection. Now we and the whale were on converging courses.

I glanced behind me where Ty hung onto the shrouds, camera around his neck. He was as anxious as I for a close-up view, but we were nervous, too. We'd both read stories of boats that had sunk to the bottom after striking a whale. Now there was one right out here with us... *maybe even under us...* and we had asked for it.

Ever since passing Cape Cod, whale-watching boats had zipped past us, their rails lined with eager tourists. Rather than pay forty bucks a head to be jostled by elbows, we held out for a private show from our own boat's deck. In town after town, from New England to Nova Scotia, signs advertised guaranteed sightings. But without local knowledge, our own whale-hunting guaranteed nothing but frustration and disappointment.

Admittedly, we'd seen a few pilot whales along the way, but they were nothing more than oversized dolphins. A minke in the distance off Casco Bay was smaller than our boat -- nothing to write home about.

I wanted Jacques Cousteau.

Day after day I'd peered out at the endless ocean, hoping this would be The Day. A ripple on the horizon would cause me to raise the binoculars, wondering if I'd seen a dorsal fin or merely the shadow of a wave.

Now off the coast of Newfoundland, ten miles west of Fortune Bay, our fortune turned.

It was my watch. Ty was facing aft, his head buried in a book. We'd raised the sails, but the winds were light, so we were motor-sailing to put some miles under the keel. I checked our position on the GPS and compared it with the paper chart by my side. Over a thousand miles of ocean lay between us and our home waters of the Chesapeake Bay.

I casually checked the radar. As usual, there were no contacts in these remote waters, and the screen was blank. We hadn't seen another boat since the day before, but I lazily scanned the horizon just to be safe. Suddenly, my eyes stopped mid-sweep. Lulled by the warm sun and the drone of the engine, my immediate reaction was less than coordinated.

I jumped up, arms waving overhead like a groupie at an Elvis concert, and sputtered, "Flukes! FLUKES!"

Ty dropped his book and sprang to his feet.

"A whale?"

"Yes! And if it showed its flukes, it's gotta be a humpback!"

It was the mother lode of mammals. A Kodak Moment in the making.

Now that I'd seen it, I knew this was no mere shadow on a wave. There was no mistaking the curved black tail of a real, live whale.

"Where was it?" Ty asked, just as a plume of water spouted into the air half a mile ahead.

"Does that answer your question?" I answered excitedly.

Ty nodded toward the throttle. "Give it a little more juice and head over that way."

I increased speed and reset the autopilot. While Ty went below for his Nikon, I grabbed the digital camera we kept in the cockpit for just such a moment.

We both peered anxiously at the spot where the whale's spout had dispersed into a wispy curtain of mist. Then, off to the right, a shiny body surfaced. Rolling in slow motion from head to tail, it seemed to go on and on, like one section of a giant, undulating sea monster.

"See how he's arching?" Ty asked. "That means he's getting ready to sound.

Sure enough, the whale's back curved even more sharply. As it did, those flukes I'd waited so long to see flicked out of the water and paused just long enough to give us the perfect postcard pose. I squealed loudly and we snapped our shutters like paparazzi on Oscar night until the tail slipped beneath the waves.

"Did you get a good shot?" Ty asked.

"Perfect! How about you?"

"Awesome."

"Do you think our engine scared him away?" I asked, disappointed that he'd disappeared so quickly.

"Could be. And once they dive, they can be down for half an hour."

We stared longingly at the spot where he'd gone down, then shrugged our shoulders. The show was short, but it was a gift to treasure.

Resuming our course, the excitement lingered, and I chattered on like a school kid. Finally settling down, I stared at the horizon and laughed at myself, remembering my spastic reaction and the high-pitched squeals I'd made when the whale dived.

Some mature, retired naval officer you are, Suzanne.

I shook my head. My unflappable husband had enjoyed the show as much as I, but unlike me, he had kept his dignity! A Captain, retired several years now, Ty certainly fit my image of a distinguished naval officer. He still kept his hair trimmed to military standards and exuded an aura of authority. Now, after one of the most exciting moments of our cruise, he was back to reading his book as if nothing had happened. I knew he wouldn't rehash the experience in his mind a hundred times like I would.

Call me greedy, but one sighting was not enough. I wanted more! I'd heard that whale hunting could be addictive, and now I understood why.

Ty glanced up and caught me looking at him. He laid his book in his lap, crossed his hands, and announced matter-of-factly, "I want more whales."

I grinned back at him. Our styles might be different, but we were two of a kind.

Settling back behind the wheel, I reveled in the warm, fresh breeze. Cooler weather had been creeping in lately, and the frightening fall gales that battered the unforgiving Newfoundland coast were just around the corner. But today was warm enough to take down our boat's canvas and vinyl cockpit enclosure and soak up the sunshine.

I realized how lucky I'd been to catch a glimpse of those flukes in one tiny degree of our 360 degree horizon. We'd waited weeks for such an experience. Expecting more whale sightings in the short time we had left in these northern waters didn't seem reasonable. But the poor odds didn't keep me from focusing my attention outside the lifelines much more than normal for the next few hours.

I should have bought a lottery ticket.

Not one mile away, a geyser of mist shot straight into the air. I instantly grabbed the throttle and pulled it back. The change in engine noise elicited a predictable reaction from the captain.

"What's wrong?" Ty asked worriedly, instantly jumping to his feet.

I pointed to port. "A spout!"

"More?"

"Yeah! Let's go, okay?"

These little detours delayed arrival at our destination, but what was the hurry? This kind of sighting was one of the reasons we'd come here – for an experience most people only dream about.

"Absolutely, but let's turn the engine off this time," he suggested.

Now in stealth mode, we altered course and trimmed the sails for a broad reach. I willed the winds to stay steady, propelling us silently toward the spot where not just one, but *two* enormous bodies were now swimming on the surface!

"Those aren't humpbacks," Ty announced. "They're not showing their flukes when they dive."

I pulled out our field guide for help.

"They look like minkes, but minkes are medium-sized and you can't see their blow very well."

We'd seen these guys spout straight up from a mile away, and they were huge, easily larger than our boat. According to our book, a large whale with a straight blow, curved dorsal fin, and arched back with no tail visible was a finback. I quickly turned to the section on fins, and the picture exactly matched the two creatures that were growing closer with each passing wave.

"Holy mackerel, Ty! Fin whales average 70 feet long! They're the second largest in the world, after the blue whale!"

He peered through the binoculars. "Those two are easily that big."

I had to remind myself to breathe.

A flash of motion caught my eye close abeam. Dolphins!

We'd seen plenty of porpoises on this trip, but they'd been strangely standoffish. Every attempt to take their picture had resulted in photos of empty water as they disappeared too quickly for a shot. But today was not your ordinary day at sea.

At least ten white-beaked dolphins decided our boat could join their parade as they, too, swam toward the whales. I clambered to the bow, holding tightly to the lifelines while Ty stayed aft to tweak the sails and steer. Stepping in front of the forestay, I climbed out to the forward-most point of the boat and sat on the small perch that jutted over the water. Now I had an unimpeded view of these striking creatures.

Unlike the all-gray bottlenose, these guys were an eye-catching mixture of dark gray, black, and white. We'd never seen dolphins with these markings before, but we hadn't sailed in their North Atlantic habitat until now. The dolphins weren't used to spotting species Homo Sapiens, either. They reacted to our presence with equal enthusiasm, zipping back and forth under our keel, then bounding in front of us as if to say, "Come on! The show's up ahead!"

And indeed, it was. Suddenly the water before us churned with not just ten, but dozens of dolphins. In their midst the two whales lolled on the surface. Beneath them must have been one heck of a big school of fish, because we were witnessing a feeding frenzy. In their excitement, several dolphins vaulted completely out of the water, twisting and somersaulting in moves that would make an Olympic diver jealous. Our chorus of oohs and aahs accompanied the amazing acrobatics.

As we approached to within a hundred yards, the whales arched higher and disappeared. Hoping they wouldn't stay down too long, Ty altered course to the right so our paths would meet when they came back up. We looked at each other warily, neither sure this was a good move, but neither willing to miss getting as close as we could to these giants.

Now we were in the midst of the excited dolphins, so close we could lean over the side and touch them, but there was no sign of the whales. Time seemed to slow. Where and when would they come up? I'd thought I wanted an intimate encounter, but how close was too close?

"There! To starboard!" Ty shouted. One of the finbacks had passed us unseen and was now a safe, but disappointing hundred yards on the opposite side.

"Should we tack and try to catch up to it again?" I asked.

Before Ty could answer, a *whoosh* as loud as a wave crashing on a reef pierced the air. Whipping our heads to the left, Ty gasped and I couldn't help but scream. The sucker was one whale-length from our hull, swimming parallel to our path. He'd surfaced just close enough, as if he knew our personal comfort zone, then stayed beside us long enough to show off his bulk in all its grandeur. When he was satisfied we'd snapped enough pictures, he spouted one last time and slid out of sight.

Just as quickly as we'd come upon the scene, the show was over, leaving us high, yet drained from the adrenaline rush. We resumed our course, but left the engine off, content to soak up the silence as the wind filled our sails.

I checked our position on the GPS and compared it with the paper chart by my side. Then, I casually glanced at the radar. Just like before, there were no contacts. The screen was still blank, but that no longer meant there was nothing out there.

One

CHANGING TACKS

November, 1999; Puget Sound, Washington

The snow-capped Olympic mountains provided a majestic backdrop for our late Fall sail. The air was crisp and cool. A harbor seal poked his head out of the water and warily watched as we glided past on a fast beam reach. It was about as perfect a day as you could ask for.

Then Ty turned to me and said, "Suzanne, we need to talk."

That is one of those phrases that can't possibly be followed by anything good.

"I know, I know. I need to put about two more coats of varnish on the handrails," I said, using humor to mask a feeling of impending doom.

"The handrails are fine," he said, easing the jib sheet and filling the foresail as we rounded a point. "The problem is, I need a job."

This, I knew, was nothing to joke about. Ty had given up a challenging job as a defense analyst in Washington, DC to accompany me to my command tour on the Naval Base in Bangor, Washington. Unfortunately, there were few executive jobs for him in this mainly blue collar area.

"Marine surveying's not cutting it, huh?" I asked the question, already knowing the answer.

"I enjoy that," Ty said as he adjusted the sails, "but it's not steady work. Most of all, it's not very mentally stimulating."

I nodded my head, having sensed how restless he'd become, rumbling around our large Navy quarters while I interacted with my colleagues all day.

"So what do you have in mind?"

"I want to see what's available back in DC."

I took a deep breath. We loved the Seattle area, and had bought a home here. I had lined up a follow-on assignment at Puget Sound Naval Shipyard, but I didn't have orders in hand yet.

"If you're not happy, then Washington, DC it is," I said. My marriage came first.

He nodded his head solemnly.

Approaching our marina, we headed up into the wind. Working together, we furled the jib, then Ty went forward to lower the mainsail. No doubt about it, we were a good team.

"Whose turn is it to take her in?" Ty asked.

"I think you did it last time."

"Then you've got it," he smiled.

"Aye, aye, Sir!"

"You call your husband 'Sir'?" We both laughed at the private joke. Years earlier someone had asked me that same question after overhearing me talking to Ty on the phone. I answered with, "Yes, and he calls me 'Ma'am.'" These courteous forms of address were ingrained in both of us after full Navy careers, but they'd become terms of endearment as well. There was no one I respected more than my husband.

As Ty stood on deck with a dock line in hand, I pulled into the narrow fairway between two piers. Turning the rudder hard to starboard, I carefully maneuvered the 36-foot boat into her slip. Ty stepped onto the finger pier, looped the spring line around a cleat, then did the same with the bow line while I handled the stern.

"Well done," he said.

"I had a good coach," I said, beaming. I was lucky to have a former destroyer captain to teach me boat handling. With twenty six years of training junior officers, Ty was a skilled and patient teacher. Unlike most private vessels, where husbands under stress were known to yell at their wives, we rarely raised our voices on *Liberty*.

I stood back and looked at our beloved boat. She was aptly named, representing not only our patriotism, but the freedom that came from being on the water. It was also a great play on words. In the Navy, if you're not on duty, you're on *Liberty*. All my sailors knew if they couldn't find the skipper, she was probably on *Liberty*.

"We can't sell this boat," I said.

Ty stepped beside me and appraised her. "I know. I thought of that."

"Too bad we can't sail her around."

"I thought of that, too," Ty said, and I knew he'd like nothing better.

"It would cost a fortune to truck her across."

"Yep."

We looked at each other. Ty's two daughters were grown. I had no children of my own. The boat was our baby. Fortune or not, she was going with us.

"Ok. You got the lines?" I asked, knowing it was a rhetorical question.

"Got 'em," Ty replied.

We usually worked together to secure the boat, but setting out extra dock lines and tying them off just-so was Ty's thing. Everybody has their own way of doing things, and this was one area in which my husband was meticulous. I knew that once he was done, he would check the lines at least one more time before leaving.

Sure enough, as we walked away from the boat, heading for the parking lot, Ty stopped. "Gimme a minute. I want to check the lines one more time."

Rolling my eyes behind his back, I set my bags on the dock and waited. One minute turned into two as he tweaked the ropes, then stood at the bow to make sure the boat was perfectly centered.

All right already! I thought the words, but kept my mouth shut. The lines looked good enough to me!

Ty wiped his hands and picked up his gear. "Good to go!"

"Roger that, Captain!"

* * *

Finding a job proved far too easy. Within a month, Ty had accepted an offer with a company who wanted him to start right away. I was happy for him, but depressed at the thought of being separated for the four months until I was due to transfer. We arranged to spend no more than three weeks apart at a time, even though the expense of flying cross-country would be high.

The first weeks apart were the worst. I rattled around the cold house, missing his smile and warmth. Email and the telephone kept me sane.

"I used to look forward to weekends," I told him on our nightly call, "but they drag on forever when you're not here."

"I know what you mean. At least you can go sailing."

"Yeah, right. Without you?"

"Sure. Why don't you take a couple of your girlfriends out this Saturday?"

I stared at the phone, dumbfounded. *Is he for real?* I couldn't imagine any other man who would suggest such a thing.

"You can't be serious? You'd trust me to take her out without you?"

"Of course! You're a Coast Guard licensed captain, too, you know."

"I know, but…"

"Go ahead, Suzanne! You'll have a ball."

He was right. There wasn't a thing I couldn't do on the boat. I was a sailing instructor in my spare time, for goodness' sake, but for some reason it had never occurred to me to take our own boat out without him. Now that he'd suggested it, the idea started to grow on me. What a confidence builder it would be!

"Ok! I'll do it!" I agreed, no longer dreading the coming weekend.

I had no trouble finding two friends who were as excited as I about "girl's day"on the water. Diane and Julia were glad for a chance to go sailing. After an uneventful departure from the slip, we were on our way.

Diane had done some sailing in the past, and didn't need much instruction. Everything was new to Julia, but she was eager to learn. I showed her how to tell which direction the wind was coming from, then put her at the wheel.

"Keep the bow of the boat pointed right into the wind while I raise the sails. There'll be a lot of flapping and banging at first, but that's normal."

She did just fine. By the end of the day, everyone had trimmed the sails and taken a turn at the wheel.

Both women were also naval officers, and they were interested in my plans to get assigned near Ty.

"Have you called your detailer yet?" Julia asked.

"Not yet," I answered. "There's probably no shortage of jobs in Washington, but I don't think I want to leave it up to her."

"Wise decision," Diane answered. We all knew how the system worked. I could sit back and hope my detailer offered me something I'd like, or I could pull a few strings. It wasn't something I was totally comfortable with, but I was willing to do anything to get back in the same house with Ty as soon as possible.

"Do you know anyone who can help?" Julia asked.

"As a matter of fact, I do." I turned to Diane. "Remember Captain Fry?"

"Of course I do!" Diane and I had met while serving in the Pentagon five years earlier.

"What's he doing now?" she asked.

Before answering her question, I turned to Julia to explain. "I was the Chief of Naval Operations' protocol officer and Captain Fry was his Executive Assistant." Looking back at Diane, I explained, "Captain Fry is now *Vice Admiral* Fry, and he's Director of Operations for the Joint Staff."

Both women whistled. The Joint Staff was the organization with members from all Services that coordinated military planning at the highest level. If the three-star admiral was willing to intervene on my behalf, my chances of good orders were very high.

"I'd say you'll have no trouble at all finding a job." Julia laughed.

"Cross your fingers," I said. "Now, if you'll give me a hand, we'll get these sails down and head in."

Rounding the turn at the end of the marina piers, I took a deep breath. It was slack water, so the current wouldn't affect my landing. The wind would be blowing me off the pier, though, so I'd have to come in fast and flat. Gripping the wheel, I said a quick prayer, and headed in.

"This is a little different than parking a car," I said, talking to ease my nerves.

"Yeah. No brakes!" Diane replied.

Any landing where you don't hit something is a good one, and I smiled with a mixture of pride and relief as we snugged in the dock lines. *Safe and sound.* I shut down the engine and successfully fought the urge to shout, "I did it!"

As I secured the boat, I went through the familiar checklist, leaving everything exactly as I'd found it.

"All set?" I asked my friends, when I'd handed up the last duffel bag from below.

"Ready," they replied.

I locked the hatch and stepped ashore. We made it ten feet down the pier, when a niggling doubt made me hesitate, then stop.

"Gimme just a second, ok? I want to double check the lines."

Hearing my own words, I winced. *Did I really say that?* I sounded just like Ty!

With my girlfriends waiting on the pier, I walked back and looked over my work. Suddenly I understood. It was easy to leave without a thought when someone else accepted responsibility, but it was a whole different ball game with the weight on my own shoulders. If strong winds came up and she wasn't secured well enough, any damage to the boat would be all my fault. Double checking that *Liberty* was perfectly centered in the slip, I laughed at myself and swore I'd never roll my eyes at Ty again.

Two

DREAM JOB

I stood on my toes, trying to see over the crowd in front of me as the passengers filed far too slowly off the plane. The thump in my chest followed only a nano-second behind the first sighting of Ty's smiling face as he came into view.

"Hey you!" I said as we greeted each other with a hug and kiss.

"This living apart stuff stinks," Ty said.

"You're telling me!"

Ty took my hand and we walked toward the baggage claim. "Have you heard back from Admiral Fry?"

"As a matter of fact, he called while you were somewhere over Kansas."

"And?" Ty stopped and waited expectantly.

I was all smiles. "I report to the Joint Staff in May."

"Are you serious? Ty asked, hugging me a second time. "What's the job?"

"Well, that's the thing. I'll be doing protocol again, but at least it gets me back to Washington."

Ty nodded his head in understanding. While protocol could be an exciting job, he knew I didn't really care for all the picky rules. Most of my Navy colleagues were driving ships or flying airplanes, but as a protocol officer, my biggest concern would be who should be invited to official dinners and who got to sit at the head table.

"It's an important job, Suzanne, and you'll be directly supporting the Chairman of the Joint Chiefs of Staff."

"I know, but *protocol…*" In my mind, it didn't command respect.

I'd spent my whole Navy career struggling to feel worthy. When I joined, women had only recently been authorized to serve on ships, and sea duty assignments were hard to come by. Eager to be an officer in any capacity, I gladly accepted a commission to serve ashore as a General Unrestricted Line Officer.

Imagine. My male colleagues were *warriors*. I was a *GURL*.

In the politically-correct years that followed, somebody wised up and gave us a more suitable name: Fleet Support Officers. Soon women were allowed on all surface ships, but by this time, I was too senior to start at the bottom of the shipboard hierarchy. Going to sea was not an option for us, and over the years we FSOs became dinosaurs – a dying breed.

No matter. I continued to serve ashore and wore my uniform proudly. I joked that I was a jack-of-all-trades and master of none, having worked in intelligence, plans and policy, training, administration, public affairs, operations…and protocol.

"Yep, it's back to guest lists and place cards again," I told Ty

*   *   *

When you're a Commanding Officer, you are king. Even though the Pentagon was impressive, I hadn't counted on the let-down of moving from my private office back in Bangor to a small cubicle in "the pit," working side-by-side with five other protocol officers. The autonomy and decision-making authority I'd had as CO was a thing of the past under the close scrutiny of the Director of Protocol, Lieutenant Colonel Earl Wallace. He was an Air Force officer the same rank as I, and his leadership style made be bristle.

In a previous assignment as protocol officer to the Chief of Naval Operations, the Navy's top officer, I'd been a one-woman show. I called the shots and made things happen. I spoke to Admiral Boorda multiple times a day, discussing his desires and preferences. Now I had a lieutenant colonel telling me how to do my job and jealously guarding access to the Chairman like a pit-bull.

I'd been in the new job a month when Colonel Wallace announced, "You've been planning Major General Harris' promotion ceremony, so I want you to brief the Chairman on his role in it."

I was finally going to meet the Big Man. And he was truly *big*. General Shelton stood six feet five inches tall and was 210 pounds of solid grit. An Army Special Forces officer with a chiseled face, he was an intimidating figure in any setting. Sitting in his cavernous office with four silver stars on each shoulder, he caused even senior officers to take a deep breath before addressing him.

Now it was my turn. Having been given little notice and no guidance about how to brief the general, I stood in his doorway and hesitated. With Colonel Wallace standing behind me, I squared my shoulders and strode across the plush burgundy carpet. I stopped directly in front of the large mahogany desk covered with folders marked "Top Secret" in bright red.

General Shelton didn't look up, so I plunged in. "Good morning, Sir. I'm Commander Giesemann, one of your new protocol officers. I'm here to brief you on General Harris' promotion ceremony which you'll be presiding over in five minutes."

As I spoke, the general's aide slipped past me and opened a closet door next to his private washroom. She pulled out a green uniform coat weighted down with glittering insignia and colorful ribbons, and held it in front of her expectantly. The coat came down to her knees.

The general looked up from his papers, glanced at the colonel, then nodded at me.

"Go ahead."

I had briefed plenty of senior officers in my career, and vowed not to let this giant of a man fluster me, even if he was the leader of the entire United States Military. With a confident voice, I began, "Sir, you will be promoting Major General Harris to Lieutenant General today. Chaplain Bates will give the invocation, then you will deliver your remarks, which the speechwriter has placed on the podium. Following your remarks, I will read the promotion order."

Nobody seemed to find fault with my approach, so I pressed on.

"Sir, the plan in your daybook states that next you and Mrs. Harris will pin the third star on his shoulderboards. But there's been a change. General Harris has asked that his wife and his mother pin the stars on instead."

I waited at attention while the Chairman digested this last bit of information. Finally he spoke.

"So he doesn't want me to pin on the star?"

"No, Sir."

He thoughtfully nodded his head, then stated with finality, "Then I'm not going to do it."

The air in the office evaporated.

My mouth momentarily pursed, but I gave no other outward indication of my shock. Inside, my mind was racing.

What do you mean you're not going to do it? There are fifty family members and senior officers standing across the hall sweating in that crowded room, waiting for you to preside!

My military training held me back, but I wasn't about to just cave in and say, "Aye, aye, Sir!"

Instead, I stood there, staring dumbly at those four glittering stars.

Out of the corner of my eye I could see that the aide's eyes were as big as plates.

General Shelton looked from me to Colonel Wallace, and back again, expressionless. He reached over, picked up a fresh file from his in-box, and stated, "Let's get on with it, then," effectively dismissing me as he got back to work.

I stood frozen in place, glancing at Colonel Wallace, whose face mirrored my surprise. The aide shifted her weight from one foot to another, undecided if she should hang up the coat or not.

Just as I was beginning to pray for the floor to swallow me up so I wouldn't have to face the crowd across the hall, General Shelton looked up from his papers. Leaning forward, he squinted at me and drawled slowly in his thick North Carolina accent, "I got you *good*, didn't I?"

If I was dumbfounded before, you could have knocked me over with a feather now.

It was all a joke? He was just messing with me?

The Chairman of the Joint Chiefs of Staff was enjoying himself. "You were speechless!" he laughed, as he stood and took his enormous coat from the greatly relieved aide.

Now smiling, I followed the general out the door to the ceremony, having learned a valuable lesson about the man: he may seem bigger than life, but he was human and enjoyed a good joke.

Colonel Wallace fell in step beside me. "I knew he was kidding all along," he whispered.

Sure you did, Earl. Sure you did.

* * *

Once a month the Chairman hosted a visit by his counterpart from a foreign country. These visits paid huge dividends in military relations and were given great attention by all concerned. There were impressive honor ceremonies to welcome the guest, followed by briefings, tours, and luncheons, all of which had to be planned with precision.

The culmination of each visit was a formal dinner, hosted by General and Mrs. Shelton. The guest lists included senior officers from the Joint Staff, VIPs from the visiting country's embassy, and a smattering of Congressmen, journalists, and influential businessmen. I was regularly assigned to plan these visits from start to finish.

When hosting these important dinners, General Shelton preferred to have a Master of Ceremonies run the evening. The MC followed a set script, inviting the guests to their seats, introducing the major players, and presenting General Shelton when it was time for his remarks. It seemed to me that the officer who planned the visit and was most familiar with the guests' foreign names, should be the one to stand at the podium.

Colonel Wallace wouldn't hear of it. He took over once a dinner started. If the event was held at a major hotel instead of the Chairman's residence, he would greet General and Mrs. Shelton as they came in the door. He, not the officer who had done all the leg-work, explained the evening's plan to the general before the guests arrived. Then, as the MC, the colonel and his wife would dine among the guests while the protocol officer sat in the kitchen.

After half a year of this routine, I'd learned to accept the status quo. Then, on the morning of a visit by the Chilean Chief of Defense, the tide turned. Colonel Wallace arrived at work looking like death warmed over and called me into his office.

"Suzanne, I have the flu. There's no way I can make the dinner tonight. You're going to have to take charge. You and Ty can have our seats if you want, but I need you to be the MC."

Once again my military bearing kicked in, preventing me from jumping up and down and whooping. I thanked the colonel for his trust and assured him everything would go smoothly. Then I dialed Ty's office.

"You doing anything tonight?" I asked.

"Why? You have to work that official dinner, don't you?"

"Yeah, but I was thinking you might want to join me and the Sheltons for some filet mignon at the Hay Adams. But if you have other plans…"

He was as pleased as I was and casually informed his colleagues that he was dining with the Chairman of the Joint Chiefs of Staff that evening.

I spent the rest of the afternoon making sure everything was perfect. I slipped away several times to the private ladies room down the hall to practice my script out loud. Others might have laughed at my excessive preparations, but I didn't like leaving anything to chance.

Ty and I arrived at the elegant hotel well in advance so I could make sure everything was in place. I'd worn a slimming navy blue and cream pant suit and felt sharp. I conferred with the maitre d' and made sure the table arrangements and place cards matched my carefully designed seating chart. Ten minutes before the guests were due to arrive, I greeted General and Mrs. Shelton at the door.

"Colonel Wallace was unable to be here this evening, Sir, so I'll be taking care of things in his place."

I sensed a flicker of doubt cross the general's face. After all, he was used to having Lieutenant Colonel Wallace run things, but I knew I could do just as well.

"If you'll follow me, Sir, I'll show you where you'll be sitting and explain the sequence of events. Would you like a drink?"

I could feel the general relax as I guided him through the dining room and back to the foyer just in time for the first guests to arrive. Ty mingled in the ante-room, sipping a glass of wine and chatting with the Chileans while I stood behind the Sheltons at the door. Once everyone had a drink in hand, I kept an eye on my watch. When the designated cocktail hour was over, I whispered to the Chairman that it was time for dinner. He gave me the nod, and I directed one of the servers to ring the dinner chimes.

After ensuring that everyone had found their seat, I stepped to the podium. Having practiced in the restroom, I needed no notes. Instead, I smiled at each table and greeted our South American guests in Spanish with my best Chilean accent, then shifted to English and repeated my remarks. There were smiles all around, and I returned to my seat, flushed and quietly excited. Ty patted my leg under the table cloth.

"You're doing great."

The rest of the dinner went off without a hitch. I had strategically placed my seat so the Chairman was in my direct line of sight. By all indications, he was enjoying himself. From past experience, however, I knew that any success would be instantly wiped out if the guests overstayed their welcome. With his busy schedule, the general placed high value on his free time. 9:45 was the witching hour.

As the Master of Ceremonies, I ran the show, so at precisely 9:30, I rose from my seat, walked to the podium, thanked the guests for joining the Sheltons, and wished them *buenas noches*. Even though Latinos are used to partying late into the night, they got the message, and by 9:40 the Sheltons were the only ones remaining.

I walked with them to their sedan. The driver opened the door, and General Shelton turned to me before getting in. "Good job tonight, Suzanne."

"Thank you, Sir."

It was Mrs. Shelton who dropped the bombshell. As she walked around the car, she leaned over and whispered in my ear, "You may have just talked yourself into a permanent job."

The car pulled away from the circular drive and I stared after it. I was practically vibrating with excitement, yet one question dominated my thoughts:

What is Colonel Wallace going to say?

*   *   *

The Chairman's driver approached me in the hallway. "Heard you did really well last night."

"Why? Did the general say something on the way home?"

He looked left and right. Things overheard in the sedan were not to be repeated.

"He and Mrs. Shelton talked about it. There might be some changes around here, but that's all I can say."

I shivered again with the anticipation of being the permanent MC, but I couldn't share my excitement with anyone. I certainly wasn't going to say anything to Earl! There was another counterpart visit planned for the next week. It would all come out before then.

The day of the next big dinner rolled around, but no one said a word about my taking over as Master of Ceremonies. It was as if the Chilean dinner had never occurred. I'd had no opportunity to interact with the Chairman all week, and I couldn't bring up the subject even if I had. I looked at the seating chart, and noted that Colonel and Mrs. Wallace were prominently shown among the other guests.

"Suzanne," Earl barked, "Make sure you have those place cards on the table by the time I get there."

I sat in my cubicle, fuming.

"Commander Giesemann, you have a call from Kris Cicio on line three," someone shouted across the office.

I picked up the phone and shocked myself by answering with a very nasty, "What?"

"What?!"

Kris was the Chairman's personal assistant and scheduler, and even though we were friends, my phone manners were inexcusable. I rushed across the hall to apologize in person.

"Kris, I can't believe I answered the phone like that! I have never talked to anyone like that in my life. Please believe me! It's just that Colonel Wallace is making me crazy!

"Say no more."

Luckily, Kris understood my working environment, but there was no excuse for my manners. I would just have to hang in there. One thing I'd learned about the military was if you had problems with your boss, either he or you would be transferred within a few years.

Figuring that Colonel Wallace's long tenure as Master of Ceremonies outweighed my single successful evening, I pushed any aspirations to the back of my mind and got back to work. It was a good job, with moments of excitement, and I got to go home each night to my husband. It was more than many naval officers had. What more could I ask?

* * *

The green dress emblazoned with rose-colored flowers was just a tad brighter than the khakis I usually wore from Monday to Friday. Ty glanced up as I walked into the kitchen. He took one look at my outfit and lowered his mug to the counter.

"Wow! Nice uniform! Let me guess… you have a ladies' program today?"

"You are so smart!"

"They used to trust me with nuclear weapons."

"I can see why," I said, giving him a quick kiss.

"Who is it today?" Ty asked.

"The Turks. The Chief of Defense will tour the Pentagon, meet with the heads of the Army, Navy, and Air Force, and be briefed on vital national security issues. Meanwhile, I'll be taking his wife to tea."

"Your enthusiasm is overwhelming."

Ty knew I didn't relish my duties as ladies' escort, but when the Chairman's counterparts came to town, their wives came with them. If another protocol officer was in charge of a visit, I would often be assigned to plan and execute the wives' portion. These ladies' programs were important in their own rights, but as a former "GURL," I silently resented doing the frilly events.

The saving grace was Mrs. Shelton. Not only a gracious hostess, she was a beautiful, warm, and approachable woman who treated me as an equal and a friend. I'd heard horror stories of other senior officers' wives, and knew I was blessed.

This day, like the others, was actually quite enjoyable. It was unusual for me to spend a whole day with a group of women, and it was a nice change of pace. Best of all, it got me out of the office.

After we dropped off the last guest, Mrs. Shelton and I were alone in the back of the small van.

"Suzanne, I want to ask you something."

"Yes, Ma'am?"

"Hugh is looking for a change, and we'd like to know how you'd feel about being an aide."

The van could have hit a wall and I wouldn't have been more jolted.

This was not the way aides got their jobs! There was usually a formal announcement for applications, followed by a lengthy selection process, complete with interviews of multiple candidates, until a final decision was made. Suddenly, I realized that the "permanent job" I'd talked myself into was not the Master of Ceremonies for an occasional fancy dinner. That was small potatoes compared to this. I was being offered the chance to be the aide-de-camp for the senior ranking officer in the United States armed forces!

And he wanted *me*, a female non-warrior.

Mrs. Shelton continued to speak as if she hadn't just brought my world to a screeching halt.

"Not everyone can handle being an aide. It's very demanding, you know. There's a lot of travel involved, and long hours, and Hugh doesn't want to shake things up unless you're interested in the position."

Infused with energy, I felt like I could jump out of the van and lift it over my head. *Interested in the position?* I thought of the places we would travel: Europe, the Middle East, Asia, South America… places I might never again have the opportunity to visit on my own. And we would travel in *style*.

I would accompany the Chairman to gala events, to Capitol Hill, and to the White House! I would ride in the limo and have daily contact with the general, witnessing first-hand how national-level decisions were made. As for the long hours, I knew Ty would understand. After his years at sea he was well familiar with the call of duty. We might not get to sail as often as we'd like, but he would be as thrilled as I was.

I took a deep breath. "Ma'am, I'd be honored."

She nodded her head with a smile. "I'll talk to Hugh."

The next day, the phone rang. One of my colleagues yelled to me across the office, "Suzanne, Kris Cicio on line three."

Unlike the last time Kris called, this time I answered properly, "Commander Giesemann. May I help you?"

"Suzanne, it's Kris. General Shelton would like to see you."

I took a deep breath and raised my eyes to the heavens in thanks.

This *GURL* had made it.

Three
9/11

September, 2001; Washington, DC

I glanced down at the cheap sports watch on my wrist. The black nylon strap didn't exactly go with my pretty green pantsuit, but the fashion police were low on my list of concerns. With my job, having an accurate digital read-out with an audible alarm was much more crucial than being in vogue.

I noted the time and date: 0640, September 11th, 2001.

"Looks like you picked a great day to fly," Ty said as he drove across the Woodrow Wilson Bridge. The sky was already a brilliant blue, full of puffy, white clouds.

"It's not like I had any say in the matter," I laughed, rifling through the briefcase wedged between my feet.

"Yeah," Ty agreed. "But I guess when the Queen of England decides to knight your boss, you give a cheery 'aye aye' and go."

"Right. I just wish I didn't have to leave you again."

"It's a tough job, but somebody's gotta do it."

I squeezed his knee. In the past nine months I'd visited eighteen countries and the same number of U.S. cities. As aide-de-camp to the Chairman of the Joint Chiefs of Staff, that kind of schedule was expected, but it was still tiring. I was looking forward to a slower pace after the general's imminent retirement, but for now, my attention was focused on the present.

I pulled a small book from my bag and opened the slightly tattered cover for the umpteenth time. Inside was the schedule that would guide my every step for the coming week, and my preparations had turned it into a coloring book. Large blocks of text were highlighted in bright yellow, others in neon-green. My hand-written notes filled the margins with bright blue ink, and certain critical events, like our 0715 departure were underlined in red.

I'd told the rest of the staff to be on the plane ninety minutes before take-off. As soon as the general arrived, we'd take off. Studying the schedule in my hands, I frowned. Something didn't seem right. I looked back at my wristwatch. The air in the car grew suddenly hot as I stared in horror at the trip book.

"Oh, my God! I am in *so much trouble!*" I shouted, my panicked cry rising high above the traffic noise.

"What?! What is it?" Ty couldn't imagine what had caused my outburst.

"I totally miscalculated the time! Drive faster! I should have been there a whole hour ago!"

In spite of my careful preparations and clear instructions to the staff, I had confused my own departure time from the house. I had gone through my morning ritual, showering, dressing, and loading my bags with no sense of urgency, unaware that the rest of our party was already on the flight line at Andrews Air Force Base.

I often joked that math was not my strong point, but this was no laughing matter.

How could I have made such a mistake? I pounded my fist against my thigh, as we sped east on route 495 at 85 miles per hour. The Chairman's sedan would be pulling up to the plane in less than half an hour, and we weren't even close to the base yet!

I picked up my cell phone and dialed Frank Angelo, the Chairman's communicator. I knew he'd be loading the staff's luggage and wondering where I was.

"Frank, it's Suzanne." I said, trying not to sound as shaken as I felt. "I had a little trouble this morning, but I'll be there in fifteen minutes."

There was no sense telling them not to leave without me. General Shelton waited for no one – not even his aide.

The rest of the ride passed in lip-biting silence as I flipped through the pages of the trip book. What else had I screwed up? What would I do if I missed the plane... go back to the Pentagon and sit in my office for a week? Who would assist the Chairman? Everyone assigned to this trip already had their own job, from the speechwriter, to the doctor, to the communications sergeants. I would surely be fired. This was not a good way to start a trip.

Luck was on my side. The traffic lights on the way to the base were blessedly green. Once inside the gate, Ty successfully delivered me to the flightline without attracting the attention of the military police.

The gleaming jet sitting on the tarmac was a welcome sight. Ty helped carry my bags as I sprinted to the plane's boarding ladder. I'd made it with six minutes to catch my breath before the Chairman was due to arrive.

Frank Angelo was there to greet me, wearing the silly multi-colored cap he saved for our trips. He took my bags, giving me an off-color smile. "You and Ty get a little carried away saying goodbye this morning, Commander?"

As a civilian, Frank could wear his crazy hat and make risqué remarks. In the post-Tailhook Navy, my uniformed colleagues wouldn't have dared.

"Very funny, Frank, but this was not a fun morning, I assure you."

I turned and kissed Ty, upset at having to say goodbye for a week when I was so rattled and distracted. The frequent separations were the downside to this job, but having done his share of sea-duty, Ty understood that the mission came first.

I boarded the plane and looked around at the strange configuration. Our normal aircraft, a VIP 757 often used by the Vice President, wasn't available, so we were using the head of the Air Force's plane, nicknamed "Speckled Trout." The unfamiliar surroundings only added to my sense of disorientation.

I squeezed past the other staff members who were milling about the aisles. To my surprise and relief, no one commented on my late arrival. I greeted Marshall, the Chairman's personal security agent, and the rest of our team with a forced smile, grateful not to have to explain my stupidity.

Frank's voice rang down the aisle, "Five minutes out!"

He'd gotten the call from the general's driver that they were passing through the main gate. I dropped my briefcase on the blue leather seat and hurried off the aircraft. Taking my place at the foot of the ladder, I turned to greet the Chairman's senior enlisted aide, Master Sergeant Mark Jones.

"How're you doing this morning, Ranger?" I asked, using his familiar nickname.

"Livin' a dream, Ma'am, livin' a dream!"

It was Ranger's standard reply, and I expected nothing less. He was the most impressive soldier I knew, having worked his way up from Army cook to his current trusted position. Always upbeat and squared away, Ranger's attitude was infectious. I began to relax as we settled into our familiar roles. My screw-up would be transparent to our boss, and that was all that mattered.

The sleek, black Cadillac carrying General and Mrs. Shelton and his executive assistant, COL Lute, drove into sight. I felt the normal shiver of excited anticipation mixed with nervousness as Ranger and I snapped to rigid attention in perfect unison. The sedan glided to a stop in front of us and we brought our hand to our brow in a sharp salute. Dropping my arm, I opened the doors for the general, gathered his briefcases, and quickly followed him up the boarding ladder. Five minutes later, right on schedule, the lumbering Speckled Trout lifted into the sky. We were on our way to Europe.

The Atlantic Ocean spread beneath us like an enormous blue carpet. As I relaxed with a magazine, one of the flight crew approached Colonel Lute across the aisle. I listened as he reported that a small aircraft had crashed into one of the World Trade Center buildings in New York City. The Colonel and I exchanged wary glances.

"That doesn't sound good," he said, as he rose and walked to the general's private compartment at the rear of the plane.

Minutes later, as the colonel returned to his seat, the crewman reappeared and reported another plane crashing into the second World Trade Center building.

"That can't be an accident," I said, recalling with a shiver the speech the Chairman made at a conference on global terrorism just a few weeks earlier. His parting words to prepare for a terrorist attack at any time and any place seemed suddenly prophetic. I followed the colonel with my eyes as he went back and told the general of the latest incident.

When Colonel Lute returned, we put bulky headsets over our ears and placed calls through the plane's communications technician back to the Pentagon. The Chairman sat silently in his compartment, awaiting further details. I was able to get through to Kris Cicio, the general's personal assistant. The urgency in her voice was evident as she relayed that these were not small airplanes, as had initially been reported, but two jetliners full of innocent passengers.

"Oh, Suzanne," Kris cried, "We're watching it on the television. It's awful, just awful. Both towers are burning, and they're—" her voice was cut off, and I badgered the comms tech to re-establish the connection. While he was trying, I listened to BBC news reports through the headset, passing on what I learned to the rest of our staff as they listened anxiously from their seats. I told them that every aircraft across the country had been ordered to land, and that they weren't allowing any international flights to come in.

Across the aisle, Colonel Lute was on a different circuit, conferring with someone in the Pentagon's National Military Command Center. Even the aircrew, who normally stayed in a separate section of the aircraft, stood in the aisles to listen in.

When he finished his call, Colonel Lute removed his headphones and walked to the Chairman's cabin. He immediately returned, nodded at me, and said, "We're going back."

The news was no surprise.

I ducked my head into the cockpit and delivered the orders to the pilot. "Major, take us back to Andrews."

"Yes, Ma'am."

"Will you have any problems with the controllers?" I asked.

"Not with the passenger we're carrying," he confirmed, "but those authentication drills we do all the time to identify ourselves won't be an exercise today."

I returned to my seat and put the headset back on. I was able to get through to our office again and this time spoke with the Vice Chairman's executive assistant, another Army Colonel.

"Suzanne, this is really bad," he said. "The scenes on TV are unbelievable. You guys need to get back here right away."

"We're coming now," I answered, as the big plane completed a sweeping turn and headed back toward the coast. Every other passenger plane across the nation now sat on the ground, but with the uniformed leader of the United States military aboard, our aircraft flew on unimpeded.

Through the headphones I heard shouting in the background.

"What's all that commotion, Colonel?" I asked.

"I'm not sure. Stand by, Suzanne."

When he returned, the anxiety in his voice had gone up a notch. "Something's happened here at the Pentagon," he said. "I think a bomb exploded, but we're still trying to find out what it was. I have to go."

General Shelton now stood at the communications console, speaking with head bowed into the mouthpiece to Air Force General Richard Myers, the Vice Chairman, who was standing in for him at the Pentagon until we got back.

We continued to gather news from the BBC reports and phone calls, frustrated at the lack of complete information we were used to getting. Colonel Lute turned to look at all of us, putting a hand over his mouthpiece. "It wasn't a bomb at the Pentagon. It was a third airliner."

The previous news was distressing enough, but this was like a physical blow. Now it was personal.

To outsiders, the Pentagon was an impressive yet imposing five-sided fortress --the symbol of our military might. To those of us on that aircraft, it was the place where we worked, ate, shopped and exercised. To hear that it had been violated was inconceivable. All of us spent more waking hours there than in our own homes.

Rather than an impersonal structure with nameless faces, the Pentagon's halls were filled with friendly co-workers. These were not just soldiers, sailors, airmen, Marines and government civilians, but good family men and women -- parents, spouses, sisters, and brothers who went to church, coached little league, and volunteered in their communities.

I prayed that few had been killed, all the while calculating how many of the twenty-three thousand who worked at the Pentagon would be in any of the five-storied wedges at any one time. It was a number I didn't want to think about.

"Where did it hit?" I asked Colonel Lute.

"They're saying it was near the helo pad."

I pictured the spot in my mind. It was two sides away from my own office, but close to many of the Navy's spaces, including their new command center.

A thickly accented British voice came through my headphones reporting that now a fourth airplane had crashed into the ground somewhere in Pennsylvania.

The disasters were stacking up in unprecedented fashion. I parroted the news to the assembled group, and we stared at each other, nearly speechless. How many more hijacked aircraft were out there?

The boss' bodyguard, Marshall, looked uncharacteristically nervous. A large, intimidating black man with a heart of gold and an infectious smile, his brows were knitted together in concern that seemed to go beyond the shock most of us were feeling.

"Is something wrong, besides the obvious?" I asked.

"My wife started a new job this morning in that part of the Pentagon," he said softly.

My heart sank and I thought of my husband. Some things were too painful to even think about, and I had to push my fears to the back of my mind. Even though Ty's job as a defense analyst occasionally took him to meetings at the Pentagon, I knew he didn't have any outside commitments today and prayed he was still safe in his office across the highway.

I touched Marshall's shoulder and told him I'd try to find out about his wife.

I managed to get through to Kris again. She did little to comfort me, and instead confirmed the plane that crashed into our building was another large jetliner full of passengers, not a small aircraft as we'd all hoped.

"We can smell smoke, but so far it's ok," she said, adding that those in our front offices were going to stay in the building as long as they were able, to give us whatever support we needed.

"What's happening in New York?" I asked.

"Suzanne, the pictures on TV are horrible. You wouldn't believe it. They're – oh my God, one of the towers is falling down…" The anguish in her voice was palpable as she cried, "It's gone. It's not there anymore!"

I kept Kris on the line while I passed on this latest, unimaginable information. She asked if we wanted her to contact our families and let them know we were ok. I thanked her, grateful that Ty would receive her call, and told her about Marshall's wife. She promised to see what she could find out.

I laid down the headset and walked back to the cockpit. As I peered through the large windows, the co-pilot turned around. "You might want to tell the Chairman that our flight path will take us right over Manhattan."

I grimly realized we would have a unique and historic vantage point, as no other aircraft were permitted in the sky to photograph this sordid spectacle.

Speckled Trout had no windows in the passenger section, so after reporting the flight plan to General Shelton, I stopped by Ranger Jones' seat. One of his duties on the road was to take the official photographs to document the Chairman's travel.

"Ranger, grab your camera and come with me up to the cockpit."

We peered down through the clouds until the familiar outline of Manhattan came into view. I stared at the place where the twin towers should have been. Huge plumes of smoke blotted out the lower part of the island, making the news horrifyingly real.

Now that we were returning to Washington, I needed to change from my traveling clothes into my military uniform. Most of our trips had such varied itineraries that I usually carried everything from fatigues and combat boots to my fanciest dress uniforms. This trip to Europe was to have been nothing but ceremonial events and meetings, so I'd packed only my Navy Summer Whites.

Just great, I thought. We were headed to a battle zone, and I would be in a skirt and heels. Then I chided myself. *People are dying there, Suzanne. Nobody will give a damn what you're wearing.*

Within an hour of passing New York City, we landed at Andrews Air Force Base.

The general's sedan and driver were waiting, along with an unprecedented police escort of ten motorcycles and three patrol cars to lead us back to Washington. We were used to this kind of lights-and-sirens escort when we visited foreign countries, but not in our own capital!

All the way into the city the roads were eerily empty, save for police cars parked at odd angles across random intersections. No one spoke as we sped across the Southeast-Southwest Freeway, usually jammed with cars at this late afternoon hour. Crossing the Fourteenth Street Bridge, a heavy gray blanket over Crystal City captured my attention. And there, to the right, was the source of the thick smoke: our five-sided headquarters.

On fire.

We pulled up to the River Entrance, passing machine-gun-toting soldiers in full battle dress. I followed the Chairman into the building where the acrid smoke assaulted my nostrils, forever imprinting itself on my memory. The civilian guards who normally greeted us with smiles watched with grave faces as we made a bee-line for the general's office.

Kris stood as we entered and merely shook her head. There were no greetings nor jovial comments about not expecting us back so soon. I followed the general into his office, placed his briefcases next to his desk and took his hat and coat. Stepping out, I closed the door and turned to Kris.

"How're you doing?"

"Ok, I guess. The smoke got pretty bad for a while and we had to go outside, but it's better now."

"Did you find out anything about Marshall's wife?"

Kris shook her head, just as Marshall walked in the door, cell phone in hand.

"She's ok," he said, his face the picture of relief. "She was in a meeting in another part of the building when the plane hit."

"Thank God!" we said, both of us squeezing his arm.

The Chairman's Public Affairs Officer stepped up to Kris' desk. He was at the airport to tell General Shelton about a press conference later that day with Secretary of Defense Rumsfeld. Now Captain McCreary recommended that the general see the impact site first-hand. Hearing this plan, I took a deep breath. Wherever the Chairman went, I went. Although I had trained as an EMT, I was unprepared for devastation on the scale that we would now see close-up.

General Shelton came out of his office, accompanied by a brigadier general from the Joint Staff's antiterrorism office. His briefing now complete, it was time to see the wreckage. On the television behind Kris' desk, CNN was showing gruesome images from New York City of fire trucks and automobiles covered with ash. News reports were one thing, but I suddenly realized that those of us on the Chairman's plane would now be the only people in the world to see both Manhattan and the Pentagon with our own eyes on the very day they were attacked.

As our small group left the office, Ranger walked in, laden with our luggage from the aircraft.

"You doing ok, Ranger?" I asked over my shoulder.

"Yes, Ma'am," He answered gravely. He made no mention of livin' a dream.

The Pentagon has seventeen miles of corridors. As the aide, I always led the Chairman to his meetings, after scoping out the route in advance. Now Captain McCreary took the lead, and I followed two steps behind General Shelton. We headed toward the Pentagon's center courtyard, a shortcut to the far side of the building. The hallways were dim and deserted, save for a few people wearing surgical masks to filter the smoke. As we passed the intersection of two hallways, Marshall spied an officer in a khaki navy officer's uniform wearing an emergency vest marked "physician."

Always thinking of the Chairman's safety, Marshall snapped his fingers at the older gentleman and barked, "You! Come with us."

The officer wordlessly complied and joined our small parade. I glimpsed a flash of insignia on the doctor's lapel and my eyes widened. Marshall had unwittingly commandeered the Joint Staff's Surgeon General, a one-star admiral, but I kept my mouth shut. This was no time to worry about protocol.

Cutting across the park-like center courtyard of the Pentagon, I looked around at the odd scene. Normally filled with people chatting, smoking, or grabbing a bite to eat from the snack stand, the area was filled with men and women in surgical scrubs and camouflage uniforms.

Many were sitting on the ground, staring blankly ahead. Small, black plastic packages were laid out in rows on the grass, and I realized with a shudder that the bundles were empty body bags.

I desperately wanted to turn back, my fight or flight syndrome on full alert. I was definitely not prepared to see body parts, but my job required I stay with the Chairman. I could never ask to be excused. General Shelton was a Special Forces "snake-eater," the toughest of the tough. Duty called, and I refused to show weakness.

Having crossed the courtyard, we entered the fifth corridor. Picturing the Pentagon map in my head, I knew the impact site was only a short distance ahead and to our left. The power was out here, and the smoke was thicker than ever. I held onto Marshall's belt loop as we groped our way into a pitch-black stairwell, thinking we had no business walking into such a hazardous area.

Luckily, Marshall must have been thinking the same thing, for he suddenly recommended we approach from the outside. Relief surged through me as we turned and made our way out the Mall Entrance into the welcome sunlight.

Rounding the corner of the building was like stepping onto the set of a disaster movie. A field of tents and rescue vehicles lay before us. Fire trucks were parked on the sodden grass, spraying water onto the building's burning roof. Dozens of ambulances lined the sidewalk.

As if in a dream, I stepped around a large chunk of a jet's engine that lay in the grass, tragically out of place.

The focus of all the attention now lay directly before us: a gaping hole in a wall that had previously been just like the one outside my office. Exposed beams, broken windows, and blackened limestone created a painful portrait that my brain struggled to accept.

Office interiors lay exposed like three-sided sets on a stage. I pictured the workers at their desks only hours earlier, and prayed that most had gotten out. It was obvious that those unlucky enough to have been where now there was nothing but a huge void hadn't had a chance.

Emergency personnel scurried past us, nodding in respect to my four-star boss. Like the rest of us, the Chairman watched the rescue operation in silence and gravely shook his head. There was little to say.

**Suzanne gazes at the Pentagon devastation with General Shelton,
Captain McCreary and Marshall McCants.**

Heading back into the building, Colonel Lute informed me the general needed to go to the National Military Command Center. The Vice Chairman had been holed up there with the Joint Staff's top leadership since the morning. Now back in familiar territory, I led the way to the command post's main entrance where a security guard nodded us through.

With the general behind closed doors, I leaned on a counter next to a television and stared at the screen.

"You haven't seen this yet?" asked an Air Force officer who worked in the command center.

"Just a few pictures."

"Keep watching. They'll show a clip of one of the planes actually flying into the second tower."

I watched in horror the scene I would later turn my head to avoid whenever it came on. When it was over, I picked up a phone by the door and called home.

"Hi," I said when Ty picked up.

"Hi," he answered, his voice flat.

"We're back."

"Good. Kris called me earlier and told me you were ok."

"I knew you'd know we were safe. What an awful day, huh?"

"The bastards," Ty said, then shared with me his unique idea of how to eliminate terrorism once and for all. Unfortunately, the realities of politics precluded the kind of drastic measures my husband envisioned, no matter how satisfying.

Any proposals for a response would come from Secretary Rumsfeld and my boss, the President's principal advisors on defense. But how could we respond when we didn't know what inhuman animals were behind this unthinkably evil plot? I pictured the scene I had just witnessed and choked back my frustration.

"I don't know how late we'll be here tonight, but I'll keep you posted."

"Call me when you're ready for me to pick you up."

"Will do."

The door opened and General Shelton stepped out.

"I gotta go. I love you, Ty."

"I love you, too, Suzanne."

Back at the Chairman's office, someone had left a box of pizza. It was after seven and I realized none of us had eaten all day. Colonel Lute stepped away from his desk and told me the boss was needed in the SECDEF's teleconference meeting room in just a few minutes. Having never been there, I grabbed a slice of cold pizza and left to scope out the location.

Hurrying back and checking my watch, I peered through the tiny peep-hole in the Chairman's door. The general was alone at his desk. I reached in a drawer and pulled out the remote access device that allowed me access. I pressed the tiny button, and hearing a click, pushed the door open a foot.

"Time for your teleconference with SECDEF, Sir."

Never much for words when working, General Shelton nodded and rose. I retraced my steps and lead him to a small room behind a heavy, vault-like door. While we awaited the Secretary's arrival, the Senate Armed

Services Committee's two most powerful senators entered the room. I'd seen Senators Warner and Levin at numerous hearings on Capitol Hill. The two normally gregarious men were uncharacteristically quiet. They moved to the far side of the room and sat in silence.

Secretary Rumsfeld entered the room, and I lingered a moment to see what I could learn. Three large screens dominated the room, each broadcasting different news networks. One of the screens showed footage of a fiery explosion at a foreign factory. The words "LIVE" blinked boldly in the lower corner as the newscaster speculated that the explosion might be some sort of U.S. retaliation for the attacks on our country.

Secretary Rumsfeld and General Shelton exchanged a puzzled look, and the Secretary asked, "Did we do that?"

I blinked in surprise. *If he doesn't know what that was all about, we'd better NOT have done it!*

General Shelton denied any knowledge of the report, which later turned out to be an unrelated and accidental incident.

Secretary Rumsfeld settled into his chair at the head of the table, and I slipped out of the room as the others took their seats. While I waited in the hallway, Captain McCreary approached and informed me the press conference would follow their meeting. I hurried to the Chairman's office to retrieve his dress uniform coat, thankful to fall back into my familiar role in the midst of such uncertainty.

I returned and waited with Secretary's Rumsfeld's military aide outside the conference room. A young Army officer with bandaged hands walked by, escorted by a senior officer. The aide whispered to me, "That guy was driving by when he saw the plane hit. He jumped out of his car, ran right into the hole, and started pulling people out."

He was the first of many heroes who would later be recognized for their incredible selflessness.

Victoria Clarke, the Assistant Secretary of Defense for Public Affairs, nodded as she walked past me into the meeting room and announced it was time for the press conference. I handed General Shelton his coat as he came out, then followed the pensive group down the stairs to the press corridor. Outside the room where reporters from CNN and the major networks were waiting, Torie Clarke stood like a coach in a huddle and gave a serious pep talk. Her assertiveness when addressing the two most powerful men in the Department of Defense was impressive.

"Gentlemen," she stated, her face stern, "you are about to address 320 million Americans who have witnessed an unspeakable tragedy today."

The reminder was unnecessary, but neither man appeared to take offense. Both took their places at the podium in front of the familiar oval Pentagon sign and reassured the nation that the government was still operating, and that our nation was strong. I stood off to the side, my heart aching, but swelling with pride in our country and its leaders.

It was after eleven PM and there was little more to do until more information was available. General Shelton told me to have the driver bring the car around. I summoned the driver, then made a quick call to Ty and asked him to come and get me. He informed me that all the entrances to the Pentagon were blocked.

I thought of my luggage and looked down at my high heels. It was dark out and late. We agreed that he would wait across the highway near the shopping mall. I would get there somehow.

I hung up, checked that the driver was out front, then notified General Shelton that the car was ready. Picking up his briefcases, I followed him to the car, and opened the door. While he climbed in, I put the bags in the trunk and returned to deliver a sharp salute as the car pulled away from the curb.

I stood on the granite steps in the darkness and looked at my watch. It was 2330. The parking lot was deserted. How was I going to get to the mall? Luckily, a police officer came out of the building and stopped.

"Do you need something, Commander?"

"Yes. A ride to my husband!"

It was one of those nights when any American would help a fellow citizen. My problem solved, I ran inside to grab my luggage.

We drove past South Parking, normally near-empty at this time of night. Now the lot was awash with the bright lights of emergency flood lamps, like a night game at a football stadium. Underneath an enormous Army field tent, rescue workers toiled on.

Approaching the appointed rendezvous, I saw our familiar green Honda Civic and pointed it out to my escort. Thanking him, I got out of the car and retrieved my bags.

Ty stepped from the driver's side as I approached. We hadn't expected to see each other for a week, and now we were together again in less than a day. Unfortunately, there was no joy in our reunion.

Anger was etched on Ty's face. He hugged me, but his arms were tense. I knew that men and women process events differently, but this emotional day proved it beyond question. In response to the worst tragedy in our nation's history, Ty wanted to launch nuclear weapons. I just wanted to be held.

Taking my cue from him, I locked away my emotions and held back my tears.

You have to be tough, Commander.

Just like a snow day, only essential personnel were required to report to the Pentagon immediately following the attack. In the past, I'd jokingly commented that it was great to be nonessential if it meant a day off. As the aide to the Chairman, there was no question that I would return to work. Ty's office was open for business, so we drove in together.

Remembering the roadblocks, we left extra early, but it wasn't early enough. Although only a small percentage of the Pentagon's work force reported in, all entrances were clogged. With policemen checking IDs of every vehicle's occupants, the traffic was backed up from the parking lot onto the highway.

For the second day in a row I found myself sweating a late arrival. It was my duty to stand at the curb and assist the general with his bags when he pulled up. There was no way he wouldn't notice my absence.

After moving only a few feet in five minutes, I couldn't stand the slow movement a second longer. I kissed Ty goodbye, got out of the car, and trotted down the highway's off-ramp. It was too late. I saw the Chairman's black limo pulling up to the curb as I scurried up the curved drive to the River Entrance.

Son of a bitch! I cursed the fates as I watched Ron, the driver, get out of the car and do my job for me.

Breathless from the unexpected run, I tossed my hat on Kris' desk and entered the general's office just as Ron was leaving. He raised his eyebrows in question and I shook my head with disgust. I went straight to the small credenza by the general's desk and poured a cup of coffee for him. I placed the mug on his desk, but didn't bother to speak. General

Shelton had no time for excuses. He was already engrossed in the reports on his desk, and didn't say a word. With all that was going on, it was clear he didn't care who carried his bags in.

But I cared. For me, there was security in familiar routines. In the past twenty-four hours, however, nothing was routine. I wondered if it ever would be again.

I checked the tiny 3x5 card on Kris' desk that showed the day's schedule. Unlike most weekdays when we were in Washington, the card was nearly empty. After all, no one had expected us back until the following week. It would no doubt fill up quickly, and there was already one new meeting on the page. It was no surprise that he was scheduled to go to the White House.

I rarely accompanied General Shelton to meetings of the National Security Council. He knew his way around the White House, and had no need for my assistance. Once I got him into the sedan with all his papers, I was free to take care of other business until his return.

I delivered my boss to the car right on schedule, then walked back into the building. The smoke still hung heavily in the air, seeping into my clothing and hair. How I wished I were anywhere else! Unable to sit still, I aimlessly walked the deathly quiet hallways with leaden feet. Approaching the innermost corridor, I peered through the ceiling-high windows at the surreal scene across the center courtyard.

A fireman stood at the tip of an extension ladder, spraying water onto the roof where bright orange flames shot skyward. It was almost twenty-four hours since the attack, and the Pentagon was still burning! How many fire drills had I participated in these past two years, knowing there was no danger? We'd evacuated the building and stood outside in the rain or snow to practice. Now, here I was in a building that was actually on fire, and we were expected to continue working.

What few people were in sight walked past me in a daze. I felt like they looked.

Walking past the River Entrance on the way to my office, a single file of young soldiers in fatigues paraded soberly past. I recognized them from their impeccable bearing as members of the elite Army Honor Guard, the 3rd US Infantry. These were the soldiers who marched on the parade field at our honor ceremonies and conducted dignified military funerals at

Arlington Ceremony. It was strange to see them in fatigues instead of their spotless dress blues.

In response to my inquiry, I learned they'd been tasked to search through the rubble for victims of the attack. It was no wonder their faces were stony.

I returned to my office and sat at my desk, staring at the schedule from the trip we hadn't completed. Suddenly I heard shouts in the hallway. Someone banged on the door and frantically yelled, "Get out! Get out of the building now!"

Heart racing, I opened the door to find a torrent of people rushing toward the nearest exit, many of them running.

"It's another plane!" Someone shouted. "Hurry!"

I joined the panicked crowd and hurried to the nearest exit. The guards shooed us along, convinced an attack was imminent. I stepped out into the blessed sunshine and moved to the far end of the parade field. Standing among the edgy group, I searched the sky, dreading what I might see, and praying there would be no more carnage.

"It's a false alarm!" a guard announced from the steps. "You can come back in now."

Going back into the building was the last thing I wanted to do. I returned to my office with a sense of vulnerability I'd never before experienced.

It was no easier going to work in the days that followed. I could turn off the television, but there was no escaping the constant reminder that the place we thought was invulnerable had been unthinkably violated. Working in the very building where 189 innocent people had been killed was hard for me to come to grips with.

These were people just like me… men and women I had worked with, some of whom I'd known, like the man with the Santa Claus beard who spent his lunch hour passing out candy to unsuspecting strangers. If it could happen to good people like that, it could happen to any of us.

I tried to lessen the stress I felt the best way I knew how, by running. The exercise was little help, however, when my daily jog from the Pentagon Athletic Center took me past a growing pile of debris. It was impossible to ignore the swarm of men in white coveralls and masks combing through the dust for human remains and evidence.

It was my job to escort the Shelton's to the memorial ceremony at the National Cathedral at the end of that long week. While I felt I'd been exposed to more grief than I could handle, the service turned out to be the start of my own healing process. I led the Chairman and his wife to their seats, then found a seat in the front of the cathedral where I could respond quickly if my boss signaled.

Sitting with an unimpeded view of the President, his strength gave *me* strength. I was stirred by his remarks, and proud that we had a man with such firm faith and high morals at a time when we needed strong leadership. I found surprising comfort in Billy Graham's words, and left the service feeling less heavy-hearted than I had going in.

With a clearer mind and a day off that weekend, I talked with Ty about how to spend it.

"Do you think we could go out on the boat?" I asked, feeling slightly guilty for even suggesting it.

"I don't see why not," he said. "The city's shut down, and it'd be good to get away from the news."

"Exactly," I said, relieved he understood. Other people could turn off their TVs when they reached their limit of witnessing tragedy, but I had to keep going back into the Pentagon. To both of us, the boat was our escape, our refuge.

Sunday afternoon, we followed through with our plan. There was little wind, but it didn't matter. Sitting in the middle of the Chesapeake Bay, we were free. Ty took the wheel, and I lay on the deck, staring at the sky.

"Don't you wish we could just turn south and keep on going?" I asked dreamily as the boat cut a silent path through the water.

"Sounds good to me."

"Then let's do it," I said, sitting up. "As soon as possible."

We'd talked about making the break for years, and our shelves were lined with books to help us prepare for it. Thick volumes like "The Voyager's Handbook" and "Heavy Weather Sailing" taught us the practicalities of long-term cruising. Others like "The Self-Sufficient Sailor" and "A Sea Vagabond's World," kept us motivated for the lifestyle we dreamed of.

The only thing holding us back was my job. Ty had already retired from the Navy and was working until I, too, was retirement eligible. That date was less than two years away, but until now we hadn't made a firm commitment to the plan.

"What about your career?" he asked, knowing I could serve another twelve years if I chose to, and possibly get promoted a time or two along the way.

"You know, some things just don't seem as important today as they did a week ago," I said, walking back to sit beside him at the helm. "I can't stop thinking about all those people who won't be around to fulfill their dreams."

It was a subject that came up repeatedly in cruising circles: "Do it now, while you have the chance." The specter of declining health and physical abilities was the usual stimulus that moved people to cut the shore strings early and set sail in search of adventure. In my mind, 9/11 added a compelling reason to make the break sooner, rather than later.

"We should be living each day as if it were our last," I said, my hand resting on Ty's leg. "When people ask me how I'm doing, I want to answer like Ranger Jones, that I'm livin' a dream. Every day."

Earlier, Ty might have said I was being melodramatic. Now, with the whole world forever changed, he nodded his head in grim agreement. "We'll need a heavier boat if we're going to go offshore."

I looked at him, my head tilted. "So you agree? I get out at twenty, you stop working, we buy a bigger boat, sell the house and cars, and sail off into the sunset?"

"Sounds like a plan," Ty said, nodding his head.

I wrapped my arms around him and squeezed, then stood up, hands on hips. That was it then. We had a lot to do. Time to get hot.

Four

THE SEARCH

September 2001, Washington, DC

Things were hopping at the Pentagon.

"General Shelton needs to be in SECDEF's conference room ten minutes before the President arrives," Colonel Lute informed me.

"Aye, aye, Sir."

I checked my watch. I had time to spare, so I stepped out into the hall to watch the fun. Any VIP visitor caused a flurry of activity and an air of anticipation in the Bradley Corridor, but Presidential visits elevated the action to new levels. The executive parking lot outside the River Entrance had been cleared the night before, and now ninja-suited guards with machine guns patrolled the perimeter. The dignitaries' entrance was unlocked and a janitor in a gray smock vacuumed the red carpet one last time.

The hallways had been emptied of anyone with no role in the visit, yet they were more crowded than ever. German shepherds and their handlers swept both sides of the corridor for bombs. Patrolmen blocked the interior entrances, standing noticeably straighter than normal. The plain-clothes officers with whom I normally chatted prior to formal visits now talked in hushed voices to men in dark suits with wires coming out of their ears. If I'd had any doubt that these intense visitors were Secret Service agents, the unique oval pins on their lapels gave them away.

I'd seen these guys plenty of times before. My first month in the job was also George W's. I'd had a close-up view of history-in-the-making on Inauguration Day, from the ceremony at the Capitol to the Inaugural Parade, where I'd been privileged to sit on the reviewing stand. I'd shaken the President's hand at White House events and shared the same conference room during military briefings. Best of all, I'd flown with him on Air Force One, a highlight of my Navy career.

Today would just be a quick glimpse in the hallway, but it didn't matter. I still felt like a tourist when he was around.

Time to go, I thought, and returned to the Chairman's office to escort him upstairs.

"What are you smiling about?" General Shelton asked me, knowing full well it was the President's visit.

"I know you see him all the time, Sir, but it's still pretty exciting for me."

The Chairman shook his head as I handed him his coat and escorted him up the escalator to the conference room.

With my boss delivered to his seat, I stepped back into the SECDEF's hallway. Just like downstairs, intimidating Secret Service agents milled about smartly. I knew I wouldn't be needed until the meeting was over and had no real reason to be there. At the same time, I didn't want to miss out on anything.

I decided to follow one of my favorite guiding principles: *look like you belong, and you'll fit right in.*

If I was going to get a glimpse of the president, I needed to stand along the route he would follow. I planted myself squarely at the top of the curved staircase I knew he'd come up. The gold-braided aiguillettes around my left shoulder clearly indicated I was an aide-de-camp. I counted on the fact that the agents knew that and had just seen me escort my boss to the room. Now, standing with authority, my hands clasped loosely behind my back, I nodded pleasantly in their direction.

It worked! They acknowledged my greeting and turned their attention to watching for intruders.

Minutes later I sensed an increase in the barometric pressure, as agents began talking into microphones clipped onto their shirt cuffs. Sure enough, a policeman bounded up the stairs, followed by a bevy of photographers, and then The Man, himself, appeared, surrounded by staffers. I'd grown used to the air of celebrity that accompanied General Shelton when we were in a crowd. That feeling was intensified now a thousand-fold, to one of reverence, as President Bush ascended the stairs.

I stood at attention, recalling the comfort his words at the National Cathedral brought to me and millions of others who were grieving the week before. Sitting off to the side of the pulpit while I kept an eye on my boss, I'd sworn the President looked right at me as he delivered his powerful message.

As if!

Now our nation's leader was only inches away, and I nodded politely.

Suddenly, President Bush focused his eyes on mine and said, just as casual as can be, "Saw you in church the other day."

My mouth fell open and I gawked, the total tourist, through and through. In church? He meant the National Cathedral! He *was* looking!

The President stopped, nearly causing a pile-up behind him, and said, "You were there, weren't you?"

Recovering my senses, I blurted back, "Yes, Sir! I saw you, too!"

George W. Bush laughed, then disappeared into his meeting.

*   *   *

"I wish I could have been a fly on the wall." Ty said. "That's way cool to be singled out by the President!"

"Pretty heady stuff," I agreed.

"You know, Suzanne, anything else you do is going to seem pretty boring in comparison to this job. I know we talked about this already, but are you sure you want to give all this up just to go sailing?"

I nodded solemnly. There was no doubt in my mind. Sure, it was exciting to work around Washington's movers and shakers. But that kind of power and excitement can go to your head pretty quickly. I'd met a lot of folks whose self-worth seemed to depend on being near important people, and I didn't want that to happen to me.

I knew my retirement would surprise a lot of colleagues who expected me to continue rising through the ranks, but I wasn't a "climber." I'd taken the aide's job for the excitement and the honor of working for General Shelton, not for what it could do for my career. The general would be retiring soon, and I had exciting plans for my own retirement. 9/11 had simply accelerated my schedule.

"Yeah," I said, "I'm really looking forward to being a homeless boat bum."

Ty laughed. "In that case, can I interest you in looking at some boats?"

My eyes lit up. He knew just the right buttons to push. "You mean right now?"

"Not now! This weekend! I printed out a few listings off the Internet."

"A few?" I said, laughing, as Ty handed me a sheaf of papers half an inch thick.

I started leafing through the pile, knowing each of the boats selected would meet our long list of criteria for what we considered our perfect cruising sailboat. Having lived aboard *Liberty* for four months while our current house was being built, we knew what worked and what didn't for a live-aboard boat. Our Freedom 36 was fast and fun to sail, but she wasn't as "bulletproof" as Ty wanted for a boat we would take out in the open ocean. If we ever were to run into a reef or sunken object, we needed as thick a hull as possible.

As for creature comforts, we wanted lots of storage space. A center cockpit boat would keep us nice and dry, and provide us with a roomy aft cabin. The interior needed to be bright and cheery, not dark and cave-like. To get all of this, we focused on boats with forty to forty-two feet of length overall.

"This one looks pretty good," I said, stopping at a listing for a Pearson 40.

"Yeah, I thought so, too, but she has 6000 engine hours."

"Yikes."

"How about this one? It's right in Annapolis."

"Hang on to that one."

We continued to pore over the listings together, separating them into two piles: rejects and possibilities.

"There's still one small problem," Ty said.

"I know. We already have a boat."

"Exactly."

I pursed my lips. Impatience was my worst fault, but if we were going to go on an extended cruise, we'd need at least a year to find the right boat and get her ready.

"We can list her with a broker this weekend when we go to look at some of these, right?"

Ty rolled his eyes and shook his head. Then he picked up one of the print-outs and said, "I especially want to see this one."

When it came to boats, he was as bad as I.

*   *   *

"You drove all the way to New York just to look at one boat?" The owner was incredulous.

Obviously, he didn't understand our affliction.

"Sure. It sounds like what we're looking for." Ty answered.

Our search was taking longer than we'd imagined. We'd inspected half a dozen boats every weekend throughout the upper Chesapeake Bay over a period of months. We knew of every forty-footer for sale from Maine to Florida. Now that we'd exhausted our local area, it was time to branch out.

Unfortunately, boat brokers are first cousins to used car salesmen. More often than not, the boats we looked at bore little resemblance to the well-chosen photos and glowing write-ups. Often, after driving two hours to see a boat, we'd know within seconds that we'd wasted our time. A bad head odor or the sick-sweet aroma of musty mildew was an instant turn-off.

Now, with four hours' wear on our tires and a hotel bill in our pocket, we'd already invested substantially in this Endeavor 42.

"Well, she's a beauty all right." The owner boasted as he leaned a rickety ladder against the faded white hull.

"Your ad says she's 'pristine,'" I said, hoping that for once we'd find some truth in advertising.

"Well, I haven't had a chance to clean her in a while, but she's in great shape. Go on up."

"Here we go again," I said to Ty, glancing warily at the deck ten feet overhead.

This late in the year, most of the boats we looked at were on the hard. Being out of the water made it easy to check the underbody, but climbing the ladders was no treat. Ty held the bottom while I clambered aboard.

"The decks are wide and flat," I observed as Ty stepped up beside me. We'd made this a priority after a charter the year before on a boat whose slanting decks were crowded with hardware.

"Yup."

Ty was in buyer-mode now, his face deadly serious, his vocabulary reduced to single word responses.

"The center cockpit is nice," I commented.

"Mm."

The owner slid open the hatch. "You can go on down below, if you'd like."

For me, this was the moment of truth. The hull, engine, and rigging were important, of course, but like most women, to me aesthetics were paramount.

I descended the ladder and looked around. Reasonably bright... No boat smell... Roomy salon... Dirty dishes in the sink...

Dirty dishes in the sink?

How long had this boat been out of the water? The guy knew we were coming to look at it. The least he could do was straighten up! I shook my head. There was no understanding some sellers' lack of business sense.

I tapped on Ty's shoulder as he descended the ladder, then pointed silently at the galley. He shook his head, and echoed my sentiments as he mouthed the word

"p-r-i-s-t-i-n-e."

The rest of the boat was relatively clean, and the layout was certainly comfortable for cruising. This one was a definite possibility, but I knew better than to make any positive remarks at this stage. Ty had long ago advised me about the importance of looking uninterested, an art he was now demonstrating with great skill as he checked out the engine room.

I followed Ty back on deck, where he carefully inspected the chain plates attaching the shrouds to the hull.

"Got a crack in this one," he told the owner.

"Really? I'm sure that's the only one."

"Mm."

His inspection of the rigging complete, I watched Ty step on the coach top and reach into his pocket.

Here it comes.

The owner's eyes narrowed as Ty pulled out a rectangular yellow box and began moving it around the base of the mast in a checkerboard pattern.

"What's that you got there?" the owner asked, leaning in closer.

"Moisture meter," Ty replied, straightening. "You've got a little delamination going on here. Deck's pretty wet."

"Oh, I don't know about that," the owner said. "The surveyor I hired didn't find anything wrong."

I winced. This guy didn't know what he was up against.

"Ty's a marine surveyor, too," I stated, while my husband hopped up and down on the deck as if it were a trampoline.

"Feels a little soft," Ty said, putting the meter back in his pocket.

The owner shrugged his shoulders, but wisely kept his mouth shut.

"Thanks for your time," Ty said, already heading for the rickety ladder down to the car.

So much for the four hour drive, I thought, recognizing the tell-tale signs of yet another reject.

I climbed into the passenger seat and looked up at the Endeavor. It had seemed pretty good to me, but I had nowhere near the experience with boats that Ty had. Having spent a lifetime at sea, he'd developed a sixth sense that alerted him to potential problems far better than dirty dishes or a meter's dial. If his intuition told him something about this boat wasn't quite right, I'd be a fool to question it.

And my mama didn't raise no fool.

Five

SIXTH SENSE

December, 1989; The Caribbean

USS JOHN RODGERS was a formidable warship -- a destroyer, Spruance class, bristling with antennas, radar, and armament. Her hangar housed an SH-2 helicopter. Her deck carried Tomahawk and Harpoon cruise missiles, two 5" inch guns, NATO Sea Sparrow missiles, anti-submarine rockets, and Mark 46 torpedoes.

You didn't want to get on her bad side.

It was no wonder Ty was proud of his ship. With her sharply raked bow, sleek lines, and awesome weaponry, she was a destroyerman's dream. As her Commanding Officer, there wasn't a day went by that he didn't check her pulse by walking the spotless decks and passageways and chatting with her crew.

This was *his* ship, earned through hard work and sacrifice aboard six others over a period of twenty years. From his first platform, a submarine, to a destroyer, an amphibious ship, two frigates and a battleship, he'd worked his way up the Navy's ladder. Now he'd been rewarded with the prize every surface warrior works toward: command at sea.

Even though COs are often compared to God, unique in their omnipotence while away from port, Ty was humbled by the trust that had been placed in him. Underlying every decision was the knowledge that he held the lives of 450 sailors and officers in his hands.

With this power came a price, though. Any casualty to the ship caused by personal negligence, whether the fault of Seaman Recruit Jones or a wet-behind-the-ears ensign, Ty could be relieved for cause. If he were nowhere near the bridge and the ship collided with another vessel, he would be fired, his naval career instantly derailed.

Officers are taught from day one that you can delegate authority, and you can delegate responsibility, but you can't delegate accountability.

It's a wonder he slept at all.

But you have to sleep sometime, and Ty knew he'd trained his officers to the best of his ability. Like a mother who instantly senses when something is wrong with her child, Ty was highly attuned to shipboard subtleties. Even a slight change in the pitch of the engines would awaken him.

It was pre-dawn in the Caribbean. The ship was steaming near the island of Vieques, long used by the Navy for naval gunfire training. She was scheduled to shoot her 5 inch guns at targets on the island after sunrise. It would be a great day!

Before hitting the sack the previous evening, Ty had written his night orders. The ship was to proceed to a position fifty miles from land to dump trash and garbage. She was to return to a position three miles south of the gun line by 0600 for visual identification of the target area. The Officer of the Deck was to wake the captain at 0500.

While in port, Ty slept in a large cabin with an adjoining office on the main deck. Because they were underway, however, he spent the night in his smaller sea cabin, just off the ship's bridge. He'd been sleeping soundly, but suddenly, he opened his eyes.

Glancing at the clock, he saw that it was only 0430. He still had half an hour of valuable shut-eye until the OOD would rouse him, but he was vaguely uneasy. Something didn't feel right. Unable to identify what had awakened him, Ty pulled on a pair of khaki trousers and left his cabin.

The bridge of a merchant ship or cruise liner is often manned by only one watch stander checking the radar and scanning the horizon as the vessel steams on autopilot. The bridge of a Navy ship is like a Las Vegas casino: active day or night and crowded. But unlike a cabaret, the bridge is bathed in a soft, red glow to preserve night vision. Sailors talk in hushed voices while they conduct their no-nonsense job of navigating the vessel.

Ty crossed the short distance from his sea cabin to the bridge and pulled open the door. He was instantly assaulted by the white glare of fluorescent bulbs. Surprise mixed with apprehension as he absorbed the scene. The OOD and JOOD were deep in conversation, their night vision non-existent. Several sailors busily swabbed the deck. The navigation team was changing charts, from navigation to naval gunfire support charts. Electronics technicians were tuning the SATNAV and radars in preparation for the gunnery exercises. No one on the bridge seemed to sense anything out of the ordinary.

Ty peered forward through the large, rectangular bridge windows into the deep blackness beyond. He saw a single, bright flashing light up high, shining through the darkness 20 degrees above the horizon. He had cruised this corner of the ocean before, and as he recognized the light from the observation post on Vieques Island, his stomach instantly clenched.

Had they been farther out to sea, where they were supposed to be, that bright white beacon would have appeared much lower on the horizon.

His first thought was, *Oh, shit!*

Then his naval training kicked in.

In a resounding voice that left no question as to who was in charge, Ty declared, "This is the Captain! I have the conn! Right full rudder! All engines back emergency!"

The Officer of the Deck and Junior Officer of the Deck went slack jawed and wide-eyed. They hastily looked left and right to figure out what was wrong, correctly suspecting they had screwed up badly. The Helmsman spun the rudder hard to the right; the Lee Helmsman yanked the handles of the engine order telegraph into his gut. Deep in the bowels of the ship, the Engineering Officer of the Watch scrambled from his seat at the operating console as the ship responded to the unexpected orders.

Within seconds of Ty's command, the destroyer's LM-2500 gas turbine engines, the same used to power commercial jetliners, screamed at full throttle. The ship's reversible pitch propellers turned at maximum speed to bring the ten-thousand-ton, 564-foot ship to a dead stop within three hundred yards, the noise and abrupt motion waking every sailor on board.

The ship had come within one mile of plowing into a coral reef at thirty knots.

Relief and gratitude washed over him as Ty considered what had narrowly been avoided. A grounding would have violently shorn the sonar dome from the hull. The jarring impact could have easily killed or injured many of his men.

Never a screamer, Ty steadied his nerves and calmly questioned his watch standers. Legs slightly shaking as the adrenaline wore off, he pieced together the string of events that had contributed to this near catastrophe.

The bridge team wanted a clean deck, so they had turned on the lights to swab it. In preparation for the next day's gunnery exercises, the Electronics Technicians were adjusting the radar and repairing the SATNAV. The team in CIC was changing their charts at the same time as the navigators on the bridge. As a result, neither station had a dead reckoning plot. Because the radars and SATNAV were down, no one knew how far they were from land. The Officer of the Deck and Junior Officer of the Deck had been discussing the next day's events, thinking ahead instead of monitoring the tactical situation around them. The entire watch section, bridge and Combat combined, had collectively lost their situational awareness.

The next day, Ty held a come-to-Jesus talk with his junior officers. He told the young men with hang-dog faces that under no circumstances would white lights be used on the bridge in periods of darkness. They would wait until dawn to swab the deck. Combat and the bridge would never change charts at the same time. One or the other would always have a solid navigational plot. He reminded watch standers that their primary focus should always be the safety of the ship.

Was it Divine Providence or the sixth sense borne of years at sea that woke him that morning, mere minutes before disaster struck? Ever the pragmatist, Ty will tell you that as the ship steamed into shallower water, he probably sensed the change in vibrations on the hull caused by the ship's pressure wave bouncing off the bottom.

Whatever the cause, he went to sleep that night knowing that navigational catastrophes can happen to anyone at any time, and thanked his lucky stars that this time it just wasn't his turn.

Six

WE HAVE A WINNER

"This line isn't moving at all," I complained.

"Glad we got here good and early," Ty said, checking his watch.

Security at Baltimore-Washington Airport was still extremely tight, even half a year after 9/11. I wasn't thrilled about flying, but I wasn't going to let my fears keep me sitting at home.

Especially not with our possible dream-boat sitting in St. Petersburg.

I pulled out the listing, even though by now I had it memorized. "I just can't believe the equipment on this one: brand new sails, new running rigging, new autopilot, new single-side-band radio, new wiring, new plumbing, new inverter… new *everything*."

"Less than a hundred hours on the engine," Ty added, as familiar with the list as I.

"It may be a 1980 boat, but this guy has basically re-built the thing," I said, sliding my luggage forward as we slowly inched ahead.

"You know what I always say," Ty said. "If it sounds too good to be true…"

"It probably is," I parroted.

But here we were, flying all the way to Florida to see for ourselves.

We'd found her on the Internet only days before, and the write-up was unlike any other we'd seen. Page after page of upgrades and amenities described a boat that so closely matched our desires, it was as if the great

Broker in the Sky had led us to her. Within minutes we were on the phone with the seller, arranging to see her before someone snatched her up.

"I see you just purchased your tickets this week," the agent said as we finally made it to the counter.

"That's right." Ty said.

"Will you be checking any luggage to Tampa?"

"No. We just have these two carry-ons." I answered.

He frowned. "I can almost guarantee you the computer's going to pick you for a search."

I looked at Ty and we rolled our eyes.

"Yep, I was right," the agent confirmed, staring at his screen. "This is supposed to be random, but certain factors automatically mark you for a check. If you'd please step over to the side, I'm afraid I have to go through your bags."

"I suppose our military ID doesn't mean anything," Ty said.

"I'm sorry, Sir."

We placed our bags on a table as the agent pulled on a pair of baby blue rubber gloves. Very carefully, as if handling nuclear waste, he opened Ty's carry-on and began pulling out items, one by one. Carefully sliding his hand into every crevice, separating socks, and unfolding shirts, he methodically inspected our belongings in full view of everyone in sight.

My pre-flight jitters turned into anger as he reached for my bag.

"I can't believe you'd do this to us, while that Charles Manson lookalike in front of us walked right through."

"I don't have any say in the matter, Ma'am," the man said as he placed my bra on the table next to my panties.

By now I was seething. "I work in the Pentagon. I was there on 9/11."

"Then you should understand better than anyone why this is necessary," the agent said, adding that he would happily refund our tickets if I wanted him to stop.

My mouth a thin line, eyes blazing, I looked at Ty and whispered, "If he starts pulling my girl-things out of that cosmetic bag, I'm going to lose it."

"Maybe you should go for a walk," Ty said, placing his hand on my back and pointing me away from the table.

"Maybe I will," I snapped, and stormed away.

Seeing a restroom across the concourse, I went inside and locked myself in a stall. Suddenly, unexpected tears were running down my face. I stifled my sobs, not wanting to attract attention from the ladies at the sinks.

Get a grip, Suzanne!

The flight, the search… all of it brought 9/11 back in a flood of memories.

I glanced at my watch. The man was slow, but surely he was finished by now. Blowing my nose on some toilet paper, I left the stall and checked my damaged face in the mirror. The hell with him. We were going to Florida to look at our dream boat. I wasn't going to let some airline bureaucrat ruin this weekend.

I arrived back at the table just as Ty was lifting our bags.

"You ok?" he asked with concern.

"You bet."

"That was so unlike you."

"And you, too. I expected *you* to have a fit."

"You took care of both of us," he laughed, then asked, "How about a drink?"

I looked at him in surprise. We usually bypassed the airport bars in favor of a cup of coffee, but his prescription sounded just right for my frazzled nerves.

"Now you're talking!" I smiled, taking my bag so I could slip my hand in his.

A beer for Ty and two glasses of wine for me later, we headed for our gate.

"Gee, looks like most of the people are already onboard," Ty said, quickly checking his watch.

"Well, glad we made the most of our time," I giggled.

"You sure are a cheap date," Ty laughed, steering me toward the skyway.

At the bottom of the ramp, I noticed three men in dark suits. The squiggly wires coming out of their ears caught my eye. Then I noticed the familiar oval pins on their lapels.

"Hey look!" I said, "It's the Secret Service!"

"Well, the secret's out now," Ty laughed.

The men looked up in surprise as I giggled yet again. "Guess I said that a little loud, huh?"

Ty shook his head in mock embarrassment as he guided me past the men toward the large door.

"Must be someone important on this plane," I said.

"Yeah, I'd say that's a pretty good possibility."

We walked through First Class, each of us scanning every seat.

Suddenly, my eyes fell on a familiar face. I turned my head and whispered in Ty's ear, "It's Rosalyn Carter!"

He nodded his head and pushed me forward.

"What? You don't want to say, Hi?"

"Not today, Suzanne."

"I'm just kidding. I didn't have that much to drink, you know!"

As we stepped into Coach, I stopped dead in my tracks. It had been ages since I'd flown on a commercial airliner. After dozens of flights on the Chairman's aircraft where there was never any lack of elbow and leg room, the scene before me was downright claustrophobic.

"Ty," I whispered, "Have these seats always been this close together?"

He rolled his eyes dramatically. "Ok, Miss Spoiled, get moving!"

"I'm serious."

"Yeah, well, you're back here with us peons now," he said as we strapped ourselves into seats so tightly packed I could barely cross my legs.

Resigned to my fate, I turned to Ty. "It's pretty cool that Rosalyn's on our plane, huh?"

"Yeah, I wonder where she left Jimmy!"

Before I could respond, the entire cabin burst into applause. Surprised to hear a sound you usually only hear on an airplane when the captain has landed safely in a storm, we both looked up.

There, coming down the aisle with his big toothy smile was Rosalyn's traveling partner, Jimmy Carter.

"Wow!" I said, a tourist yet again.

The former president walked the length of the plane, shaking the hand of every passenger aboard. As he approached our seats, I noticed an enormous silver buckle on his belt emblazoned with the letters "JC."

"Do you think those represent his initials or his faith?"

My question went unanswered as Ty reached across me saying, "Good afternoon, Mr. President!"

I reached out and grasped the man's hand, afraid to open my mouth after my previous inebriated outbursts.

The entire cabin hummed with excitement after Jimmy took his seat in First Class. I noticed that two of the Secret Service agents had joined us and taken seats in our section.

I was able to smile now, my tears and fears history. If any plane across America that day was safe, it was ours, thanks to our VIP passengers.

*   *   *

The sun on our faces was far more intense than the one we'd left back in Washington. The coral pink houses and palm trees shouted "Welcome to Florida" better than any billboard.

"I wish we could stay longer than a day," I said wistfully as we pulled into the marina lot.

"Me too, but this trip is all business. Now remember…"

"I know, I know. Be cool. Show no reaction."

"Right. Look! That must be the boat up ahead."

Ty pulled the car alongside the sea wall, where a 46 foot Morgan sloop sat glistening in the turquoise water. Neither of us moved to get out. The car was silent as we both took in the sight.

The twenty-two year old boat looked like it was straight off the showroom floor. There wasn't a scuff or a scrape on her, and the glare from her shiny white hull was blinding. A boot stripe as red as a crisp, Fall apple accentuated the whiteness. Fourteen shiny stainless steel ports surrounded a cabin top that glistened as if it had just been waxed. The tan canvas on the sails was immaculate, the modern instrumentation in the cockpit like something off a spaceship.

Finally, Ty spoke. "She's big."

"And beautiful."

I didn't trust myself to say any more.

"Shall we go take a look?" Ty asked.

"Uh huh."

The owner had been expecting us. Wearing nothing but a pair of swim trunks, he jumped onto the pier and extended his hand. "Hi, I'm Mike. You must be Ty and Suzanne."

"Hi, Mike," came a voice from behind us, and we turned to discover the source of the greeting was a large green parrot in a metal cage.

Introductions complete, we stepped aboard. Close up, the boat was even more impressive. The decks were wide and flat. The cockpit was big enough for a party. The chain plates and shrouds looked like they were right out of the box.

The wine had long since worn off, but my entire body buzzed. I'd been warned to hold my enthusiasm in check, and now it bounced around inside me like a swarm of bees. I swallowed, hoping my pie-eyes wouldn't give away how I felt.

We can actually afford this!

We'd been looking at twenty year old boats, because that was what we could afford. But older boats looked their age, many of them having been rode hard and put away wet. We occasionally tormented ourselves by looking at newer boats, but always left feeling bereft and wondering why we wasted our time.

This incredible boat could be ours!

I was excited, but strangely afraid… afraid to want something this badly at first sight.

Ty was his usual inscrutable self, in buyer-mode, as he poked around the deck. Surely he was seeing what I saw – a boat that not only matched our wildest dreams, but exceeded them.

Mike led us below and introduced us to his wife, Karla, who was busy entertaining two energetic toddlers. A small Jack Russell terrier slept on the sofa. Karla greeted us, then took the girls topside so we could have a look around.

I scanned the roomy salon and turned to Mike. "Very nice," I said calmly, while inside my mind was screaming, *Holy mackerel!*

The interior was straight out of a magazine. The honey colored teak of the walls glowed. Sunshine and fresh air flooded the spacious salon through the shiny stainless steel ports and large overhead hatches. The u-shaped galley to starboard at the foot of the ladder was twice the size of our other boat's. The double sink had sparkling faucets as modern as those in any house. The refrigerator and freezer could easily hold a month's worth of food.

The navigation table to port was large enough to spread out a full-sized chart. The instruments mounted above it were the latest on the market, not the hodge-podge of outdated models we were used to seeing. The circuit breaker panels were an electrician's dream, the wires behind them neatly bundled and labeled.

Forward was a pleasant v-berth with the first full-length locker I'd ever seen on a boat. A wider locker beside it contained shelves that could easily hold all of Ty's tools. Already, the storage on this boat was double that on our Freedom 36.

The small head to starboard was bright and cheery. Mike stepped on a pedal at the base of the toilet, and it magically flushed. No more pumping? I'd never imagined such a luxury!

Following Mike aft to the master cabin, he pointed out upper and lower sea berths in the mid-ships passageway. These would be perfect for offshore passages, when the best place to sleep was in the center of the boat. Lifting the lower berth revealed a bank of ten golf-cart batteries. This time it was Ty's turn to display some self-control.

We moved farther aft, and I was suddenly breathless. Here was an aft cabin to die for. Instead of a cramped dressing area and a bed like a coffin, an enormous king-sized berth with plenty of head-room dominated the space. Numerous drawers lined the sides, with more room for clothes than my dresser at home. At the foot of the bed, running fore and aft along the starboard side of the boat was an office-sized teak desk, complete with built-in computer stand and book shelf. The joinery work was impeccable, matching the craftsmanship throughout.

Mike explained that he had bought the boat several years before. She'd been in pretty rough shape, having been in charter service in the Caribbean. He and Karla had been told that they would never have children, so he had thrown himself into the renovation of the boat.

He quit his job and spent fourteen months working on the boat, ten hours a day, six days a week. With only two of them living aboard, he had torn out the large aft head and bathtub, a feature for which the Morgan 46 is known. Only after they were left with one tiny head forward did Karla discover she was pregnant.

And then, one year into the renovation, she got pregnant again!

Now they were a family of four, with a dog and a parrot, living aboard a sailboat with only one head. After all that work, they decided they needed a bigger boat. Mike had already purchased a sixty foot ferro-cement ketch, and was anxious to sell.

I looked around at the cozy cabin. With just the two of us, we didn't need two large heads. This boat was perfect for us.

"Very nice, huh Ty?"

"Mm."

"You'll notice I haven't gotten around to putting the floor in yet," Mike said.

I stiffened, waiting for the axe to fall. I knew there had to be something wrong with this boat.

"So if you buy it," he continued, "I'll put in whatever you like."

"Even teak and holly?" I asked, imagining how gorgeous the traditional yacht sole would be.

"If that's what you want."

"Mm." I said, afraid to look at Ty.

"Can we see the engine?" Ty asked.

"Sure."

Mike opened two large double doors in the passageway, and we all crouched down. I peered in at an engine room so large I could sit inside it, so clean a doctor could perform surgery in it, and tears came to my eyes.

Only another woman who had suffered alongside her husband as he played human contortionist just to check a boat's oil would understand my emotional reaction. I quivered at the thought of owning a boat with such easy access to the spotless engine and a spanking new generator that would power any electrical appliance we could conceivably bring on board.

Mike closed the engine room and the three of us went topside.

"I see it doesn't have a dodger, "Ty remarked, pointing to where the canvas windshield was normally mounted.

"Oh, you don't need a dodger," Mike replied.

We looked at each other. Having been offshore on other boats, we could only imagine how the waves would drench us without one.

"Ok, well, thanks for your time," Ty said.

I tried to hide my shock. Surely the lack of a dodger wasn't a show stopper! But obviously Ty had seen enough. "We'll get back to you before we leave tomorrow," I said, as we shook hands and got in our rental car.

I pinched my lips together as we pulled away, vowing not to be the first one to speak. Ty often did things just to please me, and I wanted his honest opinion of the boat before I started gushing.

We pulled out of the marina and he still hadn't spoken. Like a game of verbal chicken, I waited to see who would talk first. Finally, I squawked.

"Well??? What'd you think?"

"It's a nice boat."

"*Nice*?!" I was beside myself. "It's our *dreamboat!*"

"Yeah, but it's awfully big."

"We could handle it."

"I know, but…"

His words fell on deaf ears. I was a lost cause now. Hopeless. No other boat would match the one we'd just seen. I recognized my manic symptoms, and knew I was in trouble. I also recognized Ty's need to think things through, and decided to wait it out.

I waited all evening, and we talked around the boat, but made no decisions. It was all I could do not to scream.

That night I lay in bed staring at the ceiling while Ty breathed slowly and evenly beside me. Reasons why this was the boat for us made sleep impossible. Finally, when I could lie there no more, I slipped silently from under the covers. In the darkness I groped for a pad of paper and pen I'd seen on the desk earlier. Crossing to the bathroom, I closed the door and turned on the harsh fluorescent light.

Sitting on the lid of the toilet, I wrote a large #1, and began a list. I scribbled rapidly, producing a page that resembled the boat's listing, but personalized to fit our plans: Everything on the boat was new, so we wouldn't have to spend a lot of money on upgrades… There was very little topside teak, so we wouldn't have to do much varnishing…

On and on I wrote, listing even the inane details that I knew Ty would laugh at. Only when my brain was finally free of the racing thoughts did I return to bed. When the sun came up, I wasn't sure if I'd slept at all. Finally Ty stirred, and I pounced.

"How'd you sleep?"

"Like a rock. And you?"

"Not so well."

"No? How come?"

"I was busy."

He looked at me with a question, and I produced my night's work.

"When did you do this?" he asked, shuffling through three pages of single-spaced items.

"Last night."

"Where?"

"Sitting on the head."

Ty fell back on his pillow laughing. "You are incredible."

"And?"

"What?"

God, he was maddening. "So how do *you* feel about the boat?" I asked.

"I told you. It's very nice."

I swore I wouldn't strangle him. "Ty. This boat is magnificent. I know you think so, too. I don't understand this. What's the problem?"

"Suzanne, we already have another boat." His face was grim.

I was aware I was the impulsive one and needed to face reality, but I was not ready to listen to the voice of reason.

"I know that, but we can afford both of them for a while." I took my list from his hand, then looked back at him. "If we don't get this boat now, someone else is going to grab it."

I could hear the clock ticking across the room as he stared at the ceiling.

"Ty, just tell me… how do you *really* feel about it?"

He slowly turned toward me and took a long breath.

"I love the boat."

"You do?"

"I really do."

"It feels right to you?"

"It does."

I was no longer tired. I didn't ever need to sleep again. "And?…" I asked.

"And what?"

"Ty!"

He kissed me on the nose. "Let's go make an offer."

Seven

HELP WANTED

Buying a boat that's 1300 miles away is not like buying a car from the lot across town. The car, you just hop in and drive home. The boat, well, you have three choices: hire a trucker to ship it across land, hire a delivery captain to sail it home for you, or, of course, sail it yourself.

We chose option "C." What better way to get to know our new boat than to sail her into the Gulf of Mexico, through the Florida Keys and up the Atlantic Ocean's Gulf Stream! We figured the trip would take a little more than a week, sailing day and night.

Exciting? Yes! Daunting? You bet! At least for me.

Sail trim and line handling follow basic principles, but every boat has its own characteristics. I pictured the 46-foot Morgan with her oversized and unfamiliar equipment. I imagined trying to figure out how everything works while dealing with what Mother Nature would dish out along the way. It didn't paint a pretty picture. We could certainly handle the boat ourselves, but for the maiden voyage, I felt that a few extra hands would be useful.

I hesitantly suggested to Ty that we might consider taking extra crew along, and was amazed when he agreed. I'd forgotten that with Ty, safety comes first, superceding any macho do-it-yourself desires.

We decided to look for two volunteers. That way, we would have two watch teams of two crew each, with Ty and I on separate watches.

"Where are we going to find two people on such short notice who'll be able to take ten days off?" Ty wondered.

I'd worried about that myself, until a sign on a bulletin board at work caught my eye.

"I'll bet the Pentagon Sailing Club could help us out," I offered.

The club served sailors who didn't have their own boats. They had a well-structured training program and owned a fleet of six boats for local charters and club get-togethers. With several hundred members, surely there was someone who would be interested.

Crossing our fingers, I sent an email to the club commodore. I explained our situation and told him we were looking for two volunteers with basic knowledge of sailing who would like some offshore experience. We would provide all meals and pay for their air fare to Florida.

I heard back almost immediately. The commodore would pass our email along to the club's members. After that, we didn't have to wait long. Within hours I received an email from a woman who claimed she'd lived on a boat in Florida, and was very interested in our trip.

"Wow! Wouldn't it be nice to have another woman on board!" I said to Ty as I shared the email.

"Yeah!" He agreed enthusiastically. "And she can be on my watch team!"

"That's what you think!" I joked. "But first I'd better make sure she knows what she's getting into. Living aboard a boat doesn't necessarily mean you know how to sail!"

I hit "reply" and thanked the woman for her interest. I told her I'd made several offshore trips myself, and found them to be great confidence builders.

"While open ocean sailing is a great adventure," I wrote, "it can also be quite uncomfortable and tiring. We'll sail all day and all night in potentially rough weather, up to 120 miles from land, standing watches every four to six hours, and we won't shower every day. If you're looking for a great challenge, though, we'd love to have you along."

I never heard from her again.

The next day we received replies from two men whose sheer enthusiasm made us want to sign them up. Before making a decision, however, we invited them to dinner.

Rich was a retired Air Force colonel. Reserved and quiet, he was one of the club's instructors. He prided himself on his sail trim expertise. He'd never been offshore and was excited to experience ocean cruising.

Doug was a captain in the Air Force. He'd only recently learned to sail, but knew the basics. His military specialty was cartography, and we immediately recognized the contribution his navigational skills would bring to the trip.

Neither man seemed the slightest bit turned off by the potentially arduous duties that lay ahead, so we happily signed them on. We spent the rest of the evening discussing what gear they would need to bring, including their own foul weather gear and safety harnesses. I questioned them about their food preferences so I'd be sure to bring their favorites along.

With our crew picked and travel arrangements made, I spent the final week carefully planning the provisions we would need. The responsibility to feed our crew properly weighed heavily on me. I knew that if I underestimated quantities or forgot a vital ingredient, there would be no 7-Eleven a hundred miles offshore.

I figured on a worst-case scenario of a ten-day trip and came up with three varied meals for each day. Next I determined the ingredients for each meal based on the needs of four hungry sailors, and added in snacks and drinks. Since the boat was empty, I'd even have to remember things like paper towels and the ever-important toilet paper. The result was a grocery list four pages long.

I wrote out a watch schedule, printed out safety rules, and neatly arranged everything in a notebook. I knew I was being overly organized, but chalked it up to my aide-de-camp background. I didn't realize at the time that my excessive preparations gave me a sense of control in the face of a daunting voyage.

And then, three days before we were set to leave, Ty shattered my perfect plans.

"You know John Roe, my friend from work?" he asked me as we drove home.

"Sure, why?"

"His son, Travis, heard about our trip, and really wants to come along."

I turned to him in surprise. "But we already have enough crew."

"I know, but he really wants to do this."

"What kind of sailing experience does he have?"

"None."

This is crazy, I thought, seeing my grocery list fluttering out the window like ticker-tape.

"I have all the menus perfectly planned for four people."

"I know, but I already told John he could come along."

I was floored. He'd made a decision that would affect all aspects of our arrangements without consulting me. I no longer had control over the trip, nor my anger.

Never one to yell at my husband, I spoke through gritted teeth. "He's going to have to sleep in the v-berth, the most uncomfortable spot in the boat."

"What was I going to do?" Ty snapped back. "Tell my good friend 'no?'"

I huffed and stared out the side window. *One more body to take care of! One more person to share a confined space with for a week! How could he do this to me?*

No longer able to stew in silence, I continued my ranting aloud, "What are we going to do with another crew member? We only need two people per watch team. Who's team is he going to be on? With no experience, he'll literally be a fifth wheel."

Ty kept his eyes riveted on the road. "He can cook," he said softly.

"What?"

"John said Travis used to be a chef at the Olive Garden."

"He did?"

"Yeah."

I swear, I heard harp music.

"He could be our cook!"

"That's right."

Suddenly, the idea had tremendous appeal! Having a dedicated cook meant I wouldn't have to spend valuable sleep time preparing meals and cleaning up after four men. It was a luxury I'd never even considered!

"We'll have to invite him to dinner tomorrow so we can go over the gear he needs to bring," I said, now back in planning mode and moving full speed ahead.

Ty nodded, his face the picture of a greatly relieved man, his friend pleased and his wife placated.

The next night we were joined at our favorite sushi bar by Travis, a clean-cut and polite 27-year old who seemed a bit stunned by the suddenness of the impending trip.

"I've never been sailing," he admitted, "but I did a lot of rowing in college."

"That's ok," I said, leaning forward. "We have big plans for you, if you're up for it."

"Like what?" Travis asked.

"Your dad said you were a chef at the Olive Garden," Ty said.

"So it would be really great if you'd be the cook on this trip," I said, finishing his sentence.

Travis smiled hesitantly and poked at his sushi with a chopstick.

I sensed his reticence and assumed he wasn't enthusiastic about being stuck in the galley. I explained that being the cook was a really good deal, since he would get to sleep through the night.

Travis shook his head, "I don't mind doing the dishes and all that," he said, frowning, "but I think there's something you should know first."

I continued to smile. There was nothing he could say that would dampen my enthusiasm.

"What's that?" Ty asked.

"Well, when I worked at Olive Garden, all I did was make the French fries."

It would have been rude to laugh and embarrassing to cry.

"No problem!" I said with a big smile.

Travis was eager to please. "I mean, I can try, but…"

I was completely sold on the idea of a full-time chef. I was not about to give in easily, even if that chef didn't know how to boil water.

"Look," I said, "I have every meal all planned out. Before each one, I'll tell you exactly how to make it. It'll be easy."

He didn't look convinced and shook his head nervously, "Well, I don't mind, if you can put up with my cooking."

How bad could it be? The peace of mind of not having to feed the crew myself was worth far more than any burnt meals. I reached across the table and sealed the deal with a handshake.

We had ourselves a cook!

Eight

THE DELIVERY

May, 2002, The Atlantic Ocean off the Southern Coast of the United States

The Gulf Stream is like those moving walkways they have in really big airports. You step on and walk at your normal pace, but you end up zipping past the pedestrians on either side.

We'd been riding this magic carpet for two days, and our speed was now an unbelievable eleven knots, thanks to the three knot kick from beneath. Outside the lifelines, there was nothing but water for three hundred sixty degrees. *Liberty* was a tiny white pearl in the middle of a large blue plate. She rocketed onward, but never seemed to reach the edges.

The boat heeled over at a 15 degree angle. Moving about below decks required us to hold onto the judiciously placed handrails.

"Is this how it's going to be for the rest of the trip?" Travis asked, swinging from handhold to handhold like a kid on a jungle gym.

"Probably," Ty answered as he assumed the watch from me.

"Cool!"

I smiled at his enthusiasm. Travis had turned out to be a wonderful addition to our crew. More than just a cook, he was the Morale Officer, keeping us in stitches with his dry sense of humor and silly antics.

"Travis," I said, "spaghetti's on the menu tonight, but I don't think it's a good idea to be boiling water with all this rocking and rolling. Why don't you bake tomorrow night's meatloaf, instead?"

"Ok, no problem! I'll start on it in a minute," he said cheerfully before disappearing into the head.

I peered up through the companionway at Ty. "You got it, right?"

"Got it!"

"Ok, I'm going to try to get some rest, then."

"Roger that."

My watch partner, Doug, was already in the upper pilot berth, so I spread my sleeping bag on the lower one. It had been a long four hours, and I was ready to crash. As I awaited my turn for the head, I sat on the sofa and looked across at the spotless galley. Our cook was taking his job seriously. I wondered if he kept his bachelor's apartment as clean as he was keeping our boat.

Just then, Travis emerged from the tiny bathroom shaking his head.

"What's the matter?" I asked.

"You know, when we're heeling like this, that toilet seat is like a guillotine for guys!"

Like I said, a real comedian.

Heading for my bunk, I passed the navigation table and glanced at the chart. We'd come a long way in just a few days, and each twenty-four hours brought a different challenge.

The Gulf of Mexico had kept us on our toes dodging fishing boats. Our track through the Florida Keys had taken us between two jagged reefs. Now we were in the open ocean, where rocky ledges weren't a concern, but huge supertankers crisscrossing our path were.

The chart showed our position in a straight line east of Jacksonville, where the coast curved inward in a giant "C." The Gulf Stream, however, carried us on a track that arced outward in the opposite direction, placing us now at the farthest point we would travel from shore. I climbed into bed and closed my eyes. I still hadn't adjusted to the four hour watches and was bone-tired. In spite of my exhaustion, I couldn't sleep.

Admit it, Suzanne, you're nervous.

My rational mind knew that we were safe. *Liberty* was as sound a boat as we had hoped. Our crew had proven to be calm and competent. Still,

I found it unsettling to be a hundred and twenty miles from help, should anything go wrong, surging forward in waves far larger than we ever encountered on the Chesapeake Bay.

Hoping to relax by reading, I picked up the copy of *Guideposts* magazine that lay next to my pillow. Its inspirational stories never failed to bring me a smile and a sense of peace. Leafing through the pocket-sized pages, I settled on a story about an oil rig disaster.

I read, engrossed, about a group of men that were also far from land, but these guys were truly in trouble. The solitary platform on which they lived and worked was being consumed by an out-of-control fire. As the oil workers prayed for help, their rig began to sway, threatening to collapse beneath them. As I read, my own bed rocked back and forth, adding to the realism. Just as rescue seemed beyond hope, the men heard the sound of an approaching helicopter.

The story was so realistic; I could almost hear the blades of the helicopter going whop-whop in the sky.

Wait a minute!

I laid the book on my chest and listened, incredulous. I really *could* hear a helicopter!

Hopping out of bed, I went to the nearest port and peered out at a lone black helo flying across the horizon from north to south.

I was stunned. We were 120 miles from land, yet at the exact time I read about a helicopter coming to the rescue of a crew in need, one had flown by our boat! Raising my eyes to the clouds overhead, I smiled. I had received the message loud and clear. We were far from land, but we were being looked after.

*   *   *

It was a few minutes past midnight. With light winds and a schedule to meet, we were moving ahead under both sail and motor. Ty and Rich had just relieved Doug and me for their four-hour watch, and I was snuggling into the pilot berth. I'd barely closed my eyes when suddenly, the engine sputtered to a stop.

Lifting my head from the pillow, I waited for the predictable four words from my husband's mouth. He didn't disappoint me as he jumped up from the nav table, stuck his head through the companionway and asked Rich anxiously, "Did you do that?"

A negative reply propelled Ty into action, barking commands to grab the toolbox and flashlight. In the glow of the red lights, I could see his mind working, running through the possible causes of the malfunction. As I unhooked the lee cloth and reluctantly abandoned my warm bunk, Ty peered into the engine room, shining a light on the despicable troublemaker.

"I'll bet we're out of fuel in the big tank," I offered.

Ty didn't even bother to look up. "No way. The main tank holds ninety gallons. There should be plenty left."

Theoretically, he was right. The previous owner had told us the boat would burn one gallon of diesel per hour, and we hadn't motored more than forty-five hours so far. But maybe Mike was wrong. After all, he'd never even left the pier with his floating condo.

"Why don't we just check the tank?" I asked.

The clatter of wrenches as Ty rummaged through the toolbox was deafening.

Hesitant to question the captain, I tried a different tack. "You're the one who always tells me to check the most obvious solution first. So I think we ran out of fuel."

Unable to ignore his own wise teaching, Ty stood up from the engine and huffed his way to the tank. The dipstick came out like a dry twig.

Wise enough to keep any smart comments to myself, I thanked God that the problem was easily fixed by switching to the reserve tank. I watched as Ty turned the valve allowing the smaller tank to fill the larger one.

"We should be good to go now, right?"

"Not necessarily. We may have gotten some air in the lines," he answered, then shouted up to Rich, "Try starting it up!"

Sitting at the controls, Rich pressed the starter button to no avail. The engine wasn't going to cooperate.

After the constant drone for the past several hours, the silence was intimidating. I had to talk to myself to calm down. We were a sailboat. We didn't necessarily need an engine. The sails were up, and we were moving, albeit slowly. There were no ships within our radar's twenty-four mile range. Ty would solve the problem and have us back up to speed in no time.

If anyone could bleed a diesel engine, it was Ty. Of course, I reminded myself, he hadn't always been an engineering whiz. As he loosened the air vent screws on the governor and the fuel filter, I shared with our crew the story of how Ty reluctantly acquired his skills.

He'd been on sea duty for four and a half years, with only short breaks for training. He was due for shore duty. *Past due.* Sitting in the wardroom of the frigate USS KOELSCH, with the Chief Engineer and the Weapons Officer by his side, Ty placed a call to his detailer.

"This is Lieutenant Giesemann," he said, "I'm ready for orders."

His shipmates shared a "this-oughta-be-fun" expression as they listened in.

"As you know from my preference card," Ty said into the phone, "my first choice is the Naval Academy. My second choice is a Naval ROTC instructor billet."

Ty wasn't picky. Any university would do. ROTC would give him the break he deserved and allow him to earn a Masters Degree at the same time.

"Well," the detailer said with finality, "you're going to Peoria."

Ty pictured a map in his head. *Peoria? That's in Illinois.* "What am I going to do there?" he asked, wondering what positions the University of Illinois' ROTC unit had available.

The detailer responded with one word: "Engineering."

Ty looked puzzled. "I can't teach engineering! I'm a history major."

Beside him, KOELSCH's engineer started laughing.

"What do you mean 'teach?'" the detailer asked.

"Well, you're talking about the ROTC unit in Peoria, right?"

"No, you dumb shit," the detailer replied (this was not the kinder, gentler Navy), "You're going to be *Chief Engineer* on *USS* PEORIA."

"Chief Engineer on USS PEORIA?" Ty repeated, astounded.

His colleagues cracked up. They knew KOELSCH's Operations Officer was the last guy in the world who ought to be an engineer. Ty much preferred the bright sunshine of the bridge to the hot, dirty engineering spaces. He was right at home supervising the navigator and communications officer, and planning exercises and training. He'd be like a fish out of water in engineering.

"What kind of ship is PEORIA?" Ty asked, his brows knitted together. "I never heard of her."

"PEORIA's an LST."

"That's amphibious!" Ty yelled back, outraged, as his friends howled. An amphibious landing ship was a far cry from the sexy, thirty-knot Cruiser-Destroyer community he was part of.

The detailer was not sympathetic. He explained that the Navy had decided to transfer the top performers from the CRUDES community to amphibious ships to help improve the amphibs' maintenance and readiness. The decision came from the highest level of the Navy. There was no negotiation.

Knowing he was beat, Ty figured he might as well start learning his new responsibilities while still on KOELSCH. "What kind of plant does PEORIA have?" he asked.

"She's diesel powered."

"Diesel?!"

Ty's shoulders sagged. This was going from bad to worse! His last two ships had both been steam-powered. He knew next to nothing about diesel engines, and they wanted him to be in charge of the plant. "What schools are you going to send me to?" he asked dejectedly.

"None." the detailer replied. "You've been at sea for five years and you went to Destroyer School. That's all you need."

Ty shook his head. At Destroyer School, the only diesel engines they'd taught were an emergency diesel generator and the twenty-six foot motor whaleboat engine. These were a far cry from the huge locomotive engines that powered PEORIA.

"No schools?" Ty repeated, giving the evil eye to the Weapons Officer, who was overcome with laughter.

"Right," the detailer confirmed, then asked, "Who's making all that noise?"

"That's WEPS, Lieutenant Heyworth," Ty said, still glaring at his friend.

"Heyworth? Put him on the phone. I've got orders for him, too. He's going to be Chief Engineer on CAYUGA, PEORIA's sister ship."

For the first time since he picked up the phone, Ty smiled. "It's for you, Shipmate."

Misery had company.

Like a good naval officer, Ty packed up and moved three thousand miles from Jacksonville to San Diego. Sea bag in hand, he reported to his new ship on a Sunday night. He'd accepted his fate and now felt a shiver of excitement as he tossed his gear into the Chief Engineer's stateroom.

The room was vacant, he learned, because the previous CHENG had been relieved for cause. This was NOT a Good Sign. As the leading engineering petty officer led Ty to the belly of the ship, Ty thought of his own lack of knowledge and shuddered. This tour could make or break him.

Engineman First Class Waller showed off the three engine rooms with pride. The spaces were in good shape, thanks to a team of squared-away sailors. The six 2750 hp ALCO main propulsion diesels were enormous: twenty feet long by ten feet high and six feet wide. There were also three big ALCO diesel generators. Ty stared up at them in awe. He had a lot to learn.

"Welcome aboard," the captain greeted him the next morning. "Glad to have you, Lieutenant. We're starting Refresher Training today, so you'll be able to jump right in."

REFTRA? This six week evaluation was the most difficult set of challenges a ship would face, other than combat itself. A team of inspectors would come aboard each morning and grade the crew in a series of demanding drills and exercises. The Chief Engineer's role was key to the ship's success. Ty ran a hand through his hair. Refresher training only occurred once every three years.

His timing was impeccable.

He returned to Main Control and reached for a cup of coffee just as a lieutenant commander in a red ball cap approached. The hat immediately identified the man as an inspector. His deeply lined face and crusty swagger gave him away as a Limited Duty Officer, one of the Navy's technical specialists. This man had been an engineer since Ty was in diapers.

"Good morning, Engineer," the commander said, extending his hand. "Are you ready for REFTRA?"

"Yes, Sir!" Ty replied crisply.

"Ok, then. Show me your ECC boards."

A hot flash of impending doom spread through Ty from head to toe. "What's an ECC board?" he asked.

"What?"

"I really don't know what an ECC board is."

The inspector was incredulous. "How long have you been Chief Engineer?"

Ty looked at his watch. "About ten hours."

The officer did a double take. "What were your previous jobs?"

"I was Navigator on a destroyer and Operations Officer on a frigate."

"What schools did they send you to?"

"None."

The commander stared at Ty and shook his head. He looked down at his steel toed shoes for a moment, then back at the new CHENG. "I'll tell you what we're going to do," he said slowly. "I'm going to teach you everything you need to know to survive this tour. By the end of these six weeks, Lieutenant, you'll be a Chief Engineer."

* * *

"Ok, try her again," Ty shouted.

Rich turned the key and pressed the starter. The engine coughed, sputtered, then roared to life. Doug, Rich, Travis and I whooped and cheered. Ty would have pumped his fist in the air if we'd been alone, but now he simply packed up his tools with a smug smile of satisfaction.

"Great job, Sweetheart," I said, kissing him proudly. "Now can I go back to bed?"

"You bet. Sleep tight, and thanks for your help."

I crawled back into my bunk, where I fell into a succession of vivid, movie-like dreams, a side-effect of sleep deprivation. After what seemed like only minutes, the incessant beeping of my watch sounded next to my ear where I'd laid it. I stared in disbelief at the face: 0345 already! I had just enough time to brush my teeth and suit up before relieving the watch. I slid off the bunk and stumbled to the head. Staring at my crazy bed-head and bleary eyes in the bathroom's small mirror, I cursed the engine. Its malfunction had seriously cut into my beauty rest.

I shuffled to the companionway, still half-asleep and looked out at Ty and Rich, their faces ghostly shadows in the glow of the compass.

"Good morning," Ty said quietly.

I grunted, then said, "Guess I better go wake up that other guy."

"Who, Doug?" Ty asked.

"No, that OTHER guy." I replied impatiently, hearing my own words and knowing they didn't make sense.

"Travis?" Rich asked.

"No…" I muttered, slowly realizing there was no other guy.

Ty and Rich looked at each other in confusion.

I shook my jumbled head. "Well then, I guess I'll go put on that thing."

"What thing?" Ty asked.

"You know," I said irritated, struggling to find the right word, "that thing we wear up here in the dark. That…"

"Harness?" Ty asked, now amused.

"Yeah, THAT thing."

From their raised eyebrows, I knew I had to get my act together before I even attempted to assume the watch. I buckled my harness over my foul weather jacket and stepped up into the cockpit. Thankfully, the fog in my brain quickly cleared as the fresh, cool air flowed across my face.

"Are you feeling better now, Sleepy Head?" Ty asked.

"Yeah. Sorry about that. I'm ready now."

"Ok, then." He began our familiar watch turnover. "We had one ship pass us a couple of hours ago, about five miles off our beam, but he's long gone now. Other than that, it was an uneventful watch."

"I like uneventful," I said as Doug sleepily joined us in the cockpit.

"I've been watching the weather," Ty added, and it looks like that low they were talking about yesterday is going to be off Cape Hatteras just about the time we're due to arrive there."

"N.G." I said. A low pressure system off the notorious Graveyard of the Atlantic was definitely Not Good.

"Right, so I made the call to head in at Beaufort and take the Intracoastal Waterway the rest of the way to the Chesapeake."

The four of us shared the same glum expression. Rounding the cape was almost a rite of passage, and now we would miss it. At the same time, none of us wanted to experience the kind of nor'easter that had sent hundreds of ships far larger than *Liberty* to the bottom of the shallow waters off North Carolina.

"Sounds like Prudence helped you make that decision," I said, referring to our invisible sixth crew member.

"You betcha," Ty said. "So I plotted our new course and we're right on track. Here's our latest posit." He pointed to a spot in the middle of the chart. The dark penciled line along which it lay deviated sharply to the left of our previous track.

Doug and I peered at the chart, illuminated in the red glow from Ty's flashlight.

"Ok. Got it. Any questions?" I asked Doug.

He groggily shook his head.

"I relieve you." I said to Ty, snapping off a mock salute as I stepped behind the wheel.

"I stand relieved," he replied with an equally lazy salute.

Ty and Rich disappeared below. As they fumbled about between the head and their berths, Doug and I sat dumbly staring at the flecks of white phosphorescence shimmering in our wake.

"Travis got a good deal," Doug said wearily, referring to our cook sleeping soundly in the v-berth.

"Yeah, but so did I." Bacon and eggs were on tap for breakfast, and I could hardly wait to start smelling them waft up through the hatch as we finished our watch four hours from now. All I had to do was enjoy them, then hit the rack, leaving everything to Travis.

God bless Ty for bringing him along.

"What day is this?" Doug asked.

"I think it's Wednesday."

"Isn't it funny? Days no longer matter. It's like we're just living life in four-hour stretches."

"I know what you mean, Doug, but I'm way too tired for such deep thoughts right now," I said, only half-joking.

We sailed on quietly, occasionally breaking the silence to share a story or comment on the trip. Ty and I were truly lucky to have found such compatible crew. Not only did they have helpful hands and strong backs, but they helped us stay awake when our bodies were screaming for sleep.

The watch passed slowly, broken only by swapping our duties between the helm and the chart every hour. As I turned my navigational tasks over to Doug, I pointed to our position and complained that we'd moved less than half an inch in two hours.

Even on a big ocean, you're never really alone.

Neither of us cared for the small-scale chart. It covered such a large area of ocean that our progress seemed painfully slow. I knew that once we arrived at the ICW the next day we would see our movement across the chart far more quickly.

I slipped behind the wheel and noticed the increased strain it took to steer. "Wind's come up."

"Waves, too," Doug observed as Travis climbed into the cockpit, video camera in hand. He'd been filming our voyage for posterity, jumping to record even the most mundane occurrences.

"Morning, Travis. Getting kind of bouncy up there in the bow?" I asked.

"A little," he said, bracing himself against the companionway, "but I really got up to film the sunrise."

"Should be a good one. It's nice and clear," I said, shoving my foot against the cockpit seat as the boat rolled from one side to the other.

"Cool." Travis replied, then smiled as if a thought had just occurred to him.

"Tomorrow's the big day," he announced, adjusting his harness.

"What? We make landfall?" Doug asked.

"No, I'm going to put on a clean shirt," he replied, deadpan.

I shook my head. This guy was something else. Returning my attention to the helm, I tried to keep the boat moving in a straight line. The large waves were hitting us from our port quarter now, causing the boat to yaw as we ran with the brisk breeze behind us.

"You know," Travis said as he surrounded his camera with plastic wrap and duct tape, "I've been thinking of some new angles I want to shoot. Ok if I climb the mast?"

I stared at him in disbelief, then answered simply. "No."

"Just wondering." he said, shrugging his shoulders.

"In fact, don't even think about leaving the cockpit until things settle down out there," I said.

The nervousness that had kept me awake days earlier was gone, erased by my growing confidence in the boat. Our research had told us the Morgan 46 had a sea-kindly motion, and she proved that to us now. Her reaction to the waves was predictable, and in the increasing light of dawn I could see well enough to brace for the expected roll each swell brought.

"So are these really big waves?" Travis asked.

"Big enough," I said.

"When's it going to get really sporty?" he asked.

"Be careful what you ask for," Doug admonished, as I merely shook my head.

Glancing over my left shoulder, an especially large wave caught my eye. *This is not going to be good*, I thought, as it surged toward our beam before I could turn the wheel.

"Hold on!" I said with a calmness that surprised me.

The monster lifted us up, then dumped us on our side, sending Doug sliding onto the floor of the cockpit, the candy he'd been eating strewn at his feet.

"My gummy bears!" he cried, looking up at me in surprise while Travis cracked up.

I turned to our cook and pointed my finger, laughing. "See what you did!"

In the midst of our silliness, Ty appeared in the companionway.

"What the hell happened?" he asked.

"Just a big wave that hit us the wrong way. Sorry about that." I said, nonchalantly.

Rich joined Ty at the ladder. He'd been sleeping in the upper pilot berth, and I wondered if the lee cloth had done its job of holding him snugly in bed. If not, he had a lot farther to fall than Doug had tumbled onto the cockpit floor.

"How'd you make out down there?" I asked.

"I gotta tell you, I was laughing my ass off."

This was not the answer I expected to hear, especially from the most reserved member of our crew.

"Why?" Doug asked, still picking up the scattered red candy.

Rich informed us that when the boat heeled, he'd merely rolled against the lee cloth. Our captain hadn't fared quite so well, however. Ty had chosen to sleep in the king-sized bed instead of the sea berth. Without the lee cloth, he was at the mercy of the motion.

"I look aft," Rich said, "and there's Ty, arms and legs flyin' all over the place before he ends up plastered against the wall."

Glad he wasn't hurt, I braced myself for Ty's reaction, but the presence of an audience totally changed the group dynamic. Had there just been the two of us, Ty would have likely cursed his luck. Now, as the four of us laughed raucously at his wave-induced acrobatics, he knew he was outnumbered.

"I can see I'm not going to get any sympathy from this crowd," he harumphed, then announced, "I'm going back and get what little rest I have left."

"Which bed are you going to sleep in?" I asked innocently.

"Watch it," he said, menacing me with a pointed finger. "You're in enough trouble already!"

The grin on his face as he disappeared told me all I needed to know.

*   *   *

Once inside the Intracoastal Waterway, the voyage took on a whole new tone. No longer restrained by safety harnesses and tethers, we enjoyed the freedom of wandering the deck unencumbered. In the shallower waters with land always close abeam, however, we were forced to focus much more closely on navigation. Hopping from buoy to buoy, we crossed broad bays and transited narrow canals as eagles and osprey flew overhead.

The wind continued to increase, and I thanked Ty for making the wise decision to come inshore. As a forty-two knot gust rattled the rigging, I pictured conditions off Cape Hatteras. I shivered, but not because of the cooler northern temperatures.

Beating into frothing whitecaps, the four of us stood in the cockpit, enjoying the wildness as wave after wave rolled down the foredeck. We ducked involuntarily, seconds before gallons of water splattered against the clear plastic of our stainless steel and canvas windshield.

"You don't need a dodger," Ty said, mimicking the previous owner's words while we shared the laugh from the cozy, dry cockpit.

The sun slipped below the horizon half an hour before we popped out of the Elizabeth River at Portsmouth, Virginia. Passing the mothball fleet of Navy ships, our crew gaped at the impressive gray hulls. Ty and I smiled silently, lost in the memories the familiar ship names revived.

A radio call on channel 16 shook us from our reverie as an approaching vessel hailed the northbound sailboat off Portsmouth harbor. Looking around, I saw no other northbound boats and realized he was calling us.

"This is *Liberty*," I said.

"Uh, I just wanted to tell you your starboard running light is burned out." The voice reported.

I glanced at the bow, where our red light reflected against the left rail of our bow railing and a green glow from the starboard navigation light shined on the other side. The lights were shielded so that they could only be seen by approaching boats at specific angles, thus enabling others to judge which side of us they were viewing. "They're both working fine," I told Ty, puzzled.

He picked up the mike and relayed the status to the concerned sailor.

"Well, all I know is, I can't see your green light from here. I only see the red one."

"Are you the vessel just off our port bow?" Ty asked.

"Yeah, that's me," the man replied.

Ty and I looked at each other with a smile of amusement. "That's why you can't see our green light," Ty said, explaining what should have been obvious. "You're not supposed to see it from that angle."

There was a moment's pause, then a snippy voice came back, "Well, I was just trying to be helpful."

The five of us chuckled, marveling how anyone with a checkbook could buy a boat and drive it with no training at all. The amusing thought was somewhat more sobering, however, when Ty and Rich retired below, leaving Doug and me to find our way up the Chesapeake Bay in the dark.

Soon I wished I had as much experience as Ty as I tried to discern the lights on the shore from those on the water. Lights ashore I could ignore. Those on the water had to be identified before I could dismiss them. Unfortunately, in the darkness it was hard to tell where the water ended and the shore began.

Steering the boat along our pre-determined track, I peppered Doug with questions.

"There's a blip on the radar about 45 degrees off the port bow at half a mile. What does the chart show?"

The red beam of his flashlight illuminated the chart as Doug leaned in close. "Looks like a green daymark."

I peered into the darkness and shook my head. One more thing to worry about. Daymarks were great navigation aids in the sunlight, but they were invisible at night, except on my radar screen. Nothing more than a reflective sign affixed to a piling as thick as a telephone pole, we wanted to avoid them at all costs.

I stared intently at the radar. It had proven to be my best friend on this trip, alerting me well in advance of any obstacles in our way. Having it in my direct line of sight at the wheel gave me critical data instantly, and I marveled that so many boats mounted their radar screens below deck at the navigation table.

Interpreting the presentation as we moved through the water took some skill, requiring an understanding of relative motion with which I was slowly growing more competent. Stationary objects appeared to move, while objects going the same speed as us often appeared motionless. In the Gulf Stream, I'd learned that large ships' radar returns showed up as elongated half-inch slashes. Smaller boats and navigation aids were small dots.

Out in the Atlantic, the screen had been mostly blank, making it child's play to identify a ship when it popped up on the horizon. Now, the dark screen was filled with white blips of varying sizes, and I took a deep breath.

There was a particularly large blob on the two mile range ring in the three o'clock position. Turning my head 90 degrees, I picked out two white masthead lights and a red light, moving together as a group in relation to lights on the far shore. *That's a ship, alright*, I thought, the lights telling me that a vessel over fifty meters in length was underway, and I was seeing it from its port side.

I'd been tracking the contact for two hours, and it had slowly been getting closer. Unfortunately, it remained steadily in the three o'clock position. This was a classic case of Constant Bearing, Decreasing Range. CBDR was one of the first things I'd learned at Officer Candidate School years earlier. If a vessel's bearing in relation to my own remained constant, and its range continued to decrease, a collision was the likely result.

There are very specific maritime rules of the road to govern how ships should avoid collisions. I knew that if I could see the ship's red light, he was looking at my right side and could see my green running light. In this situation, the rules said I had to give way.

In spite of the tension, I smiled ruefully. I didn't need rules to know I should stay the hell out of this big guy's way… the Law of Gross Tonnage was good enough for me!

Looking back at the screen I noticed two large blips straight ahead, growing closer at a faster rate than the fixed daymark Doug had just identified. Peering through the dodger windows, I made out a line of three vertical white lights and a green and red light below them.

I recognized the pattern immediately, but ran through the list of mnemonic devices in my head, just to be sure: *White over white, towing at night.* It was a tug boat engaged in towing. That explained why the radar showed two blips. The second blip was whatever he was towing. And if I could see both green and red running lights, I was looking at the tug head-on.

"There's a tug and tow coming this way," I told Doug, as I started fidgeting. This was getting to be a bit much. I considered waking Ty, but reassured myself.

You know what you're doing. Take evasive action early.

Our track was taking us up the west side of the bay. We had good water off to our left, but not for any distance. I could come left to get out of the other vessels' way, but I didn't want to go too far from our track.

"I'm going to slow and turn ninety degrees to port," I informed my navigator, "just until these guys are clear."

I eased the throttle and turned the wheel to the left. As the boat came around, I found myself staring up at a fixed green light, just off our port bow. The light sat atop a dark mass, far too close for comfort.

"Doug!" I shouted, totally caught off guard, "What is that? A nav aid?"

"I don't know! I didn't see it before!"

"Neither did I! Check the chart! Quick!"

Just then, Ty stepped up into the cockpit, rubbing his eyes. "Why'd you slow? Everything all right?"

I turned the wheel back to starboard, breathing fast. "I was maneuvering to avoid a tug and tow and a ship, and out of nowhere, there's a light on a tower, right over there!"

I peered over my shoulder and blinked in confusion as the green light suddenly turned red. *What the...?*

"A fixed light?" Ty asked. "Not flashing?"

"Yeah, but now it's red!"

"Lights on navigation aids aren't fixed," Ty reminded me. "If it's a buoy, it'd be blinking."

I knew that, I thought, scolding myself. I picked up the binoculars and peered at the dark mass beneath the now red light. "Holy shit! It's not a tower, it's a sail!"

I gaped at the bobbing light, so close to our boat I could have hit it with a baseball. It was a sailboat, out here in the dark just like us, and I had cut right across his bow.

"You didn't see him?" Ty asked, stepping beside me.

"No! Look at the radar. There's nothing there!"

"He's probably wood."

It was no consolation that a wooden-hulled boat would not be detected by our radar. I should have seen his lights, but the darkness where the boat had been was peppered with lights from the Virginia shoreline.

"Well, you made the right call to maneuver away from the other vessels," Ty said, hoping to console me.

"Yeah, but I almost hit another sailboat!" The thought made me long to be back on the open sea. People thought the ocean was a daunting place to sail, but the Chesapeake Bay at night was turning out to be the greatest challenge of the voyage.

"Your watch is almost over," Ty said. "Why don't you let Rich and me take it from here?"

I looked at Doug who sat staring dumbly at the dark water. His face reflected my shock and shame.

Turning over our watch before it was time only emphasized my failure, but I'd had enough. My frazzled brain was crying for a break.

"All right. Thanks," I said softly.

"Why don't you just turn off your alarm clock," Ty suggested. "I'll take it the rest of the night."

I merely grunted and disappeared below, relieved to be away from the stress and confusion. Free of responsibility, I flopped into my bunk and fell immediately asleep.

Four hours later, I awoke, my body now accustomed to the watch cycle. I instantly remembered the close call and pulled my knees up to my chest. Hugging myself, I marveled that we'd come twelve hundred miles without incident, and I'd almost blown it in our own home waters.

I remembered that Ty had offered to take my watch for me, and I struggled with my emotions. It would be easy to stay curled up in a ball under the comforting blanket with no worries. But surely he was exhausted by now. More importantly, it was my last watch, and I was not going to give in to my fears and abdicate my responsibility. It was my boat, too.

I rolled out of the bunk and noticed that Doug showed no signs of moving. He seemed to have taken the incident more personally than I had. I left him there, put on my safety harness and climbed back into the cockpit.

"What are you doing up?" Ty asked. "I said I'd take it."

"I know. But I'm here, and I'm ready." Surely he understood my need to redeem myself.

I sat in the cockpit and watched as Rich peered over the chart with a flashlight and Ty stared through the binoculars.

"What's going on?"

"We're trying to figure out what those lights up ahead are. I think it's a tug, but I'm not sure. There are several of them out there."

He made a call on the radio, and was answered by a tugboat captain. They tried to determine each other's location, but it didn't clear up the confusion of the bright lights off our bow.

I moved next to Rich and looked at the chart. A series of yellow lights were shown grouped together in a spot marked "restricted area" several miles ahead of our track. Suddenly my brain pictured the site in daylight: a large wharf, half a mile from shore, where ships once tied up to discharge liquid natural gas. We'd sailed past it several times during day trips on the bay.

"Could those be the lights at the LNG terminal?" I asked.

Ty whipped around and bent over to look at the chart. He shook his head. "I don't believe it. I've been tracking a *pier!*"

My previous despair instantly lifted. What immediately obvious when I checked the chart, hadn't been evident to the two tired watchstanders after hours of fixating on lights. Painfully aware that my earlier blunder had almost caused a collision, I didn't feel the slightest bit virtuous, only relieved. If a salty sea captain like Ty could make a mistake, maybe I wasn't a failure, after all.

The sun rose above the horizon as we approached our final turn into Herring Bay. Its soft, golden glow erased the pall that had hung over us through the night. All hands were awake now, infused with energy as the end of the voyage neared.

Below decks, our three crewmembers scurried about, packing their belongings. Ty and I shared the cockpit alone for the first time in eight days. I steered the boat toward the familiar green daymark off Holland Point and glanced over at him. The sight made me laugh. He was the picture of sobriety, standing on the starboard seat, straight as an arrow, hands clasped behind his back, staring solemnly straight ahead.

"I can't believe we completed the mission," I said cheerily.

He snapped around and pierced me with his eyes. "We're not there yet!"

There was no use arguing. We'd come 1300 miles and could see the masts of *Liberty*'s new home in the distance. In Ty's mind, however, any number of things could still go wrong.

I shook my head and grinned. *Vive la différence.*

"How 'bout taking the wheel while I make a quick head call?"

"Sure," he muttered.

Going below, I approached the bathroom door, then stopped cold. There was Travis, sitting on the toilet seat, fully clothed.

"Do you want me to film you?" I joked. It was the only place he hadn't yet recorded.

"That's what I'm doing," he smiled, and pointed to the camera, lodged in the closet across from him.

Travis. True to form to the very end.

In spite of Ty's worries, we got the sails down and motored into the marina without mishap. It was early on a Sunday morning, but Travis' parents, John and Susan, were there on the pier to welcome us. Travis gave Susan a Mother's Day kiss and promised to fix her French Toast, his new specialty, when they got home.

I looked at Ty as he popped the cork from a bottle of Champagne. Gone was the serious face, replaced with the same happiness and pride that threatened to overwhelm me.

"Nice boat," John said. "How'd she handle?"

"Like a dream," I answered, as five salty sailors and their guests raised our glasses.

Nine

MOVING DAY

January, 2002; Alexandria, Virginia

Our 10" television, one of the few things the packers hadn't yet touched, sat atop a cardboard carton full of linens. I perched on our bare box springs, watching the news with increased interest as the local forecast came on.

"We're going to have record-breaking lows today," the forecaster announced. "You can prepare yourselves for a high of only ten degrees, but the big story is the wind. We'll see gusts up to 40 knots all day, bringing the wind-chill down to well below zero. It's going to be dangerously cold out there, folks, so be prepared."

I shook my head. We'd picked a hell of a day to move aboard the boat.

I could clearly remember the moment we'd decided to become live-aboards. It was a gorgeous Fall day on the Chesapeake Bay – sunny and *warm*. We were anchored in a beautiful cove north of Annapolis. Ty and I were sitting on the foredeck sipping rose-colored hurricanes.

Alcohol will get you in trouble every time.

"You know," I said to Ty, "We spend every weekend on the boat. We'd both rather be here than at the house. If we're going cruising next Spring, why don't we sell the house now and get used to living aboard?"

He thought it was a great idea, and we put the house up for sale within days. Unfortunately, it was several months until we found a buyer. Now, here it was, January 22nd, the coldest day of the year, and the new owner was ready to take possession.

I turned off the TV and blew warm air into my cupped hands. It wasn't much more than ten degrees inside the doggone house! I stepped over to the thermostat. It was turned all the way up, but the furnace couldn't keep up with the arctic air blowing in the front door. Trying to get the movers to close the door each time they came in or went out was hopeless.

Hugging myself to stay warm, I walked into the kitchen where one of the packers was wrapping glassware as if she were late for a hot date.

"Let me run the dishwasher so you can pack the stuff in there, too," I said.

"Oh, I already got that," she replied as she hastily scribbled our name on a box.

I gaped at her. "But they were dirty!"

She shrugged her shoulders and continued her work.

I sighed. I'd moved thirteen times in my twenty-year Navy career. You'd think I'd be used to this by now. But this was the last time. Tomorrow we'd be live-aboards. Boat-dwellers, with 360 degrees of water-front property. If we didn't like our neighbors, all we had to do was slip the dock lines.

I climbed the stairs and stepped into the only warm spot in the house: the laundry room. Closing the door behind me, I stood in front of the dryer, opened the door, and pressed "start." Revived by the hot air, I dialed Ty's office number on my cell phone.

"How're you doing, Sweetheart?" he asked cheerily from his heated office.

"I'm friggin' freezing! The movers keep leaving the door wide open!"

"I'm sorry I had those meetings today. I wish I could be there with you."

"*Sure* you do!" I said, hunkering down in front of the dryer.

We'd already loaded the things we were keeping aboard the boat, and there was no sense in Ty coming home. We arranged to meet at the marina when he got off work.

It was after six when the truck with our household goods pulled away from the curb. I had no idea where they were taking our furniture, and I didn't even care. Let the Navy deal with it! For the next few years I had no need for the nick-knacks and accoutrements that went along with living in a house.

With the back seat full of last-minute items for our new floating home, I eased the car onto the Washington beltway. There I joined tens of thousands of bumper-to-bumper commuters in the daily ebb and flow from Washington to Maryland.

Four months, I told myself. I could handle this drive until I retired. After that, the only traffic I'd have to deal with was other boats.

It was pitch dark when I arrived at Herrington Harbor Marina. The long pier of I-dock was lighted only by yellow electric lanterns on every other piling. With a black plastic bag of belongings in each hand, I struggled toward our boat, my head and shoulders bent into the howling wind.

I'd seen Ty's car in the parking lot, and the dim glow of light's from *Liberty's* salon confirmed that he'd arrived ahead of me. Aching for the warmth of the heat pump, I stepped across the dark chasm between the finger pier and the boat. The knowledge that a slip into the icy water below would mean near-instant paralysis did little to comfort me.

Safely aboard, I slid back the companionway cover and climbed down the ladder.

"You made it!" Ty said, his words visible as the breath floated from his mouth.

"Finally," I said, glancing at the thermometer on the bulkhead. It was 42 degrees. Inside.

"Heat pump's not working," he informed me. "It can't keep up when the water temperature gets below 38."

Wonderful, I thought, as the wind howled through the rigging at gale force.

"At least we have the electric blanket," Ty added.

"Yeah," I agreed glumly, heading to the aft cabin. We'd made this bed, now we had to sleep in it.

Our first night as live-aboards seemed endless as the boat tried to shake off her lashings to the pier. Sleep was next to impossible with the roar of the wind directly over our heads. I lay in the darkness, staring at the ceiling. Our normally cozy boat felt foreign and cold, like the pit of my stomach.

It will only get better, I assured myself.

The buzzing alarm at 5:00 was a relief. We pulled our clothes under the covers and did our best to warm them before stepping out into the ice-box that was our home. We'd laid out our shower bags and work clothes the night before, so there was no need to hang around the boat any longer than necessary.

Ty moved forward and kneeled down outside the head. As he lifted the floorboard and closed the valve that allowed water to flow to the toilet, I secured the inlet to the sink in the galley. Neither one of us liked leaving the boat with the valves open.

He stopped at the electrical panel and flicked off all lighted switches except the bilge pumps while I hoisted our bags into the cockpit. The familiar procedure was the same we followed after each weekend of sailing. Now it would become our daily routine.

Ty joined me in the cockpit. I shined a flashlight onto the hatchboard latch while he attached the combination lock and spun the dial. The two of us turned to step over the seats onto the side decks, when Ty stopped in his tracks.

"Suzanne! Look at the lines!"

I followed his eyes aft, where I gaped at the stern dock lines. They ran from the pilings to our cleats on either side of the boat like two sides of the letter "V". In the course of the night, the abnormally strong winds had blown most of the water out of the creek. The ¾ inch ropes were as taut as tennis racket strings.

"We must be almost sitting on the bottom!" Ty said, rushing aft to slack the lines.

I wondered how Ty could work with the stiff ropes, the blood in my fingers having fled to my torso the second we'd stepped outside. I shoved my hands under my armpits and huddled against the dodger as I waited for him to finish.

"Go to the car and get warm!" he hollered from the aft deck.

I looked up at the finger pier. When I'd come aboard the night before, it was even with our deck. Now the narrow wooden slats were a foot above my head! "I'd love to!" I shouted back, "but I can't get off the boat!"

"I'll help you in a minute!" Ty shouted.

It will only get better, I thought, repeating my mantra to keep my mind off the numbing cold.

It will only get better!

When the lines were reset to his satisfaction, Ty climbed onto the pier, his extra height making all the difference. Reaching down, he grasped my hand firmly and pulled hard. I swore silently and shut out all thoughts of the icy water below as my feet left the deck.

"Gee, this is fun," I shouted over the howling wind, as we hustled down the long, dark pier.

"You'll feel a lot better after a hot shower," Ty said. The marina's modern restrooms had been a factor in deciding to live aboard the boat. *Liberty* had a shower aboard, but rather than introducing more humidity into the already damp environment, we knew we could start each day with a long, pleasant shower ashore.

Once there, I turned the water temperature as high as I could stand it and stepped under the coursing spray. The stall instantly became a steamy sauna, and I lathered up, luxuriating in the first bone-deep warmth I'd experienced in twenty-four hours.

I tilted my soapy face toward the water and smiled. *We're live-aboards!* I thought, just as the pipes burped and the flow abruptly stopped.

The steam rolled off my body as if I were a block of dry ice. I stared at the nozzle, incredulous, fiddling with the faucets, even though I knew it was futile.

Shoulders sagging, I stepped into the chilly bathroom, my skin as bumpy as a naked chicken. Picking up the towel, I dabbed at my sudsy body and sighed.

It will only get better.

Ten

SHAKEDOWN CRUISE

May 31, 2003; The Pentagon, Washington, DC

I'd escorted plenty of senior officers in my career, but this was the first time a two-star general had escorted me. Even more unusual was having my family by my side as we walked down the Pentagon's elite, executive E-ring.

As we passed the portrait of Omar Bradley, approaching the Chairman's Corridor, Major General Harrington, the Vice Director of the Joint Staff, turned to me and asked, "If I understand this correctly, you're leaving the Navy to go *sailing?*"

I gave him a what-can-I-say face. It wasn't the first time I'd heard our plans questioned in that tone. Just the week before, the president of Ty's company had called to offer me a job as his Director of Administration. The position would have paid very well, but the money didn't matter to me. I'd tried to explain how important our cruising plans were, but I could tell he didn't understand.

I decided to give the general the abbreviated version. "Yes, Sir, that's correct. We sold our house and cars, and we head out in two days with no plans to return any time soon."

I take it you know what you're doing?" he asked, turning to Ty.

"Yes, Sir," my husband replied modestly.

"Ty spent 26 years driving ships," I said. "He's more comfortable at sea than on land."

"Yes, but how about you?" the general asked.

I laughed. "I love the water, Sir, but you know what's really ironic? I served twenty years in the Navy, and I have to *retire* to go to sea!"

He laughed. "Which one of you is the captain?"

It was a question we heard a lot.

"We both are," Ty answered, smiling at me.

"They're co-captains," my father chimed in proudly.

General Harrington didn't seem convinced. He stopped and looked me straight in the eyes. "Are you sure you want to do this, Suzanne?"

It was a little late to ask. Sixty of my closest friends, colleagues, and family members were gathered just ahead in the dining room of the Chairman of the Joint Chiefs of Staff, waiting to help me bid farewell to the Navy.

"More sure than you know, Sir."

Minutes earlier I'd finished my check-out from the Joint Staff. My final act had been to turn in the gas mask that was now standard-issue for Pentagon employees. That simple step reminded me once more how important it was to live every day to the fullest.

I turned to Ty and we shared a knowing look. Three miles away, *Liberty* was waiting to take us away from it all. Her fuel and water tanks were topped off. Her spare parts locker was full of items we hoped we'd never need. And her crew was chomping at the bit.

Since moving aboard five months earlier, our days had been filled with cruising plans and preparations. Living on the boat had allowed us to maintain our focus and organize our floating home exactly to our liking.

In spite of weathering Washington's worst winter in recent history, we loved the live-aboard life. In our townhouse, we'd been shut-ins, driving into the garage and closing the door behind us. We rarely saw our neighbors and knew few of their names. At the marina, we interacted daily with fellow live-aboards on I-dock. Shoveling snow became a social event, followed by pizza parties and pot luck suppers on a different boat every weekend.

Our slip lease ran out in April, so with a cruising departure date set for 1 June, we decided to spend our last month at Washington DC's Gangplank Marina. It was the ideal location. The commute would only be five-minutes, and we'd be able to show the boat to our friends who lived near the city.

While the marina was only one hour from Washington by car, the sail down Chesapeake Bay and up the Potomac was a four day trip. In the Navy, when a ship's been pierside for an extended period, it goes on a shakedown cruise to test equipment and crew readiness under realistic conditions. Our four-day trip from Herring Bay to the Washington Channel served as *Liberty*'s shakedown cruise.

The last time we'd been underway for more than two nights was the delivery from Florida. We'd changed a few things since then, added some equipment and lowered the waterline a couple of inches with our personal belongings. This passage would show us what worked and what we needed to modify for full-time cruising.

"Are you going to take her out?" Ty asked, as I started the engine on the first morning of our mini-voyage.

I hesitated a moment, considered my rusty skills, then answered, "Sure!"

While Ty took in the lines, I looked up to check the wind direction. It was a bit breezy, so I'd have to use some extra throttle going out. Next I glanced at the water, focusing on a leaf that drifted slowly past. There was only a slight current. No problem.

"All lines in!" Ty stated.

"Backing!" I announced.

To quote my husband, the Morgan 46 backs like a pig. Lacking the easily-controlled twin engines of most power boats, *Liberty*'s single screw sometimes seems to have a mind of its own. Because of her hull shape and engine configuration, she likes to back to port, even when we want to back to starboard. Maneuvering in reverse requires the helmsman to have a Plan "A" and a Plan "B." Many's the time, especially when there's any kind of breeze, when "A" and "B" are quickly abandoned in favor of "C."

Giving the engine about 1000 RPMs, I watched my alignment as we eased past the pilings. The open water was to my left, so my preference was to back to starboard, then pull forward into the fairway. Ninety-nine percent of my previous attempts at this maneuver had resulted in my backing all the way down the fairway, following the boat's perverse preferences.

This particular morning, *Liberty* decided to cooperate.

"Holy mackerel! She's backing to starboard!" I shouted with delight as the boat steered exactly where I wanted her to go.

"It's a sign," Ty replied, smiling.

We were off to a good start.

One of the improvements over the winter had been the addition of a new holding tank. Now our first order of business was a stop at the marina's pump-out station. The helm felt strange in my hands as I steered past the pilings on my way to A dock.

"This sure is different from driving a car," I noted.

"Yeah, but it's just like riding a bicycle," Ty replied, echoing my own thoughts that soon we'd once again be comfortable with how the boat handled.

But first I had to get the big thing alongside the pier.

I steered past pairs of red and green daymarks. They marked a notorious shoal that had grounded many a careless sailor. The wind seemed a little livelier now, and I noted it would be blowing me right off the pump-out pier.

"I'm going to take it in flat and fast, ok?"

"Sounds good."

I approached the pier bow-on, holding my breath, then turned the helm hard to starboard. Ty tossed a dockline at a tall piling, but it fell short. On the one hand, I was glad I wasn't the only one whose lassoing skills weren't always perfect, but on the other hand, I now had to maneuver the boat closer in while he tried again.

"Toss me a stern line!" Ty shouted as he leaped onto the pier.

Eyes wide at his unexpected departure from the boat, I left the wheel and ran to the aft deck.

I threw the line, then returned to the helm while he secured it to a cleat.

"Ty! The bow!" I yelled, noticing with alarm how quickly the wind was blowing it off. I tried using the engine to bring the nose in, but with the stern line cleated off, the boat had already swung out too far to get the line across. We were now completely perpendicular to the pier, and I watched, speechless, as Ty untied the stern line, tossed it back onto the boat and shouted, "Take her around again!"

Take her around again?

I had never before single-handed a boat, yet here I was, rusty skills and all, in a narrow channel surrounded by shoals, with a good stiff breeze blowing. I looked back at my husband standing on the pier and shook my head. It wasn't like I had a hell of a lot of options at this point!

I knew I needed plenty of space to make a good approach, so I powered back out into the channel. There was little room to turn the 46-footer around, so I did the backing-and-filling maneuver I'd watched Ty do so often, turning to starboard as I moved forward, backing without changing the rudder, then pulling forward again. With the wind pushing me sideways, I had to use more engine than normal. I worried that I was over-correcting, and worse yet, that Ty could hear the loud revs from where he stood.

With the boat lined up to my liking, I stared at the pier. *Lord,* I prayed, *I need you to help me bring this boat in just right. I'm going to relax now and let you guide me.*

Second time's a charm.

I brought her in a little closer this time, used a touch more power, and backed to a stop exactly even with the pump-out. I ran forward, tossed Ty the bow line, then scurried aft and handed over the stern line just as he stepped up to receive it.

"Nice landing," he said with a smile.

"Thanks," I said, beaming, "I had a little help."

After pumping the tank dry, we headed out. These were familiar waters, so we buoy hopped down the coast toward the Patuxent River with no need for electronic gadgets to guide us.

The previous summer we'd used the autopilot only sporadically. On weekend sails with no set destination, we enjoyed hand-steering. Now that we had to put in some miles in a straight line, we set the self-steering device and crossed our fingers. It had performed poorly on the trip from Florida, veering up to twenty degrees off course in both directions. We'd gotten in the habit of disengaging it whenever another vessel was nearby, just in case it wandered at an inopportune moment.

Now powering south at six knots in winds too light to sail, I noticed we were approaching a small fishing boat. Not wanting to chance a steering hiccup, I pressed the red button to turn the autopilot off. Suddenly, the boat veered hard to starboard. I spun the wheel to the left, but she continued turning sharply, now running around in a giant circle.

"Ty! Come up here!" I yelled into the cabin. "I disengaged the autopilot, and now I can't get control of the steering!"

Ty bounded into the cockpit and looked around. Our wake curved behind us in a 360-degree ring. As I franticly jerked the wheel left then right, he calmly reached up and eased the throttle back to idle. The boat slowed, then glided to a stop.

I felt like an idiot.

"Nothing like overlooking the obvious." I muttered, making a mental note not to make that mistake again.

"No problem," he answered nonchalantly. "I going to have to give the manufacturer a call. That's one piece of equipment we need to be able to trust when we're cruising."

The first evening out, we anchored in Back Creek near Solomons, Maryland, at the mouth of the Patuxent River. Since this was our shakedown cruise, I was anxious to try out the shower in the small head. We'd only ever used the one in the cockpit, but it was a bit cool for outside bathing this early in the season.

A separate shower stall was the only item on our wish list that was lacking on *Liberty*. Determined to make the best of what we had, I'd hemmed two pretty, yellow curtains to keep them off the floor. I'd chosen cotton so they wouldn't stick to us like plastic would. Now I slid the curtains around the track, protecting the toilet and cabinets from the spray, turned on the water, and adjusted the water temperature. Blissfully hot water coursed down on me with invigorating pressure.

In true Navy fashion, I let the water run just long enough to wet myself down, then I shut off the water. After I'd lathered myself from head to toe, I used only enough water to rinse off all the soap. Sliding the curtains out of the way, I toweled off and stepped out into the cabin.

"Man! That was great! You're going to love it!" I told Ty, knowing how much he enjoyed a hot shower.

"I can't wait!" he said, trading places with me.

I dressed and headed for the aft cabin. On the way, I stopped at the electrical panel and turned on the inverter which that converted our 12-volt battery power to 110 AC. With the electrical outlets now powered up, I plugged in my 1200-watt hair dryer. It was a luxury, I knew, but one I didn't want to give up. Cruising was not supposed to be camping out. I wanted to feel good about myself, and that was impossible with flat, unstyled hair.

I pressed the button and the dryer came to life. I felt guilty for running down the batteries, but thrilled that I wouldn't have to give up my shoreside comforts. Drying my hair only enough to fluff it up, I turned off the small appliance just as Ty stepped out of the head.

"Hey, my hair dryer worked great!"

Ty glanced at the Link 10 battery monitor on the bulkhead. "We're only down a few amps. You can run it even longer if you want."

"No, this is fine, believe me. What'd you think of the shower?"

"Fantastic!"

"Yeah, nothing wrong with a good old Navy shower."

Ty cocked his head to the side. "Navy shower?"

I stared at him. "Ty! You let the water run?"

"Of course."

"You bum! This is supposed to be our shakedown cruise! I took a Navy shower!"

"Suzanne, we're only out for four days. We have 300 gallons of water aboard. I'm not worried about conservation. Besides, I had to do that on seven Navy ships, and I'm not going to do it on *Liberty* unless we're in a crunch."

He was right, of course, but I harumphed for show.

"Get back in if you're not satisfied," he offered.

"No, that's ok. I don't mind missing out while you luxuriate under the running water for ten minutes," I said, my voice pitched deliberately high.

"Are you *whining*?"

I smiled. He knew me so well. "I thought you'd never ask. I'll take a Chardonnay, please."

Ty set the wine glasses on the counter, then filled them with golden nectar.

This cruising life was going to be hard to take.

Eleven

UNDERWAY

We both agreed on one thing: we would have no schedule other than our June 1st departure. We'd had enough years of regimentation. Cruising was all about freedom. The only thing that would dictate when and where we went now was the weather.

But old habits die hard. Ty was a navigator on his first ship. He was used to planning schedules down to the minute.

It was the night before we were due to leave. The last of our family who'd come to DC for my retirement had left only a few hours earlier. Now, I relaxed with a book in the salon. Ty sat at the table next to me, poring over charts. I noticed he was scribbling on a pad of paper, and something made me lean over and peek.

"What are you doing?"

He looked instantly guilty. "Nothing."

I snatched the tablet off the table. "These are *dates!*"

He hung his head like a kid caught with a handful of cookies. "I'm just doing a little planning for our first week out."

"Days 1-3," I read aloud, "Potomac River. Day 4, Tangier Island, Day 5, Solomons… This looks suspiciously like a *schedule!*"

"Okay! Okay!" Ty laughed, snatching the paper back and crossing out the dates. "You're right. No schedule!"

"And tomorrow's the last time we get up to an alarm," I said.

Our slip at the Gangplank Marina was north of the Potomac River's Woodrow Wilson Bridge. Its horizontal clearance is 50 feet, but *Liberty's* mast stands 62 feet above the water. Because the drawbridge is part of the heavily-traveled Washington beltway, openings are only scheduled between midnight and six-thirty am. We'd arranged for the latest possible opening, but that still required us to rise well before dawn.

"Right," Ty agreed. "Let's go to bed early. I'll join you in a minute."

Ty flipped on the VHF as I crawled into bed. He switched to the weather channel and we both listened intently. It didn't sound good. Unusually high winds were forecast to start around two am and gust to forty most of the day.

"I don't want to head out if it's blowing that hard," Ty said, flipping off the radio.

I groaned and flopped back on the pillows.

"Listen," he said, crawling in beside me, "It'd be bad juju to go through the bridge with forty knot winds, just in case anything went wrong with the engine."

He was right of course, but I prayed for the weather guessers to be wrong. Both of us were ready to get the heck out of Dodge. As much as we'd enjoyed the Gangplank, it was time to go, and the first of the month was the perfect day to start our new life.

The rattling rigging woke both of us before the alarm. I could tell from the low moan that it was blowing well over twenty-five knots.

"Guess we're not going, huh?" I said glumly in the dark.

"I say we wait." Ty sighed.

I rolled over and crossed my arms like a spoiled kid. *What is this going to do to our schedule?*

And then I remembered. We *had* no schedule!

It made no difference if we left today or a week from today. For the first time in my adult life, I didn't have to be anywhere or answer to anybody. It was a revelation.

Later that morning, our decision to wait out the wind proved prudent. We watched in sympathetic horror as a large sailboat that had been anchored off the marina careened out of control down the channel. Two police boats attempted to keep the wayward boat off the rocky seawalls on either side. Once the vessel was under control, an officer jumped onto the deck.

When he hauled in the anchor line, I gasped. There was nothing on the end! They got the boat under control, but it was a sobering reminder of the multitude of things that can go wrong on a sailboat.

By six PM, the wind had subsided to a reasonable level. We wandered down the pier to a visiting Irish tall ship that was scheduled to leave soon. Spying the captain of the ship, Ty approached him.

"When are you planning on heading out?" he asked.

"If she doesn't blow any harder, we'll slip the lines within the hour" the captain said in a delightful Irish brogue.

"They're opening the bridge for you?"

"Aye, at eight o'clock," he confirmed.

I could have jumped for joy!

"We can go through with her!" I said to Ty.

"I don't see why not."

A phone call to the bridge tender confirmed the plan. We were leaving June 1st after all!

At one o'clock, our small parade of boats stopped traffic on the beltway. Led by the tall ship, and followed by several tour boats and the Presidential yacht, Sequoia, we motored toward the drawbridge. With us was *Bora Bound*, a cruising boat owned by Jack and Linda Woods, who we'd become friends with during our month at the Gangplank.

A knot in my throat made it hard to swallow as I realized we were leaving our home, now truly cruisers. With all the uncertainty of the past several years, I was never really sure this day would arrive. Call me paranoid, but I had never been able to forget that one of the victims of September 11th had been a naval officer, four days away from retirement, when the terrorists struck.

With the Pentagon off our beam, I thanked God for getting us safely to this day and asked for His blessing as we headed into our new life.

The bridge opened right on schedule. Above us, people had climbed out of their cars to wave at the tall ship. We waved back as if they were wishing us a bon voyage.

With sunset just around the corner, Bora Bound and *Liberty* turned east at the first buoy south of the bridge. Within minutes after dropping our anchor, Jack and Linda joined us aboard for a celebratory glass of wine that turned into two bottles.

The next morning, we awoke without an alarm clock.

"It's Monday morning," I said to Ty.

"And we're not at work!" he replied, completing my sentence for me.

We stretched lazily, then rolled out of bed and pulled on some casual clothes.

Climbing into the cockpit, we could clearly see the traffic backed up on the beltway. It was all we could do not to gloat.

The morning air was chilly, so Ty put on the fleece jacket he'd worn the evening before. Reaching into his pocket, he looked puzzled, then smiled.

Pulling out his hand, he revealed what he'd found. "You know you have a drinking problem, when you wake up with a cork in your pocket!"

In spite of the cool air, I was glowing. It had been a long time since I'd seen my husband so relaxed and happy.

I felt the same.

Our lives had been so structured until now. Everything from showering, to shaving, to shopping was strictly scheduled around our Monday to Friday jobs. This morning I'd thrown on a pair of comfortable stretch pants and a loose shirt, waiting to shower until I felt like it. I didn't bother with make-up, and like a sixties rebel, I left my bra in the drawer. It was truly liberating!

We raised anchor at 8:30 after a leisurely breakfast. Within minutes we had the sails up.

My normally-reserved husband raised his arms over his head and shouted triumphantly, "We're sailing!"

A pleasant forty miles later, Bora Bound and *Liberty* dropped anchor in a secluded cove halfway down the Potomac to the Chesapeake Bay. We'd traveled an easy forty miles, passing historic Mount Vernon and the Marine Corps Base at Quantico, our stress dissipating with each passing wave.

While dinner cooked on the stove, I joined Ty in the cockpit with a glass of wine. Smooth jazz from our favorite CD wafted through the companionway, and I settled onto the seat between his outstretched legs.

My husband wrapped his arms around me and rested his chin on the top of my head. Neither of us said a word as we gazed at the golden sunset. We didn't have to.

We were living our dream.

Twelve

LEI-AWAY

"Do you realize we could have driven here from DC in one hour?"
Ty said.

We'd been cruising over a week and had only gone as far as Annapolis.
At this rate, New England seemed light years away. Our plan was to
explore the coast of Maine until mid-July, then visit Nova Scotia until
mid-August. Our ultimate destination was Cape Breton's Bras d'Or Lake,
known for its calm waters and scenic beauty.

Anxious to experience new waters, we could have sailed right by
Annapolis, a port well familiar to both of us, but we had to stop and pick
up our re-inspected life raft and our new Apex dinghy. Neither was ready
before we left.

The closest drop-off point for our raft and RIB was a public dinghy
dock deep in Back Creek. One of several tributaries surrounding
downtown Annapolis, its seams were bursting with the overflow of boats
from the town's main harbor. Entering the creek's narrow channel, we
overheard a German cruiser on the VHF expressing his surprise at the
congestion to a fellow countryman. Even with our limited knowledge of
German, we understood enough to laugh at the foreign visitor's surprise
about the *tausends* of boats *hier*.

With marina piers lining both sides of the creek, there was room for
only a single line of boats at anchor. Arriving at our desired location off

Jabin's Boatyard, we chose a spot that made us feel like cruising babes in
the woods, sandwiched between boats from South Africa and England.
The Virginia homeport on our transom hardly earned us much prestige
amidst these veteran voyagers.

Eager to talk to other cruisers, we flagged down the British couple off
Sea Witch as they returned to their boat in a turquoise wooden dinghy.

"Hello!" I called out. "Would you like to come aboard for a cup of
coffee?"

They glanced at each other, their lack of immediate response making
me wonder if I should have offered tea, instead.

"Right," replied the man, after getting a nod from his wife. "In half
an hour, then?"

"Splendid!" Ty responded with a clipped accent, his two year tour of
duty with the Royal Navy rushing back.

I hurried below and pulled out a box of brownie mix. I hadn't done
much baking aboard *Liberty*, save for two attempts that resulted in a
charred lemon pie and a previous pan of brownies that could have been
used for a cutting board. Emails with the oven's manufacturer served
only to inform me that our particular model had no thermostat and the
thermometer was not to be trusted. This, *I* could have told *them*.

Undaunted, I put the brownie batter in the oven and played with
the dial, pulling open the door every few minutes to check for signs of
burning. As Ty helped our guests aboard, I removed the pan and divided
the contents into 16 squares. The knife came out gooey, but Ty was
already serving coffee. What to do? I put four of the sticky pieces on a
plate and zapped them for a minute in the microwave, leaving me now
with a gummy mess that was untouchably hot.

"I'll be right up," I called into the cockpit, wondering how I could
salvage the dessert. I rifled through the refrigerator, looking for something
else to serve. Suddenly, inspiration struck. Setting the nuked brownies
aside, I carefully scooped out four new ones with a large spatula and put
them on individual plates. A dollop of Cool Whip from the fridge and a
fork on the plate left no doubt that this was not finger food.

"Delicious!" Margaret declared after the first bite.

"Delightful," Geoffrey echoed, and Ty smiled knowingly, remembering
the previous burnt offerings.

We chatted pleasantly about the couple's recent travels. Looking forward to a future ocean passage, I eagerly asked how their Atlantic crossing was.

"Dreadfully boring," Margaret replied.

I blinked at the unexpected answer, but maintained a smile.

"I guess that's better than being terrified," I said cheerily.

"It's most unpleasant, actually," she responded. "Days on end of nothing to do. Isn't that right, Geoffrey?"

Her husband didn't reply, intent upon something at the bow of our boat.

"What size is that anchor chain you're using?" he asked Ty.

"5/16th."

"I see," he said, nodding his head thoughtfully.

"It's high test. Plenty strong enough for anything we'll encounter here."

"Yes, I saw you putting it out. How much scope did you use, by the way?"

"About five to one. The bottom here is soupy mud, so I used a little more than usual."

"Right. How big is your anchor?"

"It's a 66 pound Bruce."

"And you think that's big enough?" Geoffrey asked, making no attempt to hide the surprise in his voice.

I watched Ty's jaw grind a tense rhythm beneath his cheek. He took great care in anchoring, always erring on the side of caution. We had checked the swing circle, and there was plenty of room on all sides.

"It's actually one size larger than they recommend for a 46 foot boat like ours."

"Yes, of course." Geoffrey said, smiling primly, and Margaret deftly changed the subject.

"If you were military, did you two have any play in this Iraq business?" she asked.

We described our minimal role from the sidelines in our respective jobs, praising the efforts of our colleagues who were serving in theater.

"Yes, it was quite a good show you chaps put on over there," Geoffrey agreed, then added, "but don't you think you're spreading yourselves a bit too thin? I mean, you're still in Afghanistan, but I dare say you can't be everywhere at once and continue to be effective."

As I pondered a good politico-military answer, my history major husband replied very matter of factly, "Britain had its Pax Britannica. Now it's time for Pax Americana."

Geoffrey looked as if he'd been stung, then broke into a large grin. "Right. So we did. And so shall you! Bravo, Yank!"

Margaret cleared her throat, and shortly thereafter they retreated to their boat.

The next morning, Ty and I donned tank tops and running shorts and dinghied ashore for a run. Geoffrey was puttering about on his deck as we passed, and appeared not to notice us. I wondered if perhaps the previous night's discussion might have offended him, but upon our return an hour later, he hailed us with a wave.

"Out for a jog, I see."

"Yeah. Gotta stay in shape!" Ty answered, grabbing onto Sea Witch's rub rail to hold us alongside.

Geoffrey smiled. "You athletes are going to have trouble finding places to run along the way."

"Perhaps down in the Bahamas," Ty answered, "but we can run just about anywhere there's a road."

"Right," he replied, but his face clearly stated, "You'll see…"

Margaret stuck her head out of the cockpit. "Would you care to come aboard after you've tidied up and join us for tea and biscuits?"

We happily accepted, pleased that they were reciprocating.

We returned to the boat and gathered our shower gear. Rather than deplete our fresh water supply, we'd arranged to use the facilities at Port Annapolis Marina, a short dinghy ride away. While getting towels, I noticed the Hawaiian lei I'd hung from a hook was looking pretty bedraggled. A symbol of friendship, it was a retirement gift from some colleagues in Pearl Harbor. They'd told me to keep it for good luck, so I hung it in the head to take advantage of the delicious fragrance of fresh orchids.

The orchids weren't so fresh anymore, however. In fact, the thing was downright scraggly. Wondering if I was tempting fate, I tossed the lei on top of a full bag of garbage which we bundled up and carried ashore along with our shower bags and a load of laundry.

Smelling much better after a long, hot shower, and with our dirty clothes spinning away in the washers, we dinghied over to Sea Witch for tea. Geoffrey helped us aboard and immediately guided Ty to the bow, saying, "I want to show you my anchor chain."

"Wow! What is that, half inch?" Ty gaped.

"Yes, that's right. You seem surprised."

"I just haven't seen half-inch chain on a fifty foot boat before," he answered diplomatically.

"Yes, but it's certainly stronger than the 5/16th you're using."

I chafed at his words, knowing Ty would never use less than adequate equipment. Most every sailor of a 45-50 footer we knew used 5/16th high test.

Ty merely shrugged his shoulders.

Geoffrey gave a smug smile, and as we worked our way aft, he pointed out several other ways we could improve our boat. Ty showed nothing but pleasant interest. His self-control amazed me. I gave his arm a conspiratorial squeeze that said, *your Southern manners are showing, Darling.*

All restraint was lost, however, when we stepped into the engine room.

"Oh my God!" Ty exclaimed, not even attempting to hide the surprise on his face.

Before us lay the largest diesel engine we had ever seen. It was easily eight feet long, and filled the cavernous compartment. Black oil oozed from every connection as if from sweating pores.

Geoffrey was nonplussed. "It is a bit wet, I dare say, but she runs well."

We listened incredulously as Geoffrey explained that the beast was built in 1936. It had seen thirty years of service as a British tram engine before being used for another three decades as the prime mover for a generator by a band of gypsies!

Gypsies!!!

Geoffrey proudly patted the block and boasted that he had acquired it for the bargain price of 250 quid.

"That's quite an engine," Ty said, making a monumental effort not to laugh.

We left the engine room and passed the nav table on the way to the cockpit.

"How will you check weather while underway?" Geoffrey asked.

"Well, we have the VHF, of course, plus a dedicated NAVTEX receiver."

"And we just bought some software that will allow us to link our single sideband radio directly to our laptop to view weather faxes right on the screen," I added, pleased with our recent purchase.

"You don't have one of these boxes?" Margaret asked, pointing out a large demodulator on the bulkhead.

"No, that's the beauty of it," I answered. "No other equipment is required."

"Oh, that won't work, then." Geoffrey stated.

I couldn't help but bristle. We all have different way of doing things and human nature being what it is, we like to think our way is the best, but this guy's superiority was really beginning to rankle. I wondered if Ty felt the same.

"We'll see," Ty said diplomatically, as we followed the pair into the cockpit.

Sipping steaming Earl Grey and munching cookies we chatted amiably about our plans.

"Are you going to stay long in Annapolis?" Margaret asked.

"Only long enough to pick up our new dinghy," Ty answered.

"New dinghy?" Geoffrey looked up in surprise. "What's wrong with the one you have?" he asked, peering over the side at the funky turquoise and purple roll-up that had come with our boat.

"Oh, we'll keep it as a back-up," Ty answered, "but for cruising the Caribbean, we prefer a rigid hull inflatable."

"You Americans," Geoffrey scoffed. "You have to have all the new toys."

I bit my lip. Was this guy for real?

"What size are you getting?" Margaret asked.

"Ten feet," Ty answered.

"Ten feet!" Geoffrey sputtered. "That's going to look *ridiculous* hanging off the back of your boat!"

I gritted my teeth, insulted by his haughty tone. But at the same time, I felt a small sinking feeling in the pit of my stomach as I glanced over at *Liberty*'s dinghy davits. Had we made a mistake ordering such a big tender? As with every other major purchase, we'd done our homework. Everything we read recommended buying the biggest dinghy possible, since it would be the "family car," regularly helping us transport big loads of groceries and supplies to and from shore. Ten feet was supposedly the optimum length.

Geoffrey was relentless. "How will you store it when you go offshore?"

"On the foredeck," Ty answered.

He rolled his eyes. "It'll never fit up there!"

The four of us looked over at *Liberty*'s large, flat deck. The area forward of the mast pulpits looked plenty big to me, but the crease between Ty's eyebrows told me he was experiencing the same seed of doubt as I.

My enthusiasm for our "new American toy" now deflated, I decided I'd had enough of this pair's pessimism.

"I think it's time to put our laundry in the dryer," I said to Ty, standing up without waiting for him to agree. He was right behind me as we clambered back into our dinghy, hastily thanking our hosts for their hospitality and making our getaway.

The short ride back to *Liberty* to pick up quarters for the dryer was quiet until we snugged in out of earshot behind our transom.

"Good grief, Ty, you spent two years in England. Are they all like that?"

"Well, they do speak their minds more than we do."

"I don't know about you, but I was ready to tell him to *bugger off.*"

He laughed at my anger. "That's pretty nasty language over there, you know."

"I know it is, but that guy really got in my knickers, if you know what I mean."

While Ty went to get the quarters, I stomped up to the tool locker and grabbed a tape measure. Wordlessly climbing back into our dinghy, I stretched the tape from end to end.

"Ha!"

"What are you doing?" Ty asked, climbing back aboard.

"This dinghy is exactly ten feet, and it doesn't look *ridiculous* hanging from the davits!"

"Yeah, and it's going to fit perfectly on the foredeck." Ty answered.

Our enthusiasm restored, we zipped ashore. I tied off the painter and scurried ahead to rescue our laundry in case anyone was waiting for the washer. Pulling open the lid, I stopped and stared. Instead of being plastered to the sides, all clean and sweet-smelling, our clothes were still stewing in a full tub of gray water. I noticed there was no ambient noise in the small room, and all the light was natural.

"Bad news," I reported to Ty as he walked in. "The power went out, right in the middle of our load."

"Well, that's bad luck," he replied, and my mind flashed on the scraggly lei lying in the garbage can. I dismissed the thought as quickly as it had come to me. Power goes out all the time.

"Well, when it comes back on, it'll start up automatically, so we'll just keep checking on it."

We went back to the boat and wondered why we hadn't heard from the dinghy salesman yet. It was supposed to have arrived hours earlier. Getting a little impatient, we decided to call.

"Yes, the dinghy arrived on the truck this morning," the man announced, "but it was crushed beyond repair. Some bad luck, huh?"

I fought the urge to go ashore and root through the garbage for the lei. Sure we had lots of superstitions in my family growing up, but those were just foolish traditions. Even Ty adhered to some time-honored superstitions of the sea, but just because he never let me set my hat on a table or whistle onboard didn't mean he really believed that stuff!

The salesman told us he'd paid a fortune to have another dinghy overnighted to Annapolis. One more night wasn't going to hurt our schedule. After all, we didn't *have* a schedule!

We spent the rest of the day playing with our new weatherfax software. When the isobars and wave arrows started printing out on our laptop screen, we cheered aloud. It was all I could do not to shout over to Geoffrey that we didn't need any silly box on the wall to make *our* system work!

We went ashore for the fourth time to check on our wash, but the power was still out. Thankful that we didn't have to rely on shore power on *Liberty*, we decided to leave the clothes in the washer until morning.

Cutting across the lawn on the way to the dinghy dock, I shouted, "Ty, watch out for the --" just as he stepped in a little brown pile left by a poodle.

"Oh, shit!" he cursed, wiping his shoe in the grass.

"Yep, that's what it is," I said, laughing.

Failing to see the humor, Ty climbed into the dinghy.

I untied the painter and pushed us off as he repeatedly pulled on the outboard's starter cable. He cursed even more until it finally sputtered to life.

Hoping to lighten the mood, I pleasantly pointed out the distant flashes of light in the sky and asked, "Honey, what causes heat lightning?"

"There's no such thing," he answered curtly. "Lightning is lightning."

I was sorry I asked.

A glass of Merlot and a pair of clean shoes helped improve both our moods, and we settled into the cockpit to relax with a book after dinner. As the sun slipped lower in the sky, we suddenly looked up and noticed hundreds of mosquitoes congregating under the bimini. So far none had come below, but turning on any lights would surely invite them. Not wanting to bother with the screens, we decided it was much easier to simply go to bed.

Unable to sleep, I lay on top of the sheets and reviewed the past week. Everything had gone incredibly smoothly. It was unprecedented not to have mechanical problems or difficulties of any sort at the start of our big cruising adventure.

Until today, that is. First the laundry, which was still soaking in the machine, and then the dinghy getting crushed...

"Ty," I whispered. "Are you asleep?"

"If I was, I'm not anymore."

"They say bad things come in threes, don't they?"

"That's what they say."

"Well, we had three bad things happen today, if you count your stepping in the dog doo."

"Four, if you count the problems I had getting that weather software to work."

"Yeah, but you did get it working. I was just thinking maybe I shouldn't have thrown out that lei."

"Don't be ridiculous." Ty said.

Just then the rigging rattled as if a giant hand had reached down and shaken the heavy wires holding up the mast. Our sixteen ton sloop rocked like a toy boat in a second blast of unexpected wind, and we both shot out of the bunk like bullets from a gun.

Thunderstorm!

The heat lightning was no longer silent flashes in the distance. It now split the sky around us with jagged fingers of high voltage, followed instantly by ear-splitting cymbal crashes. We scurried to secure the ports.

Repeatedly popping his head out the hatch like a prairie dog as the rain pelted the awning, Ty suddenly went rigid. "He's right on top of us!"

I peered out the port over the nav station and watched as our Brit friend's stern came within feet of out bow.

Ty lunged for the ladder to the cockpit, but hesitated as a crack of thunder split the air.

"No!" I shouted, "You can't go out there!"

Until now I'd been relatively calm, but the thought of my husband as a human lightning rod sent an adrenaline rush straight to my legs. "Please don't go out there," I pleaded, softening my order to a request. "There's nothing you can do at this point."

"I could let out more chain, so we'd drift back." Ty reasoned, his hands gripping the ladder as he rocked back and forth with indecision and frustration."

My instinct was to disagree, but I held my tongue. We were co-captains, but in a situation like this, Ty called the shots. I felt my reaction would set the tone for how we handled future crises.

Choosing my words carefully so as not to sound like I was whining, I said slowly, "My concern is that if you let out more scope and the wind shifts, then we'll hit *him*."

Ty chewed on that for a minute, looking warily at the flashing sky and the stern of the other boat bouncing just off our bow. Even in the dim light from the electrical panel I could see his jaw working as he formulated a plan.

Finally, he broke the tension and said, "Ok, let's wait until the wind changes direction enough to move us farther apart."

I let out my breath and glanced at the clock. It was midnight. "We can stand here all night if we have to, right?"

He agreed, and we went up to the cockpit for a better view. In the darkness we made out the figure of Geoffrey in his own cockpit, surveying the situation.

"We're a little close, don't you think?" Ty shouted across the noise of the heavy raindrops.

"Right." He answered calmly. "But if everything's under control here, I think I'll retire below."

Standing in a puddle of cold water in our bare feet, Ty and I stared at each other incredulously.

"He dragged into *us*, right?"

"You don't drag upwind, Suzanne."

"After all his talk about the way you anchored! And he has the nerve to just go to bed!"

"What can I say?" Ty shrugged.

The time lag between lightning and thunder was now increasing, and I knew my husband well enough to know that we certainly wouldn't be retiring to bed any time soon. Sure enough, within seconds, Ty announced, "We're going to reanchor."

"Now?"

"Yes." And with that he stepped out of the cockpit into the rain.

Shaking my head, I started the engine.

"I can't see your hand signals in the dark, so you'll have to shout." I called out.

"Roger."

Following Ty's commands, I maneuvered the boat in the tight quarters, humming my own version of an old Jim Croce tune to quiet my nerves. *You don't drag into the wind, and you don't mess around with Ty...*

The next morning, with *Liberty* swinging nicely from her newly placed anchor, I glared at Sea Witch as we zipped ashore to retrieve our soggy wash.

"That was a good drill last night," Ty said.

I had to agree. We'd weathered both a major thunderstorm and a boat dragging down on us, and I was proud of how we'd communicated. It was obvious now in the daylight that the larger boat had moved significantly from her previous day's position. Even with the half-inch chain, the soupy mud and Sea Witch's large sail area were enough to make her drag.

We tied off the dinghy and walked toward the laundry room. The first thing I noticed as we approached was the hum of a compressor. Electricity! The day was looking better already.

Ty transferred the clean clothes to the dryer while I stood over the trash can, hesitating. Glancing over my shoulder to make sure he wasn't looking, I surreptitiously lifted the lid.

Empty.

My heart sank as I realized the lei was gone forever. How could they have collected the garbage so quickly? Our cruise was doomed. What had I done?

Then, as I always do when worried, I talked some sense into myself. Everything hadn't really been perfect until I threw out the lei, after all. Little things had gone wrong every day, hadn't they? Stubbed toes, rain, the tiller extension falling over the side… I was only focusing on the bad things now because of my fears. Superstitions were nothing but nonsense!

"Ok," I said cheerily, "That takes care of the laundry. Now we'll just pick up our *ridiculous* dinghy and we'll be on our way."

"Yeah," Ty said, rolling his eyes. "Knock wood."

Thirteen

OFFSHORE

Our cruising guide raved about Cape May's ornate Victorian houses with their "mirthful colors."

We never saw them.

We spent our entire 24-hour visit standing anchor watch while waiting for a weather window. A 210 mile offshore passage lay in front of us. We needed at least two days of fair weather before leaving the safety of the harbor.

At $2.75 a foot, we weren't about to pay for a slip in a marina. Nor were we going to leave *Liberty* alone in the tiny anchorage. Hemmed in too close for comfort by other northbound boats, we listened all day as the wind shrieked through the rigging like the soundtrack to a horror movie.

While Ty plotted waypoints and played with the weatherfax, I buried my face in a book. I tried to pretend the rattling and roaring didn't bother me.

At the end of the day, Ty had a stack of pages with swirling highs, lows, and isobars. He declared that the next 48 hours would be our only chance to cross to Block Island before more bad weather closed in.

We rose early the next morning and prepared the boat for sea. Lowering the dinghy from the davits to the water, Ty climbed in and handed up the oars and small red gas tank. Attaching a rope to the outboard, he tossed me the line. As he guided, I lifted and secured the engine to its bracket on the rail. Ty climbed back aboard and went forward to untie the spinnaker halyard while I pulled the dinghy alongside the hull.

It'll never fit up there…

Our Brit neighbor's warning echoed in my ears like the Ghost of Christmas Past.

That's what you think! I thought as Ty attached the halyard to the tender and hoisted her over the lifelines. The ten-foot behemoth dangled over us, swinging in the wind until I grabbed the gray tubes and centered her over the foredeck.

"Lower away!" I shouted.

Over the winter we'd installed two stainless steel pulpits in front of the mast to brace against when hoisting sails. As Ty eased the halyard and lowered the dinghy, each of her tubes slid into the pulpits as if they were custom-made brackets to hold them there. We stared at each other in surprise. The pulpits were designed to keep *us* on deck, not the tender, but the fit couldn't have been more perfect if we'd measured with a micrometer.

"That dinghy looks *ridiculous!*" Ty said with a haughty clipped accent.

We laughed with relief as we lashed her to the handrails, pleased that the "family car" would be safe and secure for the offshore passage.

Next I pulled out the red stuffsack that held our harnesses and tethers. At the bottom of the bag were two fifty-foot rolls of blue nylon webbing. Grateful for Ty's skill at tying death-defying knots, I stood back as he ran the jack lines down each side deck and attached them securely to cleats fore and aft. I leaned over and pulled on one. We'd hook our tethers to these lines any time we went on deck while underway. They'd be the only thing between us and a swim, should we lose our footing miles from shore.

"Nice and tight!" I announced.

"Good. You ready to help me with the liferaft?"

Ours was a valise type that we stowed below decks. Big enough for four men and filled with survival gear that we hoped we'd never need, the sucker weighed a ton. I pushed while Ty pulled the orange rubber bag up the ladder and through the companionway. He set it on the coachtop under the dodger, then led its tether to the toerail. Now attached to the boat, if we threw the raft overboard it would automatically inflate.

"That should do it," Ty said, wiping his hands and looking about the deck.

"Let's put the ditch bag up here, too, just to be safe."

The bright yellow satchel was the first thing we'd grab if we had to board the liferaft. It contained a GPS, VHF radio, batteries, flashlight, and enough food and water for at least four days. Most importantly, an outside pocket held our EPIRB, the emergency locator beacon whose signal would instantly be picked up and transmitted by satellite to would-be rescuers.

Our offshore checklist complete, we raised anchor and motored to a nearby marina for diesel. The fifteen-knot wind was acceptable for heading offshore, but it made for tricky boat handling amid the maze of pilings. Pulling straight in to the fuel pier was no problem. Turning the boat around in the narrow fairway to head back out was another trick altogether.

At times like this, there was no question who would drive the boat.

The wind was determined to pin our gleaming white hull against the creosote-coated poles. While Ty backed and filled, I played human fender. Groaning like an Olympic powerlifter, I pushed against the pilings as curious bystanders stood watching from the docks.

"Toss that guy a stern line!" Ty shouted, hoping for some manual assistance to pull the boat around.

As I scurried aft to grab the line, a shaft of white pain shot through the toes of my right foot and up my leg.

"Son of a bitch! S---!" I swore like a sailor as the onlookers gaped. Hopping on one foot, I grabbed the line and tossed it ashore.

"What happened?" Ty watched me with concern as he worked with the man on the pier to maneuver the boat into position.

"I jammed my toes on the damn cleat!" I groaned, fully aware I shouldn't have been working on deck without shoes.

"Ok! Got it! Thanks a lot!" he shouted to our helper, then turned to me. "C'mere and let me take a look."

I stumbled to the cockpit and plopped down beside him. With the boat finally lined up in the fairway, Ty couldn't take his hands from the wheel. He frowned with concern as I kneaded my throbbing foot.

"Do you want to get it x-rayed?"

Breathing heavily, I shook my head. It hurt like hell, but if we went to the hospital, we could be there all day. Any delay meant we'd miss our weather window. We were headed to Block Island. That was just 25 miles from Newport. There was a Navy hospital there. If the sucker was broken, I'd just guts it out. That's what Motrin was for.

"No. It'll be fine. Let's just go."

"Are you sure?"

I stood up and tentatively put my weight on it. It was like stepping on a hot poker. *Damn!* We'd been gone nearly three weeks and were barely out of the Chesapeake Bay. I wanted to get to New England!

"Yeah, I'm sure. Let's go."

"Ok," he said, shaking his head. "You take the wheel and just sit there. I'll get the fenders and lines in."

The pain began to ease as we motored toward Cape May's narrow inlet. Surfer-sized waves rolled in rhythmically between the two rocky jetties, and my apprehension grew.

"Want me to take it?" Ty asked as he stepped back into the cockpit, the deck secured for sea.

"Sure." I was all too happy to give him back the helm.

"Looks like it'll be better once we get past the inlet."

"Good. I'll just sit here and look aft."

What I couldn't see couldn't scare me.

Staring at the receding shoreline, I recalled a video we'd recently watched about a couple who sailed from Virginia to the Virgin Islands. Their passage was rough and uncomfortable. The woeful wife shook her head and wailed, "It was awful!" Then the camera panned to her husband, who beamed from ear to ear and announced, "It was *great!*"

That simple scene convinced me that attitude is everything. I was determined to enjoy this passage.

Okay, God, I'm going to leave the worrying to You.

I grinned – the simple gesture of smiling instantly lifting my spirits – and I turned to face forward.

Perverse, but typical, the wind was coming from the exact direction in which we needed to sail. Blowing straight toward the bow, the breeze would only cause the sails to slap and flap with no forward drive. Rather than waste our time raising them, we left them furled and motored ahead.

The waves were steep, but not dangerous, rising up to seven feet. Unfortunately, the period between them was short, causing the boat to bounce and roll in every possible direction like a playground horse on a spring.

Positive attitude be damned. The motion was awful. After two hours, it was beginning to grate. Big time.

"I'm going to make a head call," I said glumly.

I descended the ladder, holding firmly onto the handrails. I'd read countless accounts of sailors getting injured when their boat lurched unexpectedly. With this crazy motion, there was no predicting which way *Liberty* would jerk next, so I moved forward slowly and deliberately.

The pain in my foot had subsided to a dull ache. While slightly purple, it hadn't swollen, so it probably wasn't broken. In spite of the uncomfortable ride, I was glad we were underway and not sitting in some New Jersey emergency room.

I stepped into the small head. I closed the door more for protection than privacy. Standing in the small space was like being in a phone booth during an earthquake. As I fumbled with my zipper, I struggled to maintain my balance. I bounced off the sink, then the towel rack. Inching my jeans down over my hips, my elbows banged into the cabinets and the counter.

Holding the lid to keep it from falling, I dropped onto the toilet seat and braced my feet against the wall. As the boat continued to gyrate, I poked my head through the door and barked angrily, "IS THIS REALLY NECESSARY?!?!"

I got no sympathy from the captain.

"Are you having fun down there?"

"Don't you dare laugh! You don't have to get undressed to do this!" I shook my head, then couldn't help but laugh with him at the ridiculous situation.

It was the nature of boats.

Climbing back to the cockpit, I noticed that Ty was no longer smiling.

"What's the matter?"

"The electronic compass just quit."

I considered his remark, then shrugged my shoulders. It didn't seam like a big deal. After all, we still had the magnetic compass and the GPS as a back-up

Then Ty reminded me that the autopilot gets its input from the electronic one. Without a course to guide it, the autopilot was useless. No autopilot meant hand steering the whole way. That wouldn't be a big deal on a nice, calm day-sail, but keeping the boat on track for a two-hundred mile voyage in rough seas was another thing. We would tire after an hour at the helm instead of our normal four hour watches, and neither of us would get much sleep.

It was going to be a *long* night.

As the day wore on, the wind slowly shifted to the southeast. The waves were now hitting us beam-on, but at least we could sail. Wearing a harness, Ty snapped his tether onto the jacklines and went forward to raise the main. The winds were blowing a brisk 18 to 22 knots, so he put in a single reef, reducing the total sail area just enough so the boat wasn't overpowered. With the main up, the ride smoothed out a bit, but we were still rolling a disquieting forty degrees to either side. Repeatedly.

The constant motion didn't do much for my appetite, but I knew we'd be more alert if we ate something hearty before nightfall. I went below to prepare a meal and found the cabin a hard-hat area. As I bent to retrieve a jar of peanut butter that had fallen from a cabinet, an apple flew out of the miniature hammock slung in the galley. This was followed shortly by a pear that splattered messily at my feet.

Fumbling through the drop bin with one hand while bracing myself with the other, I reached for a bag of dehydrated meals I'd brought aboard for just this scenario. While heating water on the gimbaled stove, I poured the dry ingredients into two oversized mixing bowls. Five minutes after adding the boiling water, the dry dust was transformed into steaming lasagna and pasta primavera that we ate straight out of the bowl.

The hot food failed to keep us warm as the sun set, so we quickly zipped the side panels onto the bimini. Not only were we now warmer and dry, but we could take off our harnesses, safe inside our plastic porch.

On we sailed, up and over the waves which failed to diminish. Relief hadn't come as we'd hoped with deeper water. We'd pegged out our fathometer hours earlier at 500 feet and were still hobbyhorsing. Thousands of miles of fetch were kicking up the water to heights unheard of on the Chesapeake Bay.

You're not in Kansas anymore, Dorothy.

I'd made at least twenty overnight passages, but each time I felt like I was starting from scratch. Sailing offshore, especially at night, was a unique experience in an environment that was alien to most humans. I had to ease myself back into the rhythm of the sea slowly. As the hours passed, I alternated between uneasiness and awe at my surroundings.

With Ty dozing inches away on the cockpit seat, I sat at the wheel, singing softly to calm my nerves and stay awake. In the inky blackness, it felt like we were hurtling through space. I peered into the darkness, checking for traffic, but all I could see was our own frothy wake illuminated by our stern light.

In spite of my singing, my mind wandered to potential dangers in the waters ahead. Even though the chances were slim, it wasn't unheard of for a boat to hit a whale or a large container that had fallen off a ship. Without headlights, it was impossible to see unlit objects that the radar didn't detect – a thought that did little to calm my nerves.

Still, it didn't do any good to worry about things I couldn't control.

Disgusted at my overactive imagination, I pushed the unproductive thoughts to the back of my mind. Instead, I focused on the red glow of the instrument panel, moving my eyes from the magnetic compass to the virtual highway on the GPS that indicated I was still on track. Every few minutes I did a sweep of the horizon, then cycled the radar through its ranges, incrementally changing the search from three to twenty-four miles to make sure I missed nothing.

In spite of the enclosure, by four A.M. the damp chill had seeped through my double layer of fleece. Wishing I were somewhere safe and warm, I pictured my office back at the Pentagon. It was bright, it had heat, and the books weren't falling off the shelves there. But it wasn't necessarily safe. 9/11 had proven that.

I realized that no one was immune to danger. I could sit in a house and never go anywhere, or I could truly live my life. As tired and uneasy as I was out here, I was right where I chose to be.

Dawn broke right on schedule, but the sun failed to make an appearance. Instead, it hid behind a blanket of nasty gray clouds.

"I'm ready to relieve you," Ty said wearily as we ticked off another hour.

"I'm ready to be relieved, believe me."

"Any contacts?"

"There's nothing on the radar but a big mass a couple of miles in front of us."

"Looks like a squall."

Indeed, I'd steered around a similar mass a few minutes earlier. By now the winds had increased noticeably, and we decided the best thing to do was to take down the sails and motor. As much as I hated the drone of the engine, if it meant getting in sooner, I was all for it.

I didn't like to see Ty go out on deck in these conditions, but I knew better than to volunteer to go myself. Co-captains or not, Ty was not about to sit inside the enclosure while I did the hard work. I started the engine and gripped the wheel as he unzipped a panel and shuffled forward to the mast.

"Hold on!" I shouted as I brought the boat into the wind.

"Don't worry!" he yelled back as the boat bounced and bucked like a rodeo bull.

I concentrated mightily to keep the boat steady. Watching the big waves, I tried not to think that it was in conditions like these that sailors went over the side. Whitecaps dotted the horizon like frothy meringue, and I shuddered, knowing it would be impossible to spot anyone in the roiling mess.

Ty slipped back inside the enclosure, breathless and red-faced. We rode in silence for only a few minutes until he shook his head.

"The ride's a lot worse with the sails down."

I'd noticed the same thing.

"Let me raise it this time."

"No, I'll do it," he said, shoulders sagging as he slipped back into his harness.

This was not my idea of fun.

Thirty-seven hours after leaving Cape May, a smudge of gray appeared on the horizon. It was Montauk Point, the northeast tip of Long Island. Our destination, Block Island, lay just two hours beyond.

I was happy to see land, but I had a hard time getting excited. I was tired to the point of exhaustion. Years earlier, I served a tour in naval intelligence, where I stood twelve-hour watches for over a year. The schedule alternated between day and night shifts every few days, leaving my body in constant confusion. I learned from that assignment that I didn't handle fatigue well.

Now, just like that year from Hell, I was punchy and irritable. Like a volcano, I was ready to erupt with little provocation.

"Ty," I warned, "if I say anything bitchy, it's not you."

"Suzanne, you're not bitchy."

"That's 'cause you can't read my mind. It's really ugly in there."

He smiled weakly.

"I don't think I'm cut out for passagemaking," I said dejectedly. "Maybe we should just focus on coastal cruising for a while before we decide on an Atlantic crossing."

His response surprised me. Sailing the Mediterranean was part of our dream. Ty was all for it. I was the one who was hesitant to cross the ocean. I realized from his change in attitude that he was as tired as I was.

Nearing the pork chop shaped island, we lowered the sails and started the engine. I studied the chart carefully as we approached the entrance to Great Salt Pond. The channel was no more than a quarter mile wide. Even though the sides were sandy, now was not the time to make mistakes. I steered while Ty stood below at the electronic chart.

"You're a little right of track," he called up. "Come left three degrees."

"I can see the channel markers," I snapped back, instantly regretting my tone.

"Come left to course one-one-zero," Ty said, as he climbed into the cockpit and moved toward the bow. "We'll anchor over there about a hundred yards ahead."

"One-one-zero. Roger."

A minute later, I put the engine in neutral, then backed until we glided to a stop.

Ty gave the anchor a shove and let it splash. He pointed one finger down at the water, my cue to back slowly. The clatter of the chain across the bow roller was sweet, but not nearly as welcome as that delicious moment seconds later when I killed the engine.

Ah, blessed silence.

Happy to leave the confines of the cockpit, I joined Ty at the bow. Together we gazed at the landscape around us. Cape Cod houses with clapboard shingles dotted the sandy bluffs, but instead of mirthful hues, gray was the color du jour. Far from drab, the starkness was alluring.

"I can't believe we're in New England," I said, no longer bitchy.

"Yeah. The passage wasn't that bad."

"Not really."

We gazed, mesmerized, as a lobster boat laden with traps motored past. In a single night we had sailed into a different world. And we had done it all on our own.

If it felt this good to make landfall here, I wondered what it would be like to sail into Gibraltar.

"Hey, Ty?"

"Yeah?"

"Before we give up on that Atlantic crossing, maybe we should sleep on it first."

"I was just thinking the very same thing."

We looked at each other and grinned.

We were hopeless.

Fourteen

GIN AND BEAR IT

The evenly-spaced lights hung like a strand of sparkling pearls across the neck of Narragansett Bay. To the average tourist, the Newport suspension bridge was little more than a picturesque back-drop for their photos of the harbor. To me, the bridge evoked a tidal wave of memories, surging with emotion.

In my mind, I was twenty-two years old again. I had just reported to Navy Officer Candidate School and stood in a column of anxious officer wannabes.

"You slugs take a long, hard look at that bridge!" a khaki clad demon barked at us. "That there is the Bridge to Freedom, and there's only one way you're going back across it: as a worthless civilian puke, or as an officer in the United States Navy!"

For sixteen long weeks that bridge was my motivation as I left old habits behind and learned to do things The Navy Way. The day I finally crossed it, heading south to my first duty station, my face shined as brightly as the new stripe on my sleeve.

In the twenty years since then, I'd had my share of Navy adventures. I'd ducked a bullet in Panama when our forces deposed a dictator. I'd zipped over deserts and jungles in Hueys and Blackhawks and been launched off the deck of an aircraft carrier. I climbed the Great Wall of China and lived in a house with straw mats in Japan. I met princes, kings, and presidents, and flew on Air Force One with our Commander in Chief.

Now, two decades of duty later, as we sailed under that monumental bridge, it was a different kind of freedom we were learning to enjoy. Four weeks into our cruising life, we were settling into the rhythm of simplicity and self-sufficiency.

Chores that we once wedged into the free spaces of our busy workdays were now adventures in themselves. A trip to the laundry meant interacting with locals, soaking up sights in new towns while the whites washed and the darks dried. Hiking to grocery stores with backpacks and street maps was an opportunity for discovery, rather than an errand to be endured.

Daily exercise was no longer a drudgery. Instead of staring at a gym's cement wall, we did our sit-ups on the aft deck to the rhythm of the waves. We checked out different ports in our running shoes, jogging past Plymouth's famous rock and threading our way through the streets of scenic Marblehead.

I thrived on our unhurried schedule, rising when we'd slept enough, no longer a slave to the alarm clock. We'd weigh anchor shortly after breakfast and travel thirty to fifty miles, depending on our mood. Early-afternoon stops left us time to go ashore and explore, followed by daily waterfront dining in the cockpit.

While a drastic change from the adrenaline-charged days in Washington, the transition seemed transparent. We were adapting easily to life at 6 knots. The post-retirement let-down so many had warned me of hadn't happened. I wondered if these first weeks were simply the honeymoon period, with the adjustment phase to follow. But so far, this cruising life was a breeze.

After a nostalgic visit to Newport, we slowly worked our way north to Maine. It was true we had no schedule, but we hoped to be in Portland by the beginning of July. Our good friend, Jim Wohlleber, a senior captain with Continental Airlines, was there on his Catalina 470. Limited to vacation days in between flights, he'd sailed *Beckoning* to Maine from Annapolis in one fourth the time it had taken us with our leisurely calendar. We'd arranged to meet on Independence Day, where Jim had reserved a front-row slip for Portland's fireworks.

"I can see the Isles of Shoals," Ty said, pointing ahead. The small group of islands marking the offshore boundary between New Hampshire and Maine was our day's destination.

"Perfect timing," I said, turning the last page of the book I was reading. I'd been going through a paperback every other day. This latest one was the chilling story of an FBI agent who infiltrated a religious cult. Preparing to anchor, I was happy to turn my attention to something more cheerful than a bunch of brainwashed cultists.

My first sight of Maine was a disappointment. Perhaps the novel had dampened my spirits, but I found the windswept islands bleak and barren. Dropping the hook in deserted Gosport Harbor, I couldn't shake the feeling that we'd stepped onto the set of an Alfred Hitchcock movie. Tiny Cedar Island lay off our beam, its few stone houses spooky and empty. Smuttynose Island, behind us, was uninhabited, save for swarms of swooping black sea birds.

Off our bow, Star Island's history told of an entire community that had been murdered by Indians more than a century earlier. Betty Moody, the only survivor, had hidden in a cave, then killed her babies to keep them from crying.

Real cheery stuff, huh?

A large white building was the prominent landmark on Star island. A former hotel, the aging structure was now owned by a private corporation that, according to our guide book, sponsored week-long religious conferences. I could almost see Mrs. Moody's ghost wandering in the shadows, and couldn't imagine why anyone would want to stay there.

Ty didn't seem to find any fault with our surroundings. He agreed with our cruising guide's five-star rating. While I went below to make dinner, he pulled out a fishing rod and contentedly dropped a silver minnow over the side.

"You having any luck up there?" I called out as I peppered a pork chop.

"If we have to rely on my fishing, we'll starve to death."

I felt his pain. He'd caught nothing but seaweed to this point, but with his manly pride at stake, he was determined to succeed.

Shaking my head, I put the meat in the pan. Seconds later, there was an excited cry from on deck.

"I got a hit! It's a big one!"

I scurried to join him, fussing like a man whose wife has gone into labor.

"What do you want me to do? Do you need me to get anything?"

"Some gin," he said excitedly.

The request stopped me in my tracks. *Some gin?* It was a strange time to crave a sundowner! Then I remembered a tip we'd read in a fishing magazine. The article said that pouring alcohol directly into a fish's gills would instantly anaesthetize it. The idea seemed far more humane than clubbing the thing with a mallet, so I hurried below to the liquor locker.

"It's a bluefish!" Ty announced.

I knew bluefish. They were really good eating if you used a spicy sauce, not oily and fishy like some people thought. They also had big, sharp teeth. Anxious to bite into him instead of the other way around, I stood ready to douse him with the gin.

When the fish neared the surface, Ty raised his rod high and flung the four pounder over the lifelines onto the deck. I waited until the gills flared, then poured a shot on in.

The fish went out like a light.

"Wow! It really works!"

"Pretty cool!" Ty agreed, standing an inch taller than normal.

Then he glanced at the container in my hand. We store our liquor in plastic camping bottles to keep the glass from clanking in the cabinet. Because they all look the same, we label each one with a marker.

"Suzanne, what did you use?"

I looked at the label. "Just some gin," I said, blinking owlishly.

"Just some gin? You used the Bombay Blue Sapphire!"

I worked my lips back and forth across my teeth. "It was the first thing I grabbed. I was in a hurry."

He shook his head. "You could have used the cheap stuff!"

Happy to change the subject, I asked Ty to pose for a picture. After the requisite trophy photo, I happily escaped below, where I set the pork chops aside for another meal. Up on deck, Ty set about gutting his prize, all the while shaking his head and muttering *"Bombay Blue Sapphire"* under his breath.

Ty has fishing down to a science.

Luckily, the thrill of the catch overcame his shock at my extravagance. One bite of the delicious filet, slathered in a jalapeno-mustard marinade, and all was forgiven.

The magnificent meal and a glass of Chardonnay did wonders for my mood. Leaning back and looking around the anchorage, I decided the place wasn't so bad, after all.

Just then, a loud, eerie wail filled the air, raising the hair on the back of my neck.

"What's that?" Ty asked.

I sat up. "I don't know, but it's coming from over there."

I pointed toward Star Island, where throngs of people began flowing out of the hotel onto the expansive front lawn. Where moments before only a handful of people had sat rocking on the porch, now hundreds of bodies moved in a strangely military fashion toward a large flag pole in the center of the yard.

I'd never seen anything like it.

"What do think's going on?" Ty asked over the mournful wail.

"I don't know, but it's really weird."

We watched as four men emerged from the white building. I picked up the binoculars and peered more closely. Each man held the corner of what looked like a sheet with a body on it. The throng parted as they walked slowly through the crowd.

I gaped incredulously. It was just like the book I'd finished earlier that day!

"My God, Ty! I think it's a cult!"

He snorted. "Suzanne, you've been reading too much."

"No, I swear! Look! They're like a bunch of sheep, following the guys with the body!"

An instant later, the wailing stopped. We watched in silence as the crowd now slowly filed back into the building, two by two.

I was glad to be at anchor, safe from the weirdos on shore.

The next morning, Ty suggested we check out the island. I wasn't thrilled with the idea, but the thought of stretching my legs overcame my hesitation.

We climbed into the dinghy and motored the short distance to the dock. Two neatly-dressed young men greeted us pleasantly and helped tie our bow line to a cleat.

"Can we ask you to sign in before you wander around?"

"Sure," Ty said, accepting the stubby pencil the young man offered. I was surprised he found nothing strange about signing a log to visit an island. I wanted to tell him to use a fake name.

While Ty signed, I held back, carefully scrutinizing the two. Their hair was short, trimmed to military standards. They were cultists, for sure.

Feeling like the FBI agent in my book, I decided to do a little investigating of my own. "Excuse me," I said, addressing the taller one. "We saw a lot of people gathering on the lawn out here last night. Was that some kind of ceremony?"

"No," he said. "That was just our weekly fire drill. We have one every Friday at 7 o'clock."

Ty put an arm around my waist and squeezed.

"Don't say a word." I hissed.

"Read any good books lately?" he teased.

I punched him on the arm. *A fire drill!*

I still didn't like the Isles of Shoals.

*   *   *

We'd looked forward to cruising Maine for its beauty, but the exhilarating sailing was an unexpected bonus. We enjoyed peaceful breakfasts on waveless water, entertained by the lobstermen hauling their traps. Then, just about the time the dishes were put away, the wind piped up, building to an invigorating twenty knots. We were used to simmering heat and zero air this time of year on the Chesapeake. Now we knew what we'd been missing. After days of motoring into the wind, finally we harnessed it and soared.

The dramatic shoreline and rocky ledges that made Maine so beautiful also made it a navigational challenge. The bobbing floats from hundreds of lobster pots added a splash of local color, but were a constant threat to our spinning propeller. Even if our autopilot had been working, we couldn't have used it in the minefield of buoys. We dodged pots, kept a close eye on our charts, and sailed on to our holiday rendezvous in Portland.

The night of July 3rd, we picked up a mooring in the Harraseeket River near Freeport. Like many harbors in New England, Freeport wasn't free. It seemed that every cozy cove was filled with pricey mooring balls. The lack of anchorages was a huge disappointment. Back home, we dropped the hook in any spot that looked inviting. Up here, there were many times we couldn't anchor if we wanted to.

We arose on the morning of the fourth to find that visibility was nil. The infamous Maine fog had finally found us. In our pre-cruising days, we wouldn't have left the marina on a day like this. Now it was just another facet of our new lifestyle. Accepting the conditions as a challenge -- one we looked upon as a rite of passage – we plotted a course for Portland.

Ty took the helm and turned on the radar. I slipped the mooring, and we headed out.

"There's something off the bow at a quarter of a mile, moving right to left," Ty said.

"I'll go forward and see if I can make anything out."

I paused to pick up a pair of Motorola radios, tossed one to Ty and put the other in my pocket. I also grabbed the foghorn and slipped its handy lanyard around my neck. Now with hands free, I headed for the bow, holding onto the rails as I went. Climbing onto the perch in front of the pulpit, I peered ahead through the water droplets that clung to my bangs.

I could have wrung the air out like a sponge.

I pulled the Motorola from my pocket and keyed the mike. "I can't see anything," I said, speaking in a normal voice. I was glad I'd thought of the radios. Using them was infinitely better than shouting, something that always made me feel like we were yelling at each other.

"Better blow the horn," Ty came back.

"Roger. Blowing the horn."

I put the mouthpiece to my lips and produced one prolonged blast. Taking my role seriously, I counted off four complete seconds to indicate we were a vessel underway. The sound was weak and pitiful, and I doubted any boat would hear me over his engine. It didn't matter. Good seamanship said fog signals were in order, so I set my watch for two minutes when the next blast was due.

Ty's voice crackled through my radio. "Contact's an eighth of a mile off now. I'm slowing."

As the engine changed pitch, I suddenly discerned movement through the mist. It was another sailboat! No wonder I hadn't heard anything. My first reaction was to wonder what the heck they were doing out in this pea soup. Then I realized we were two peas in a pod!

I waved as the boat ghosted silently across our bow like an apparition. They waved back and I noticed neither of their crew was bothering to mimic my Horatio Hornblower routine at the bow. Maybe sailing in this stuff was old hat to these Mainiacs, but to me it was a novel and invigorating experience. We were facing the elements, taking what was dished out at us. This was good stuff!

The fog cleared by lunchtime, revealing Portland's industrial skyline under an azure sky. Prices were steep where our friend, Jim, had his boat, so we picked up a mooring at the yacht club next door. By the time we secured the boat and caught the launch ashore, the party was already in progress aboard *Beckoning*.

"You guys are going to love the fireworks," Jim told us. "They really do it right up here."

Looking forward to the show, we gathered in the cockpit and faced the city. Minutes before the first roman candle was launched, the fog moved back in as if God unfurled a roll of white cotton. The thick clouds accentuated the thunderous booms that accompanied the fireworks, but we never saw a thing.

"Gee, Jim, this is some show," Ty said dryly.

"Yeah, glad we hurried to get here for this," I joked.

Jim shrugged with a what-can-I-say expression and welcomed us to Maine.

*   *   *

I didn't mind giving up my house and cars to go cruising, but leaving my hairstylist was another thing. It was hard enough finding someone I trusted with my hair when the Navy moved me to a new city every few years. Now I had to find a new stylist every five weeks!

It had been over a month since we left, and I couldn't put off the inevitable any longer. When I told Jim I needed to find a salon, he offered the services of his friend, Beth. I knew and liked Beth, and if Jim said she was good, then I was all for it.

The morning after the invisible fireworks, Ty and I returned to *Beckoning* where Beth was waiting with her shears and comb. Sitting on a step-stool on the pier, I had my first ever haircut-al-fresco. Beth snipped away while I watched boats cruise in and out of the harbor. Looking in the mirror when she finished, I was thrilled. Beth was as good as the stylist I'd paid big bucks for back in DC. But no amount of money could match the priceless picture of my very manly husband, next in line, sitting on the stool with a bright pink cape around his shoulders.

Jim had two weeks of vacation left, so we arranged to meet *Beckoning* in Boothbay later in the week. Leaving Portland in our wake, we raised our sails and headed for the open waters off Casco Bay.

Several hours into the sail, the Coast Guard broadcast an urgent weather alert on channel 16. Turning up the volume, we learned of a thunderstorm forming not far from where we were. This kind of news always got our attention, but when they warned of winds up to sixty-five knots, we looked at each other in alarm.

Off the port quarter, far in the distance, we could see the dark clouds gathering. Sixty-five knot winds put this storm in a whole different league from anything we'd previously encountered. Without saying a word, we sprang into action. We'd been through this drill before and each knew what to do.

Fueled by a sense of urgency, we took the sails down in record time. Ty wrapped extra ties around the boom, making sure the mainsail wasn't going anywhere. Then he put a lock through the furler so it couldn't accidentally unroll. While he finished up on deck, I ducked below and grabbed the hatch boards and our foul weather gear. I didn't allow myself the luxury of worrying. There was no time for that.

Back in the cockpit, I tossed cushions, charts, books, binoculars, and the boat hook through the companionway. They fell onto a heap at the foot of the ladder, but now was not the time to be concerned with neatness. Anything on deck that wasn't tied down went below.

I kept glancing over my shoulder, wondering if the storm would pass over us or pass us by. Then I recalled how I'd been able to see rain squalls on the radar on the trip to Block Island. Stepping over to the screen, I didn't see anything abnormal until I increased the range to 24 miles. There, just outside the third range ring, was an enormous black mass.

"Ty! The storm is fifteen miles out and moving this way!"

He stopped working and looked at me, surprised. "How do you know?"

"I can see it on the radar, clear as day!"

I stared, fascinated, as the mass migrated toward the center of the screen. The storm was moving fast, and it was coming right at us.

"Ten miles!" I announced as Ty joined me in the cockpit.

I handed him his foul weather gear and began putting on my own bright yellow overalls and jacket.

"I want you to go below," he said sternly.

I took a deep breath. If he was going to be up here, I should be, too. We were co-captains, after all. I decided I'd fight that battle when the storm actually hit. In the meantime, I wasn't thrilled at the thought of him standing with his hands on the wheel in a thunderstorm, and I told him so. He agreed that he'd stay in the cockpit, but wouldn't take the helm unless he had to.

The ominous clouds moved toward us like a mile-high purple wall. Ty's furrowed brow reflected my tension as I ran through a list of mental "what-ifs." I tried to consider everything that could possibly go wrong, and hoped we'd covered all the bases. One item we hadn't thought of came to mind, and I quickly ducked below. Worried I was getting carried away, I popped back up and handed Ty a pair of foam earplugs.

"In case we get hit by lightning," I explained in answer to his puzzled look.

This wasn't just catastrophizing. Our mast was the tallest thing around for miles. I could only imagine how loud the ensuing crash of thunder would be if we were struck.

Instead of dismissing my excessive preparations, he surprised me by popping the plugs in his ears. I did the same with an extra pair, and as if on cue, the sky opened up around us.

I'd never seen rain fall so hard. It was as if we were a toy boat in a bathtub, sitting directly under a wide-open faucet. Ty eased the throttle back to idle. If there was anything outside our lifelines, we couldn't see it through the downpour. We were completely blind, with no way of knowing what was around us. The radar that had helped us earlier in the fog was now useless, its screen obliterated by the mass of water-soaked clouds directly over us.

Ty had told me to go below, but I sat on the sill of the companionway, not quite in the cockpit, yet not in the cabin, either. It was a good compromise, and I was glad to part of the experience, rather than hiding from it. I was awed by the display of power and fury, more amazed than afraid.

All around us, the thunder boomed, letting us know the lightning was out there, even if we couldn't see it. Ty tersely called out readings from the wind speed indicator. I tensed as he reported gusts of 30, 32, and 38 knots, but none higher. Time seemed to stop as we waited for the assault to pass, and I prayed we'd seen the worst of it.

The radar had shown it was a fast moving storm, and sure enough, as quickly as it came upon us, it was over. The 65 knot winds were a no-show, and that was okay by me.

Liberty stepped out from under the faucet into a picture-perfect summer day. It was as if the whole event had never happened. Our foul weather gear seemed suddenly out of place, and within seconds we were back down to shorts, soaking up the sunshine.

With our anchorage now just a few miles ahead, Ty drove while I went below to make order out of the chaos in the cabin. Looking around at the disorder in my home, I was struck by how vulnerable we were out here. If it wasn't fog, it was blinding rain, high winds or waves. Sure, there were days of peace and serenity, but we were certainly at the mercy of the often unpredictable weather.

One thing was for sure, being on the water was never boring. I'd signed up for this life willingly, knowing what I was getting into, and I had no regrets. But right now, all I wanted to do was sit in a quiet cove and unwind.

"Hey, Ty," I called up into the cockpit, "You think you could catch another bluefish when we get in?"

The unexpected question surprised him. "Well, I could try, I guess. You're hungry for more fish?"

I poked my head through the companionway and grinned at him. "Nah, but I could sure use some of that Bombay Blue Sapphire."

Fifteen

INTREPIDITY

The cruising life was all we'd dreamed of. It was exciting, yet relaxing. We were exploring places off the beaten path, challenging ourselves, and having fun. But one thing was missing. Where were all the other cruisers?

I was far from tired of Ty. Few couples get such quality time together. But still, the stimulation of some new faces would have been welcome. In the workaday world, we'd grown accustomed to being around other people. That abruptly changed the day we set sail. Spending most evenings at anchor or swinging on a mooring ball resulted in a self-imposed isolation we hadn't anticipated.

We'd heard great things about the highly social community of cruisers and looked forward to joining it. But if other cruisers were out there, they weren't near us. As we worked our way north, we saw no boats from south of New York, save our own. Sure, Florida and the Caribbean were the cruisers' Mecca, but did no one sail north for the summer? Maybe we were just too early in the season…

If we were feeling lonely in Maine, it didn't look likely we'd find big crowds on our way to Cape Breton's Bras d'Or Lake. The Nova Scotia cruising guide warned us of bold shorelines, strong currents, high tides, and frequent fog. Distances between ports where a boat could do repairs were long. Marinas were few and far between. Coast Guard assistance was limited, and commercial towing services were non-existent.

But we were excited about cruising Canada. If it wasn't a little challenging, what was the point? We had the skills, the know-how, and the equipment to handle the conditions the book warned about. The only thing limiting our explorations was the weather. We wanted to start heading south before cooler weather set in, and figured mid-July to mid-August would be just the right window for our Canadian odyssey.

We motored out of Bar Harbor on July 15th for the overnight passage to Nova Scotia. We'd made all our offshore preparations, and were ready for sea. Yarmouth was the closest port of entry, but it was on the wrong side of Nova Scotia. We were anxious to see the east coast, so we set a course for the town of Shelburne, 160 miles away.

Fog was in the forecast, and sure enough, within two miles of leaving, we found it. Like passing through a door, we went from clear skies to sea-level clouds in a mere boat-length.

"What do you think?" Ty asked.

I wasn't comfortable crossing the Gulf of Maine with zero vis, and said so. Ty concurred. We had an agreement that prudent decisions about weather would always take precedence over our desire to move on. One more day in Maine wasn't going to make a difference.

Neither of us cared to return to Bar Harbor. Unlike the rest of beautiful Mount Desert Island, it was far too touristy for our tastes. That, and a miserable night rolling from side to side in the harbor's rocky anchorage made Bar Harbor our least favorite port call to date.

Putting the engine in idle, we checked the guide for a suitable place to await clearer weather. Nearby Flanders Bay offered no facilities, but got a high rating as a good place to visit, if you liked seals and bald eagles. We were all for watching wildlife, and didn't care about going ashore. With our dinghy lashed to the foredeck, it would have been too much trouble, anyway.

Flanders Bay it was.

I enjoyed lay-days. We were on the move far more often than we spent in port or at anchor, so a day off from driving and navigating was a nice break. While Ty played with the weatherfax, I baked an almond cake and read a book. Home-made pizza and a DVD on the computer rounded out the relaxing day.

July 16th, we arose to find the fog was still hanging around, so we did, too. A loon entertained us for most of the afternoon, warbling and diving every time we tried to get a good photograph. Other than that, we'd caught up on our reading, the weatherfaxes were all beginning to look alike, and the previous day's baking had exceeded my weekly quota of domesticity.

We were starting to itch.

July 17th, the infamous Maine weather was losing its novelty. While it was still foggy, the forecast called for some improvement. We decided to go for it, then hesitated. Were we breaking our rule about weather? It wasn't like the seas or winds were high. Fog was manageable if you had a radar and knew how to use it.

The crossing was like night and day from our Cape May passage. As soon as the last of the lobsterpots bobbed in our wake, we tried out the autopilot. Ty had installed the new compass the week before, and we cheered as *Liberty* plowed ahead in a perfectly straight line. With our first course change a whopping hundred and ten miles off, after six weeks of hand-steering, I was more than happy to let Auto-Otto do the driving.

Winds were out of the southeast at two to five knots. That meant that once again we'd be in trawler mode, but at least we'd be comfortable. Instead of the steep, short-period waves we'd endured off the coast of New Jersey, these seas were only three to four feet high and widely spaced…"swell," in both senses of the word!

The only challenge was the fog. Yes, it cleared for a while, but twenty miles out to sea it was back like a bad neighbor. Out here in the open water, navigating was much more manageable than threading blindly between islands close to shore, but it was still nerve-wracking.

I assumed the watch and assessed the situation. I couldn't see a thing beyond the bow, and suddenly understood what my Navy colleagues who drove submarines went through. It was like driving with a blindfold on. I was completely dependent on my instruments.

According to the GPS and compass, we were right on track.. Depth was not an issue out here, but other boats were. It was times like this when the radar was my very best friend. Turning the situation into a game, I imagined the radar's screen was a bullseye, with *Liberty* at the center of the target. The objective was to keep anything that showed up on the screen away from the center at all costs.

Most of the blips remained outside the two mile safety circle I'd set around the bullseye. When one contact tracked steadily toward the center, I disengaged the autopilot and altered course thirty degrees away from it. The course change instantly widened the contact's closest point of approach, and I breathed easier.

It was eerie knowing there were things out there big enough for the radar to detect, yet I couldn't see them. Because we were moving, even stationary objects appeared mobile. They moved across the screen in relation to our own boat's speed. For all I knew, the contact I was maneuvering to avoid was a lobster pot float. But it could just as easily b a steel fishing boat. In either case, I wasn't about to lose the game, and I kept my guard up the whole time I was on watch.

When the sun went down, the darkness made no difference, except now I had to use a flashlight to plot our position on the paper chart beside me. Other than that, blind is blind.

The big difference was the cold. The thermometer in the cockpit fell throughout the night. The enclosure shielded us from the frigid air blowing off the water, but I still needed boots, jacket, hat and gloves to stay warm. Rubbing my hands together, I hoped Nova Scotia's August was noticeably warmer than July. This was not my idea of summer weather!

Earlier in the passage, we'd raised the main to give the engine a boost. But as the sun came up the second morning, the winds shifted aft, causing the large sail to slat and bang noisily. Ty wasn't due to relieve me for half an hour, but he climbed into the cockpit scowling.

"I'm going out and take that down."

The seas had built a bit. I didn't want him going out on deck, but my suggestion to snug in the main sheet and tie the boom off at centerline fell on deaf ears.

Ty reached to unzip the enclosure.

"Hey, put your harness on!" I said, the bite in my voice fueled by fear.

He gave me a disgusted look. I hated to nag, but harnesses offshore were part of our deal. I'd been monitoring the instruments for the past four hours and had watched the sea water temperature steadily drop. I knew he had no idea how cold it really was.

"Ty, the water is forty-three degrees."

That got his attention.

When we sailed Puget Sound's chilly waters, we thought fifty-two was cold. Forty-three was a whole new ballgame.

I didn't need to voice my concern. We both knew if he fell overboard, hypothermia would set in quickly, and with fog this thick, it would be nearly impossible to find him. Needless to say, he put on the harness.

We'd been told the fog often hung offshore, then cleared quickly once you approached land. The information proved quite accurate. Twenty-eight hours after leaving Flanders Bay, we entered Shelburne Harbor. As quickly as we'd sailed into it, we emerged under bright blue skies. Instantly, the grayness that had enveloped us the whole way was gone, giving us a 20-20 view of rolling green hillsides, white sandy beaches, and crystal-clear water.

The sensory stimulation wiped away our tiredness, and we bustled about the boat, preparing for our first foreign port call. With Otto steering down the five mile channel, I went below for our passports. Ty picked up the cell phone and dialed Canadian Customs. Most boats were allowed to check in over the phone, and we looked forward to an easy entry.

Only able to hear one end of the conversation, I listened as Ty answered, "Yes, Sir. Yes, Sir. No, Sir," and gave the Customs agent our vital statistics.

"Alcohol?" he asked, and I winced. Foreigners were only allowed to bring in two bottles of wine per person. Anything over that would be assessed an outrageous 165% tax. We'd done our best to whittle down our supply over the past month, but we were still a couple of bottles over our limit. What little hard stuff we had was in with the fishing supplies. After all, it served a dual purpose.

"No, Sir," he said into the phone.

I bit my lip.

"Weapons? Yes, Sir, one shotgun."

We'd debated the gun issue long and hard with our sailing friends before leaving. The arguments went both ways, and according to the magazines, the cruising community was fairly evenly split. In the end, both of us decided we'd sleep better knowing we had some sort of protection onboard. It wasn't an issue in Canada, of course, but we were ultimately headed for the Caribbean, where piracy hadn't ended in the age of sail. We settled on a Remington 12 gauge pump with a legally short barrel.

The short barrel seemed to concern the Customs agent, and when Ty hung up the phone he was frowning.

"What's the matter?" I asked.

"They want to check out the gun in person. They're sending two agents."

"Aren't they in Halifax?"

"Yep. It'll take 'em three hours to get here, and we're not supposed to get off the boat until they've cleared us."

Not going ashore right away wasn't a problem. We were both pretty tired from standing watch all night and could use a little rest. The extra bottles of wine were what bothered me. I didn't want to pay the duty, but I didn't care to pour it down the drain, either.

The Shelburne Harbor Yacht Club was our chosen destination. They were reputedly a friendly bunch who welcomed overnight guests either alongside their new piers or on one of their mooring balls. Ever mindful of our limited budget, we didn't even consider getting a slip.

Two sailboats were already hanging off moorings. As we headed up into the wind toward the bright orange ball we'd chosen, I noticed with delight that the boat alongside us was not only American, but from Annapolis, Maryland!

I was excited about meeting our new neighbors, but first we had to secure the boat. I picked up the boat hook. When Ty brought us alongside, I snagged the pendant with the hook, hauled it under the lifelines, and slipped it over the starboard bow cleat. Just like that, we were home. No fuss, no muss.

Ty killed the engine, and we "aaah'd" in unison at the blissful silence. We congratulated each other with a high-five for another successful passage.

Within seconds of securing, the noise of an approaching outboard grabbed our attention. A small open skiff, driven by a smiling man with a round, red face pulled alongside.

"Hallo! I'm Harry, the yacht club ambassador," he said, handing up a card with his title embossed in black. "Welcome to Shelburne!"

We offered to tie off his bow line and invited him aboard, but Harry was content to putter back and forth, all the while filling us in on the yacht club amenities. For the bargain-basement price of $7 a night, we were welcome to stay on the mooring and have full use of the club.

Ty and I shared a knowing smile. The cost was a mere fraction of what we'd paid in the States. We liked Canada already!

After settling up with Harry, we straightened the boat and prepared for the inspectors. Ty retrieved the shotgun from its hiding place and laid it on the table along with a box of shells. I opened the liquor locker and stared at the wine. I wasn't going to lie about it, but paying the duty would be like buying it all over again.

Suddenly, inspiration struck. With Ty's concurrence, I went out on deck and called across to the other American boat. Up popped two heads, and I explained our predicament. True to the cruising community's reputation of rendering assistance when needed, the two were more than happy to dinghy over and help us whittle down our wine supply.

Tom and Barb, on *Gosi,* were even newer to cruising than we were, but they'd already learned an important rule: never visit another boat without your own drinks or snacks. Since we were supplying the wine, Barb came prepared with chips and dip. She told us she'd learned this requirement from Dee, a seasoned sailor on a catamaran named *Vagabond Tiger.*

Gosi had been in Shelburne for several days already. I was disappointed to learn that *Vagabond Tiger* was long gone. Now that we'd met another cruising couple, it would have been nice to meet more.

Knowing the Customs agents were on the road by now, the four of us took our mission very seriously. By the time the officials arrived with their briefcases and clipboards, *Liberty* was legal, and her crew was as relaxed as rag dolls.

Tom and Barb made a hasty retreat back to *Gosi.* Having been known to say silly things when my tongue is lubricated, I stayed in the cockpit. Ty went below with the men to show them the shotgun.

Watching from the companionway, I held my breath as one of them carefully measured the barrel. He conferred with his partner, then dialed his cell phone.

"Why do you need a shotgun, anyway?" the younger one asked Ty.

"In case we're attacked by polar bears in Labrador," Ty answered, deadpan.

I stifled a laugh and didn't dare to look at him. The Bras d'Or Lake was as far north as we planned to go, and we sure weren't going to see any polar bears up there. We might possibly see a moose or two, but we weren't about to shoot them!

The agent shook his head with great sobriety while he considered Ty's reply. I guess he found the answer quite reasonable.

By now his partner was off the phone and pronounced that our shotgun was just within the legal limits. Their duty done, they closed their briefcases and thanked us for our cooperation.

I stared at them, dumbfounded, as they climbed back to the cockpit. What about the liquor? After guzzling two bottles of good wine, they weren't even going to check? Ty shot me a don't-say-a-word look. I smiled innocently as we shook hands goodbye and held my breath. I didn't dare breathe on them.

I stayed on board while Ty dinghied the men ashore. The town's historic buildings looked appealing, but I was too tired to do anything but collapse into bed.

The museum and shops would still be there the next morning, and indeed, they looked even more quaint and inviting after eleven hours of dreamless sleep.

We spent a full day sight-seeing. Our plan was to continue on to Lunenburg, another historic fishing village, the next day, but Ambassador Harry wasn't willing to let us leave so soon. He intercepted us at the dinghy dock and invited us to the club's barbecue the following night.

We looked at each other and nodded enthusiastically. Why not?!

Wayne, the yacht club manager, wandered by and asked if we wanted to bring the boat alongside the pier for the night. When we learned a slip was only $20, no more than the cost of a mooring in Maine, we happily accepted.

Wasting no time, we zipped out to *Liberty*, rigged fenders and docklines, and moved to the docks. No sooner had we settled at the pier, than two couples wandered by and stopped to chat. A steady stream of curious visitors followed. The contrast from being at anchor was striking.

I realized that our sense of isolation wouldn't have been nearly as intense if we'd splurged on a slip more often.

There was no shortage of hospitality on the club's outdoor deck the next evening. Far from snooty, these yacht club members handed us a beer and treated us like family. They were genuinely interested in our plans for touring their province.

When we mentioned we were going as far as the Bras d'Or Lake, they nodded with pleasure. Those who'd been there said it was well worth the trip.

A man with curly red hair stepped up. "You thinking of going up to Newfoundland, too?"

I looked at Ty and shook my head. The province of Newfoundland and Labrador wasn't even on our scope. His comment to the Customs agents about Labrador had been simply a joke.

"We hadn't given it any thought," Ty said.

"They say it's beautiful. Lots of fjords with water so deep you have to go back miles 'til you can anchor. One American couple that sailed there liked it so much they stayed. Even bought a Newfoundland dog."

We laughed at the thought. No, we'd made our plans, and the Bras d'Or Lake was far enough for us.

*   *   *

We left Shelburne the same way we arrived: in the fog. Plowing through clouds that would ground a jetliner, we could only shake our heads at Environment Canada's less-than-helpful forecasts. Every half hour they dutifully announced that "visibility is fair in rain and poor in fog."

What an amazing grasp of the obvious.

The seas off the coast were large, five to seven feet, but described in meters by the weather guessers, they didn't seem quite as intimidating.

Our first night out, we dropped the hook off a secluded beach. It could have passed for a Caribbean isle with its white dunes and crystal clear water. Unlike the coast of New England, signs of civilization were few and far between. The houses we could see in the distance were modest, not the ostentatious mansions so prevalent in Maine.

Day two was more of the same, weather wise. At least I was getting used to this sailing-blind thing. Harry had jokingly warned us there was a fog-making machine off Lunenburg, and as we approached that picturesque town, I figured they must have had that machine going full speed.

Five miles out of the harbor we picked up three small blips on the radar screen. The contacts were a couple of miles in front of us and moving relatively slowly.

"I'll bet they're sailboats, going the same place we are," Ty said.

Sure enough, as we entered Lunenburg Harbour and got in the lee of the land, we now had a clear view of three other boats.

"Look! It's *Gosi*!" I cried, pointing to her familiar hull. "They're going to Lunenburg, too!"

It was the first time we'd seen the same boat twice, and I was excited to find out where they'd been for the past three days.

We'd been motoring all day, but had the jib up for a boost. With the extra speed from the foresail, we gradually caught up to the three other boats. Soon, we passed *Gosi* and one of the others.

Ahead of us remained a large catamaran, the name *"Vagabond Tiger"* emblazoned on its hulls.

"That's the boat *Gosi* shared the crossing with," I said as we inched closer to the big cat.

"I can't believe we're catching up to him," Ty said. "Catamarans are usually a lot faster than monohulls."

As if he'd heard the comment, the catamaran's captain looked over his shoulder. Within seconds, he unfurled his large jib and his boat took off like a shot.

"Would you look at that guy!" Ty said. "He saw our sail out and wasn't about to let us pass him!"

I shook my head and laughed. "Yeah, he did the same thing you would have done."

Ty gave me a sheepish look.

No sooner had we dropped the hook in front of Lunenburg's bright red fishing museum, than *Gosi's* crew hailed us on the VHF. They invited us aboard for a sundowner as soon as we were settled. Remembering what

I'd learned from Barb, I grabbed a bag of chips before we hopped in the dinghy.

Tom welcomed us and offered a hand when we pulled alongside. I passed him the chips and apologized for not having any dip.

"That's okay," Barb said, taking the bag of snacks and pointing behind us, "Frank and Dee on *Vagabond Tiger* are coming. I know they'll bring some."

We turned and watched as a couple in a large, hard dinghy zipped toward us. Instead of sitting on the seats, both were standing up, one behind the other. It was a strange sight.

"Yeehah!" the man shouted as the dinghy screeched to a halt next to ours.

Tom introduced us to Frank and Dee. His voice held a note of awe when he informed us the couple had been cruising for fourteen years.

"Do you always ride your dinghy standing up?" I asked.

"Always," Dee said in a velvety voice.

"Only way to ride in the Caribbean if you want to stay dry," Frank boomed.

I made a mental note to try it some time when no one was watching.

The six of us settled into *Gosi's* cozy cockpit. While Tom handed out drinks, Dee produced a blue, soft-sided cooler and took out a glass bowl filled with dip. Barb gave me an I-told-you-so smile while Dee methodically filled a basket with crackers and arranged the food neatly on the table. It was clear she'd done this a time or two before.

Ty and I listened while Frank animatedly discussed the day's sail. I noticed the others seemed to hang on his every word. This man exuded energy and joie de vivre, but there was something else. He had an air about him that I instantly recognized – the same self-assurance and command presence as my Navy Captain husband.

This guy was former military. I was sure of it.

As if on cue, Frank nodded at the distinctive emblem on my polo shirt and said, "You were on the Joint Staff, huh?"

I smiled and said, "That's right. And you're a retired Army Colonel."

He looked stunned, then quickly recovered. "How'd you know?"

"You have The Look."

"And the haircut," Ty added.

Frank ran a hand through blond hair that was so short it was spiky on top. It was shaved to mere stubble on the sides. "Yeah, well, that's Dee's fault. She cuts my hair."

These guys were real cruisers all right. In our quest to be self-sufficient, I'd studied a book on home haircuts. It didn't take long to decide that some things were best left to the experts.

Ty and Frank began comparing military backgrounds. Soon they took off on a spirited conversation that bounced from politics to religion, and every socially taboo subject in between. Listening to their strong opinions, I couldn't help but think that if the two of them were ever in a small boat alone, it would lean decidedly to the right. They were as like-minded as any two men I'd ever seen.

There was a twinkle in Ty's eye as he sipped contentedly on his beer. Taking advantage of a moment when the others were talking, I leaned over and quietly whispered, "Quack."

He nodded his head in agreement, knowing immediately what I meant. We had a saying that "ducks like ducks." It meant that like people attract like people. Frank was most definitely a duck.

"Where are you headed from here?" Dee asked, turning to us.

We told them of our plans to spend a couple of days in Halifax, then press on to the Bras d'Or Lake, still two hundred miles away. We hoped to spend a week there before heading south.

After fourteen years of cruising, Frank and Dee's plans were much less structured. They weren't yet sure where they were headed, Frank said, gesturing vaguely to the north. Tom and Barb surprised us by saying they were going to spend a week in Lunenburg, then another week just around the corner before heading back south.

I was surprised at the variety of styles. Ty and I certainly enjoyed relaxing, but we had far too much wanderlust to stay anywhere more than a few days. After the long passage to get here, I wanted to see a lot more than Lunenburg. Saying our farewells, we wished Tom and Barb a safe sail south, and told Frank and Dee we hoped to see them along the way.

Heading out the next day, bundled in layers of fleece, I could understand the appeal in *Gosi's* more leisurely pace. With large ocean rollers rocking *Liberty* from side to side, it definitely would have been more comfortable to stay in port.

But I was getting used to this by now. The fog was so commonplace, we didn't even hesitate to get underway. Heck, we'd been in Nova Scotia nearly a week, and had yet to see the coastline!

Lacking visual distractions, I entertained myself trying to picture what was really out there as we sailed along. Was that medium-sized dot on the radar screen a sleek motor yacht headed for the big city, or a rusty old fishing trawler surrounded by squawking gulls? It was fun for a while, but soon the mental images lost their importance. Big or small, I just wanted to steer clear of all contacts.

After standing my watch, I turned the helm over to Ty and pulled out a road map of Nova Scotia. The coastal route was dotted with towns whose names made me smile. No question about it, we had to add Ecum Secum to our list of stops. Mushaboom was another possibility, as was Necum Teuch, a name I didn't even want to try and pronounce without some local knowledge.

Folding the map, I slid in beside Ty at the helmsman's seat.

"How're you doing?"

"Fine, but I'm sure glad we have this radar."

I nodded in agreement. I couldn't imagine leaving port without it. Being able to rely on our equipment allowed me to relax.

Suddenly, a large fishing boat with outriggers the size of telephone poles popped out of nowhere, just off our to port. I gasped and clamped a hand on Ty's thigh as the boat cut right across our bow.

"What?! What is it?!" Ty asked, jumping to his feet.

I was so shocked, I could only point.

"Damn!" Ty shouted, jerking the wheel to the left as the ghost-boat slipped back into the fog off to starboard.

"Where did he come from?" Ty sputtered, staring at the radar screen.

I leaned in for a look, too.

"There's nothing there."

This was not good news. For days now I'd been sailing blithely along, secure in the knowledge that the radar would tell us when danger was near. Now this dragger as big as a house had come within a boat length, and he had no radar signature.

So much for trust.

As was our habit after any close-call, Ty and I dissected the situation in great detail. We hadn't heard the boat coming over the sound of our own engine. We figured he was made of wood and had no radar reflector, a fact that amazed us in these fog-prone waters. *Liberty* carried not just one, but two reflectors, hoping to make our signature as prominent as possible on other boats' screens. In the end, all we could hope for was that the phantom boat had known we were there.

I felt let down by our instruments. Cheated. But there was nothing wrong with them. They worked fine, given the proper input. Just like worrying about whales, there was no sense agonizing over things I couldn't control. I'd just have to continue to trust, and leave the rest to prayer.

Having sent up a special request, I began to relax. I glanced over Ty's shoulder and noticed an especially large blob at the top of the radar screen. We were approaching Halifax Harbour and traffic was picking up.

"That must be a big guy," I said, checking the chart as I prepared to take over the wheel.

"I've been tracking him for the past hour," Ty said. "He was moving for a while, but now he seems to have stopped outside the inbound traffic lane. I'll bet it's a ship going into Halifax, and now he's waiting for a pilot."

The channel into the harbor was just ahead. In this kind of situation, the safe thing for a small boat to do was cut straight across the channel and get out of it right away. The water was plenty deep enough for us to the east of it, so we kept going in a straight line until the chart said we were clear. Then we turned ninety degrees to port and paralleled the busy shipping lane in.

As we made the turn to the left, the large blip we'd been tracking slowly moved around the screen to the right.

"Yeah, he's just sitting there," I confirmed by studying the relative motion.

We continued toward the harbor and I monitored our progress in relation to the blob. It appeared to move down our starboard side, but that was only because we were moving and he wasn't. Another contact off our bow attracted my attention when it ghosted down the left side of the screen, just touching the half-mile range ring. Passing distances were closer than we would have liked in this busy harbor, especially when we still couldn't see a thing outside our lifelines.

Up to this point, the only sound in the strangely silent world was the mournful moan of a fog horn well west of us. Now the close-passing vessel's engines throbbed loudly through the mist, the rumble greatly amplified in the thick air. Ty and I glanced at each other warily. I wasn't at all happy with this situation.

Suddenly, a wall-shaking "WHOMMMMMMM" blared straight up our transom, making both of us jump as if we'd been kicked in the behind. Whatever it was, it was right behind us!

Eyes like saucers, our heads snapped around in unison. Seeing nothing through the blasted whiteness, we turned like conjoined twins to focus on the radar screen. Judging by the volume and the deep bass of the sound that nearly knocked us off our feet, this was no little hand-held fog horn. There had to be one *hell* of a big ship behind us, but all that showed up on the screen was the same contact we'd been tracking for over an hour.

"Yep, he's a big guy, all right!" I gulped, triple checking that the large blip was still a mile away and growing no closer.

Every so slowly, the distance between the contact and the center of our screen widened. There were no further blasts, and I couldn't help but wonder why the ship had blown the horn, other than to get his jollies out of scaring me half to death!

Ten minutes later, now in the lee of the land, the fog lifted. Before us lay the largest city we'd seen since Portland. After spending several days in the sticks, a weekend of hustle and bustle would be fun. I turned the wheel over to Ty and busied myself preparing for our arrival.

"Look at that!" Ty said, interrupting my chores.

Thinking he was pointing out something on the skyline, I casually peered around the dodger.

"Oh my God!" I exclaimed, as a container ship the length of ten football fields passed us to starboard.

I noted that this ship's return was identical to the vessel that had blasted its horn at us minutes earlier. Even though we'd been in no danger, I couldn't help but shudder. We were a speck in the water compared to these monsters, yet we were all out here together. I was really happy for the clear skies, but now that I'd seen what we were dealing with, I almost wished the fog was back.

*   *   *

The Royal Nova Scotia Yacht Squadron was the oldest in North America. While in a different league from their brethren in Shelburne, the members welcomed us with the same warm hospitality. Having learned how much staying pierside increased social opportunities, we decided to splurge on a slip.

Sure enough, our first evening in Halifax we were invited to partake in a cook-out on the well-manicured lawn. As often happens when sailors get together, weather was a major topic of conversation, with the fog at center stage.

"This is so unusual," the locals told us. "It's never lasted this long."

Uh huh. Likely story.

They insisted the skies almost always cleared by early July, and assured us some beautiful days lay ahead. When learning of our plans to head south by mid-August, a minor uproar ensued.

"But September's one of the best sailing months of the year!" they insisted.

This was news to us. All we had to go by was what we'd read. Now we were surrounded by a group who warned us we were missing out if we left too early.

Ty and I looked at each other knowingly. We were in no real hurry to go south. Once we got off the water, the temperature was quite nice, and our enclosure made it bearable underway. If the fog was truly going to end soon, we'd love to spend more time in this beautiful, friendly province.

"Have you thought about sailing to Newfoundland?" someone asked.

This was the second time we'd been asked the question.

Our charts only went as far as Cape Breton, Ty told them, causing another minor uproar.

"Oh, you can buy all the charts you need right up the road!"

"You should go there if you have the chance. The scenery is spectacular!"

The seed was starting to sprout.

Back on *Liberty*, we pulled out our Seven Seas Cruising Association Bulletins. While I scoured them for stories from others who'd traveled farther north, Ty opened an atlas to the Canadian Maritimes and whistled softly.

"It's pretty far north."

I peered over his shoulder and my eyes widened. "Wow. Aren't there icebergs there?"

"Not this time of year, but I imagine it starts getting nasty pretty early in the season."

He pulled a pair of dividers from the nav kit and took a rough measurement. It was another 260 miles from Halifax to Newfoundland's southwestern-most city, Port aux Basques. But after doing some quick calculations, he announced the trip was doable, if we didn't spend too long in Cape Breton.

I pulled out a calendar.

"We'd have almost all of August up there and could catch more of the lake on the way back."

Ty nodded thoughtfully, then pulled out the cruising guide, recalling it had some words on Newfoundland at the back.

If the guide's warnings about Nova Scotia were grim, the section on Newfoundland was dire, indeed. Where Nova Scotia was remote, it's northern neighbor was downright isolated. It certainly wasn't for the faint of heart. "Newfoundland," the book advised, "was best explored "by only the most intrepid."

I thought of what we'd sailed through to get this far: big offshore waves, forty-degree rolls, bold, rocky shores, frigid water, and of course, the ubiquitous fog.

I looked at the map. I'd never dreamed of sailing so far north and knew no one else who had. But that was part of the appeal. Newfoundland stood out on the map as if highlighted -- a whole new world, waiting to be explored!

My chest was tight and my ears buzzed with a growing excitement. I raised my eyebrows and grinned at Ty.

"We're intrepid…"

He pursed his lips and looked down at the map. Then, looking up at me, he smiled back and nodded.

"Let's go buy some charts."

Sixteen

DUCKS

Once we left Halifax, we saw a whole new part of Nova Scotia. Namely, the coast! The maddening fog that had followed us for a full week was finally gone. With a clear view of the shore, we found that this area was even less populated than west of the city.

The southwesterlies that prevailed along the coast sent us surfing at top speed as we ran with the wind. Up and over the seven foot swells, *Liberty* rejoiced in the freedom of coastal sailing. The intensity of the sun shining on our white canvas was enough to warrant sunglasses, but it did little to warm the chilly ocean breeze. It looked like the cockpit enclosure would be a permanent fixture for as long as we remained in the Maritimes.

Mornings were the coldest. It was hard to believe as we stepped from our warm bed into the frigid cabin that our friends back home were sweltering. As I wiped condensation from inside the lockers and along the cabin sole, I shook my head. It was like home, alright – in January! If Nova Scotia was this cool in July, what would Newfoundland be like?

We hoped to find warmer conditions once we reached the sheltered waters of the Bras d'Or Lake. Cape Breton, while part of Nova Scotia, is an island all its own. Shaped like a large fist with the thumb pointing up, the huge lake lay in the middle of that fist, protected on all sides from ocean winds and waves.

A pod of pilot whales escorted us across the choppy Canso Strait to the shores of Cape Breton. At St. Peter's Canal, we tied up inside the lock and waited for the water to rise. Minutes later, *Liberty* was at lake-level and free to proceed. Motoring through the gates, the lack of waves wasn't the only pleasant surprise. The lake water was a full twenty degrees warmer than on the other side of the lock.

The difference was astounding. Suddenly stifling in our fleece jackets and long pants, we rushed below and pulled out the summer clothes we thought I'd seen the last of for the season. While I pranced around the deck in shorts and a tank top, Ty rolled up the panels on the enclosure.

Under sail alone, we slowly wound through St. Peter's Channel, soaking up the warm breeze and enjoying the scenery. It truly was lake-like, ringed by small mountains, and lined with tall trees.

The voices of two fishermen interrupted the silence as the VHF came to life. We normally tuned out idle chatter, but this particular conversation caught our attention.

"By, it's hot out here ta'day," the first man said.

"Yer right," the other came back. "Hateful day."

Ty and I stared at each other, unsure we'd heard what we did.

"Did he say 'hateful?' Ty asked, raising his palms to the cloudless blue sky.

I nodded my head and we burst out laughing. We'd take this hateful weather any day!

We decided to spend a few days on the lake before heading farther north. No longer concerned with getting from point A to point B, we were free to raise the sails and go wherever the wind blew, no matter how slowly we sailed. Lucky for us, there was a strong, steady breeze. With little fetch to kick up waves, we enjoyed exhilarating, yet comfortable sailing.

We'd heard that fishing on the lake was excellent, so before going to anchor the first night, we stopped at the mouth of a river and tossed over a line. This time, it was my turn to get lucky. Within minutes I had a three pound cod flopping on the deck.. We weren't the only ones catching, however. In a moment straight out of National Geographic, a bald eagle swooped down from a tall treetop and plucked his dinner from the water just off our bow.

It was obvious the Bras d'Or Lake was special, yet this was the height of the season and there were few other boats in sight. Approaching the largest town in the area, we discovered why we'd had the water to ourselves. It was Regatta Week, and all the boats were here in Baddeck.

We called the marina to ask for a slip, only to learn they were full. Because they were holding some mail for us, we'd intended to stay there. Now that we had no choice, we happily anchored for free just down from the busy town wharf.

Within minutes of dropping the hook, we dinghied ashore for mail call. Gregor, the manager of Baddeck Marine, was friendly and helpful, but he was unable to find our package.

"How long ago'd you say it was sent?" he asked with a delightful, lilting accent.

When we told him the box was mailed Priority, eight days earlier, he laughed.

"Ya won't be seein' that fer three weeks at least. This is Cape Breton, ya know."

I frowned. Infrequent mail was one of the down-sides of cruising. Part of our reason for hanging around the last few days had been to wait for this special delivery. The box was from my parents – a care package full of news magazines and favorite foods we'd been unable to find. Mom and Dad had spent two days searching for our wish-list of goodies and were as anxious for us to receive the large box as we were.

It looked like we'd be stopping in Baddeck on our way back from Newfoundland.

As we turned to go, Gregor shook his head gravely. "Ya know, ya picked the worst day of the year ta visit."

I cocked my head. Surely he wasn't talking about the hateful weather!

The problem, Gregor explained, was the annual Poker Run. The maritime version of a scavenger hunt, local boats raced from point to point, accumulating cards until they had a winning hand. With a grim expression, Gregor told us the race started at eight AM the next morning, and that every cigarette boat on the lake would start warming up as early as five o'clock.

Ty and I exchanged a grimace. Worse than biting flies or tiny no-see-em's, the ear-splitting thunder of a cigarette boat's oversized engines had spoiled many a peaceful moment back on the Chesapeake. How many times had we sat at a pierside restaurant as a Donzi cruised by the dock, preening his stripes like a peacock and revving his engines to decibel levels far higher than necessary.

We considered raising the anchor and moving. But we'd come a long way to see Baddeck. We decided we weren't going to let a noisy race ruin our visit! In fact, we realized, it might even be fun to see just how loud forty speed boats could be! Adopting an "if you can't beat 'em, join 'em" attitude, we hit the sack early, prepared for the pre-dawn wake-up call of Mercuries and "Ever-rudes."

The glare of the sun through the port woke me from a dead sleep. I opened one eye and peered at the clock on the bulkhead. It was seven thirty and no roaring engines had awakened us! Did they cancel the race?

We dressed quickly and climbed on deck. Across the water at the town wharf, a couple dozen sleek hulls bobbed in front of the yacht club. Instead of sitting behind the wheels, the racers were casually milling about, sipping… yes… *coffee*! I was shocked. Where was the Budweiser? Sure, it was early, but that never stopped any powerboaters back home!

Around a quarter to eight, the first entrants started drifting toward the start line. We waited expectantly for the ear-splitting revs, but each boat puttered past as if his throttle were stuck in low gear.

"Sorry for the noise!" one skipper called over.

"Did he just apologize?" Ty asked incredulously.

"I think so," I said, gawking in disbelief. "And look how the women are dressed!"

It was warm on the lake, but we didn't see a single halter top or skimpy bikini. These babes had pig tails! Ty shook his head in utter dejection.

By eight o'clock, thirty-six racers had motored by so slowly that we barely bobbled in their wussy wakes. At eight-ten, when all had leisurely lined up between two large orange buoys, a loud gun went off. There was a moment's hesitation, as if no one dared to go first, then the engines roared to life. Finally, we were treated to a taste of home, as the water churned and the peace was shattered by a short-lived, but deafening roar. We hooted and cheered as the boats sped off.

So much for the worst day of the year in Baddeck.

The town was a nice change of pace from the sleepy fishing villages we'd visited on our way east. A major stop for tourists en route to the Cabot Trail, Baddeck was bursting with colorful B&Bs, restaurants, and cute, nautical gift shops. We wandered the main street, then stocked up on groceries and checked email at the library. While Ty stayed behind to check weather on the Internet, I visited every beauty salon in town, hoping for an appointment.

It had been over five weeks since my dock-side cut in Portland and I was past due for a trim. Unfortunately, it was the height of tourist season in Cape Breton, and none of the shops had any openings for at least a week. Normally, I would have been content to try at our next port call, but in this case, that was Port aux Basques, Newfoundland. Although I'd never been there, I'd seen photos. Dominated by fish plants and stark, unadorned houses, it didn't look like the kind of place to get a stylish cut.

Hair hanging in my eyes, I found Ty and poured out my troubles.

"You could always go see Joey," he offered.

I punched him playfully in the arm. Joey was the barber Ty had visited the week before in St. Peter's. The young shop owner asked if he wanted his hair cut medium or short. Ty said medium, and Joey got to work. By the time he was finished, Ty looked like a recruit, fresh out of boot camp. I'd never seen his head so bare. Rubbing my hand over the stubble, I couldn't help but wonder what would have happened if he'd asked for it short!

No, thanks. Even Newfoundland couldn't be as bad as Joey.

Zipping back to *Liberty*, we noticed a new boat anchored next to us. It only took an instant before we recognized the large, white catamaran. It was *Vagabond Tiger*! The ducks were here!

We pulled alongside and called out a greeting. Dee came on deck, her pretty Asian eyes smiling a warm welcome. When we invited the two of them to join us for dinner, she promised to ask Frank as soon as he returned from an errand ashore.

Back on *Liberty*, we spied a small boat racing toward us. Even from a distance, there was no mistaking Frank as he rode his dinghy like a surfer on a board.

"Good to see you guys!" he thundered as he pulled alongside.

The air came alive with his vibrant energy as Frank filled us in on where they'd been since Lunenburg. When we'd finished catching up, I repeated the dinner invitation.

"Cruisers never turn down a meal!" Frank said. "I'll go tell Dee."

Within the hour, we were helping them aboard. Already predictable, Dee came prepared with her familiar blue cooler. We enjoyed the cream-cheese and roasted pepper dip, then moved below for the main course.

After finishing every bite of the chicken I'd prepared, Frank thanked us for the meal. He told us that some cruisers would go to any lengths for free food, including frequenting only bars that served snacks with happy hour. I wasn't sure if he was referring to himself, but it did seem that he had perfected the art of saving money. As if to prove my assumptions, he asked if we were interested in sharing the cost of a rental car the following day to drive the Cabot Trail.

Ty and I didn't even need to discuss it. We'd seen postcards with stunning views from the trail's switchback roads. The scenes were far different from the sea-level perspective we were used to. Sharing not only the cost of a car, but the good company of our new friends, was a win-win situation.

For the rest of the evening, Frank and Dee, both magnificent mentors, entertained us with over a decade of their cruising experiences. Their stories were both amusing and educational. Faced with rising crime against cruisers in Venezuela, the two had started a security net during their extended visit there.

Frank was full of suggestions of how to protect both ourselves and our boat. It was no surprise that a soldier like Frank would be armed just like we were, but in the event of trouble while at anchor, his best advice was to call attention to ourselves in whatever way possible. Fog horns, flares, or flashing lights, he claimed, would summon help from fellow sailors.

Wishing them a good night, I promised to raise a ruckus if we were boarded by any crazy Nova Scotians.

The weather the next morning truly *was* hateful, but not even the cool drizzle and gray skies could dampen our spirits. Joking and laughing in our little green rent-a-wreck, the four of us stopped at every one of the Cabot Trail's scenic overlooks.

One spot in particular was on our list of must-sees. Ingonish Harbour, halfway up the east side of Cape Breton's protruding thumb, was the perfect jumping-off point for the passage to Newfoundland. By pre-positioning there, we could cross the Cabot Strait in one long day and arrive before sunset.

The red-roofed Keltic Lodge, perched high at one end of Ingonish's horseshoe-shaped harbor, was the perfect vantage point from which to survey the entrance to the only anchorage on this part of the coast. On our charts, the channel had looked narrow. In person, it was even more intimidating. Our bird's eye view showed an entrance no wider than a two-lane road.

I surveyed the scene with my hand over my mouth. Twenty-five knot winds were gusting in from the sea, pushing surfer-sized waves against the pebbly beach and through the narrow inlet. The dramatic sight would have been thrilling, if we'd been mere tourists. Not so for us sailors.

"Unless the wind's blowing from the west, there's no way we're going in there," Ty said.

I agreed. I'd rather sail straight from the lake to Port aux Basque, than risk being bashed on the shore at Ingonish. The extra six hours were well worth the peace of mind.

We invited Frank and Dee to sail with us to Newfoundland, but they were used to cruising in the tropics and were ready for warmer weather. They planned to explore the Bras d'Or Lake for another week or so, then start heading south.

Regardless of where we were headed, both boats needed fuel and water. The contrast in how we got it was striking. On *Liberty* the next day, Ty and I rigged lines and fenders, raised the anchor, and pulled alongside Baddeck Marine's fuel pier. Half an hour later, with tanks topped off, we returned to the anchorage to await fair weather.

Being a catamaran, *Vagabond Tiger* was nearly as wide as she was long. Whether they wouldn't fit at the fuel pier, or because they wanted to economize, Frank and Dee chose to purchase their diesel from a nearby gas station, where the price per gallon was slightly cheaper.

Just after we had *Liberty* securely re-anchored, the drizzle turned to steady rain. I watched as our friends, clad in yellow foul weather gear, made trip after trip from shore to their boat, their dinghy loaded down with as many jerry cans as it could carry each trip. Dee was so petite she had to scrunch her shoulders to keep the containers from dragging on the deck. I marveled how such a small woman could handle two of the heavy jugs at once. Chalking it up to their fourteen years of practice, I shook my head and gave them credit. I wasn't sure I would have enjoyed cruising as long as they had if such basic tasks as refueling and taking on water were such an ordeal.

The rain continued overnight and was forecast to last another day. Our Newfoundland weather window was steadily decreasing, but this was no time to cross the Cabot Strait. Shrugging our shoulders, we settled in for another day at anchor.

Ty had just poured a cup of coffee when the VHF came to life.

"*Liberty*, this is *Vagabond Tiger*."

His eyes lit up as he reached for the radio's mike. "*Vagabond Tiger*, this is *Liberty*. Shift to six-eight?"

"Six-eight."

Frank told us they were going to sit out the rain, too, then invited us to come over when we got tired of being cooped up.

There was only one problem. I didn't have any dip.

Ty passed along my predicament, and we were instantly forgiven. Frank was far more interested in making a trade.

"If you have any CDs or books we might like, bring 'em along!"

Entertainment was to Frank, as dip was to Dee.

With grocery bags full of goodies, we suited up in our foulies for the short ride across the water.

Boarding the dinghy, I looked at Ty. "Wanna try standing up?"

He was game. I held onto the painter and flexed my knees. With one hand on my shoulder and the other on the tiller, Ty stood behind me and steered. It was definitely different… a little bouncy… but kind of fun!

"Look at you two! You're learning!" Frank crowed as he took the painter and cleated us off.

We scrambled aboard, shook off our wet coats, and stepped inside. *Vagabond Tiger* was a beauty. As much as I loved *Liberty*, there was no ignoring the increased room and visibility on a catamaran. As Frank showed us around the boat and described her comfortable, non-heeling ride, I could tell even Ty was a tad envious.

"She'll do up to what? Twelve knots?" he asked.

"Yeah, but nobody sails," Frank said.

His statement caught me off guard. The biggest disappointment I'd had this whole trip was the lack of sailing. The winds were usually either too light or right on the nose. We had the best of intentions when we started out. We were going to take our time and sail as often as possible. But if we'd stuck to that plan, we'd still be back in New England. Our summer weather window would have closed before we even got to Nova Scotia.

"So it's not just us?" I asked.

Dee shook her head. "Most cruisers motor much more than they sail.".

It wasn't the most encouraging news, but at least I no longer had to feel guilty that we used the engine so much. Sailing was still our first choice over motoring, and unlike trawlers, at least we had a choice. Most often, we compromised and motor-sailed.

In spite of the dreary weather, we spent a pleasant afternoon sipping coffee and swapping CDs. Ty and Frank talked engines and batteries, while Dee quenched my growing thirst for girl-talk.

By the next morning, the sun was out and the winds, now light, had shifted to the west. Conditions were perfect to enter Ingonish. Frank and Dee appeared on deck to wish us bon voyage as we excitedly departed Baddeck.

"Looks like we'll be motoring again," I shouted across.

"Like I told you," Frank yelled back, "nobody sails!"

With wishes for safe trips all around, we promised to look for each other on the way south.

Like sporadic mail, leaving new friends was another down-side to cruising. But at least we had the chance to meet them in the first place. In the short time we'd known Frank and Dee, we'd created lasting memories.

As *Vagabond Tiger* grew smaller in our wake, I felt the same tug at my heart as I had each time the Navy moved me. Focusing on the future rather than dwelling on loss had always helped, so I turned and faced northward.

It was Newfoundland or bust.

Seventeen

Ahoy, Mate

They didn't call Cabot Strait "the Chuck" for nothing.

While we didn't lose our lunch on the all-day crossing from Ingonish to Port aux Basques, the notorious channel lived up to its reputation for disagreeable conditions. Gone were the protected waters of the lake. Along with attention-grabbing rollers, the fog was back, but thankfully, there was little traffic.

In spite of the conditions, with a strong wind behind us, we moved along smartly. Regular checks of our progress showed us averaging an almost unheard of nine knots.

About half-way across the strait, a large, elongated blip appeared in the lower right-hand corner of the radar screen. Its size earned my instant respect, and I watched it closely. Even with our good pace, this vessel was going twice as fast as we were.

"I have a large contact off the starboard quarter," I told Ty. "From the course and speed, I'm willing to bet it's the ferry from Sydney to Port aux Basques."

"Okay," he said, barely looking up from his book.

I continued to monitor the vessel's progress, wishing I could see it. No matter. Within an hour, it had overtaken us and was no longer a potential threat. By the time Ty relieved me, the contact had disappeared from the screen.

Now off watch, I decided to try and make lunch. We'd been up since five-thirty, underway with the sunrise at six. We were both getting hungry, but the boat was rolling too much to stay below for long. On days like this, PB&J sandwiches were the most I could manage.

Grabbing a loaf of bread, the peanut butter, jelly, a knife, and some napkins, I returned to the cockpit and plopped down on the floor. Ty laughed as I assembled the sandwiches at his feet, but it was better than chasing jelly jars around the galley or wiping peanut butter off the bulkhead.

Our stomachs satisfied, I tried to relax with a book, but put it down minutes later. Even the gripping mystery couldn't help me escape from the incessant drone of the engine that was chugging away directly beneath me. With the enclosure back up, the noise was annoyingly amplified. I ducked below and dug out a portable CD player we rarely used. Slipping the headphones over my ears, I hit "play." Enya's soothing voice instantly transported me into my own little world.

By the time I relieved Ty at the helm, even he was looking a little frayed around the edges. When I suggested he try out the headphones, he surprised me by agreeing. Usually one to keep an eye on things even when he was off watch, Ty turned up the volume and checked out of the net.

With Otto steering and nothing on my scope, I opened the Newfoundland cruising guide. According to the sections I'd highlighted in yellow, the Canadian Coast Guard closely monitored maritime traffic in and out of Port aux Basques. All vessels, no matter what size, were asked to hail Traffic Control on channel 11 when approaching the harbor.

A trio of red arcs on the chart showed the three distances at which vessels should call in: 15, 5, and 2 miles out. I plotted our latitude and longitude and perked up. According to our position, we were now approaching the first arc. The entry procedure was a novelty for me -- all part of the fun of cruising.

I tapped Ty on the foot. When he pulled off the headphones, I told him we were approaching the reporting zone.

"Ok if I make the call?" I asked.

Ty rolled his eyes and snorted.

"What?"

"I've taken ships into some of the busiest harbors in the world without any help. We're perfectly capable of finding our own way into Port aux Basques, Newfoundland."

I could see his point. Looking at the empty radar screen, this could hardly compare with the teeming Straits of Malacca. But in this fog, I was happy for any assistance the Coasties were willing to give us.

Ty may have scoffed at the requirement, but I knew he wasn't one to overlook written rules. I pulled out our documentation number, noted our course and speed, then picked up the microphone. Port aux Basques Traffic answered my call immediately. After a brief exchange of information, we were cleared to enter the zone.

The radioman asked that we remain on channel 11, and shortly a new voice came through the speaker. With the bored tone of someone who'd made the same report a few hundred times, the man informed the controller that the vessel *Caribou* had arrived at the pier.

Recognizing the name, I brightened. "Ty! That's the Sydney ferry. I was right! That's who passed us out here earlier on her way into Port aux Basques."

"Good."

I frowned. I knew it had been a long trip, but his enthusiasm was underwhelming.

I listened as Traffic Control asked *Caribou* what time they'd be heading back to Sydney. When the man answered, I stiffened. One glance at the chart confirmed my fears.

"Ty, the ferry's going to be coming out the channel just about the time we're heading in."

Again he shrugged. "No big deal."

No, it *was* a big deal. I'd seen post cards of the ferry. This was no little ten-car carrier, and I told him so. He was unconcerned.

The closer we got to the entrance buoy, the more agitated I became. I recognized the familiar symptoms of fatigue, and fought to keep my cool.

"I think we should take the sails down now," I said.

Ty shook his head. "No, it's too exposed out here. Let's wait until we're in the lee of the land off the entrance."

I looked at the chart. It made sense to wait for calmer waters, but I wanted to get the sail handling over with before we had to deal with the ferry. His manner told me Ty was tired, too, though, and I decided not to push it.

As soon as we cleared the point, I spoke up again. "Ready to take the sails down now?"

"Not *yet*. Let's get inside a little more."

I took a deep breath. I did not like this one bit. I was just beginning to make out the shoreline through the fog, and from what I could see, they didn't call Newfoundland "The Rock" for nothing.

"Ty, I think we should take them down now."

I'd pushed him just a little too far.

"Suzanne," he snapped angrily, "I know what the hell I'm doing!" His tone was one he'd never used with me before.

I was instantly remorseful for nagging. Of course he knew what he was doing. He had years of experience at sea -- far more than I. But I was also annoyed. We were both tired, and I was frightened about encountering the ferry. He didn't need to bark at me like that! Fighting the urge to retreat below and let him handle the sails alone, I stayed behind the wheel, stone-faced and silent.

"All right," he said tersely, "bring her up into the wind now."

I complied wordlessly, my lips a thin, straight line. Some co-captain I was.

Ty went forward to lower the main. The boat bounced around in the sloppy seas, and I struggled to keep her steady while he worked. As difficult as it was, I knew we were better off here than where we'd been a few minutes ago. It was a good call on Ty's part, but still, that ferry…

I'd already notified Traffic Control that we were inside the two mile arc, and now they hailed us on the radio. "*Liberty*, Port aux Basques Traffic. This is to notify you that the ferry *Caribou* is exiting the harbour."

Right on schedule.

Ty was just returning to the cockpit when the Coast Guard called. I knew he heard them say the ferry was coming out, but he didn't say anything. Now I was squirming. We needed to answer back! I nodded at the mike and questioned him with my eyes. He merely shrugged his shoulders.

"Roger," I said to the controller. It was a stupid thing to say, but I was stalling for time.

I pointed at the chart. "Ty, the channel's really narrow here where the breakwater comes in from both sides."

"I saw it. There's plenty of room for both of us."

I have to tell you, I'd make a lousy poker player. When I realized he wanted us to head on in, my eyes widened in a mixture of disbelief and fear.

The radioman was anxious for an answer.

"*Liberty*, Port aux Basques Traffic. This is to notify you that the ferry *Caribou* is exiting the harbor. What are your intentions?"

I stared at Ty, my mind racing. Never a risk-taker, this was totally out of character for him. He was glaring now, not at me, but at the intrusion of the traffic controllers. Finally, he shook his head, and grumbled, "Tell them we'll stand by just north of the entrance buoy."

My sigh of relief could have filled the mainsail.

I relayed the message, then listened as the controller addressed the ferry.

"*Caribou*, Port aux Basques Traffic. Be advised, the forty-six foot, white-hulled sailing vessel, "*Liberty*," will be standing by at the entrance buoy until you are clear."

"Roger."

I willed myself to relax, knowing that the ship now knew we were here. Suddenly, movement off our port side caught my attention. I turned my head, and in spite of my best intentions I gasped sharply.

"What?" Ty asked, clearly annoyed with me.

"There's your ferry," I said tersely, nodding my head at an enormous blue behemoth, no less than six-hundred-feet in length, charging down the channel at a very respectable clip.

Ty casually turned to see the little boat that everyone was making such a fuss about. Taking in the scene, at first he blinked, then his eyebrows went up ever so slightly.

"Oh… Well." he said, ever Mr. Cool. "That's some ferry."

Even though I now knew we were in no danger, my hands shook so badly that I asked Ty to take the wheel. Huddling in the lee of the dodger,

I willed myself to calm down. Everything was perfectly under control, except my frazzled nerves.

"*Liberty*, this is *Caribou*."

"This is *Liberty*," Ty answered calmly.

"Yes, Captain. I see you off my starboard bow. I'm just going to swing hard to starboard out here and pass astern of you."

"Roger."

Had I not overheard their exchange and known what was happening, I would have been tempted to jump over the side as the ocean liner changed course and turned toward us, no more than three hundred yards away. In spite of my jitters, I recognized a unique opportunity and grabbed my camera. Snapping the shutter, the digital picture showed a view no sailor ever wants to see – that of a very large ship, emerging through the fog, coming straight at us.

That's some ferry, all right!

Thankfully, photos can lie. The frozen image failed to capture the movement of the graceful *Caribou* as she continued her turn and passed smoothly astern of us, exactly as agreed.

Like a choreographed dance, Ty put our engine in gear and pulled into the now-empty channel. Before us, two long walls of giant stones jutted out, perpendicular to the shoreline. I tried to imagine *Liberty* and *Caribou* going through the narrow breakwater at the same time.

It wasn't a pretty picture.

"Suzanne, I didn't realize the ferry was going to be quite that big."

"I'd seen a picture of it back in Baddeck," I told him.

"Yeah, but I hadn't. I was picturing some little ferry."

"I know you were."

"And I'm sorry I snapped at you earlier."

I touched his arm. "We're both tired, Ty. I know you know what you're doing."

"And so do you."

I nodded my head. I was grateful for the apology, but with the public wharf just ahead, any further discussion would have to wait.

Two long, tall piers, each painted bright yellow, stuck out into the harbor next to an abandoned fish plant. Three fishing boats and a Canadian ketch were tied up already, but there was still plenty of room for us.

Three men in ball caps and jogging suits watched from under the eaves of a nearby building. When we started heading in, they sauntered over and stood with hands in their pockets at the edge of the pier.

"Hello!" I called out, tossing a dock line to each of them. They gave a silent nod of acknowledgement, then expertly cleated off the lines.

"Thanks very much!" Ty said, coming to stand beside me.

He got the same subdued response.

"Not very talkative," I said softly as the three remained on the pier, staring at the boat.

Looking forward to meeting our first Newfies, we climbed the pier's rickety ladder and joined our welcoming committee.

"Bit foggy out there today," Ty said.

All three nodded thoughtfully, and finally one spoke. "Where'd ya come from, by?"

"Ingonish," I answered.

The three nodded again and continued to stare at the boat.

Then the oldest one in the group turned to Ty and said, "Ah da wye fer Ingnish?"

I could tell from the man's inflection that he'd asked a question, but I wouldn't have sworn it was in English. Not sure what to say, I turned to Ty. Knowing he was expected to answer, he nodded enthusiastically and said, "That's right!"

I stifled a laugh, knowing he could no more understand the thick Newfoundland accent than I could. We struggled through a few more pleasantries, picking out only forty percent of the words, then excused ourselves to tidy up from the passage. The three stared quietly for a few more minutes, then returned to their bench.

Ty stayed out on deck to add a couple of spring lines, and. I went below to put the cabin back in order. Minutes later, Ty joined me.

"We have more company."

I peered through the small port over the nav table. Two men, again with hands in their pockets, stood staring down at the boat.

"They like to look, don't they?"

"Yeah, and they don't seem to care that it's starting to rain."

Sure enough, a steady drizzle had dampened the deck, but these latest onlookers were undeterred. They gazed silently at the boat as if they'd never seen one before.

Having been aboard all day, we were anxious to take a walk and have a look around. The rain didn't look like it was going to stop any time soon, so we decided to do like the locals and just ignore it. With no way to dry our clothes, we suited up in full foul weather gear. Looking like a team of hazardous waste handlers in our yellow rubber boots, pants, jackets, and hoods, we drew a few sideways glances from the local residents.

We'd chosen Port aux Basques not for its aesthetic appeal, but because it was the closest port to Cape Breton. It was a working town – plain and functional. Under the drizzly, gray skies, it was obvious the small city was merely a transit point for tourists headed to other parts of the province.

In the residential section just south of the wharf, faded turquoise, green, or red buildings added a splash of color to the otherwise stark surroundings. The small, humble houses were mere boxes with roofs, devoid of architectural adornment.

North of the wharf, the locals had gone to great effort to liven up the otherwise dreary harbor. A line of sailboat-shaped banners flapped from tall flagpoles along a waterside boardwalk. Designed to attract the daily influx of tourists before they rushed out of town, the promenade started at the off-ramp of the ferry. At the far end of the walkway was a group of gaily-painted, shed-like kiosks. Signs over the doors advertised local food, clothing, and crafts

None of the shops were open, so we returned to the boat and enjoyed dinner aboard. Several times during the meal we stopped to converse with the steady stream of curious visitors who wandered by to check us out. Just as were clearing the dishes, the sounds of lively folk tunes drifted in from the nearby park.. Hoping for an introduction to Newfie culture, we left clean-up until later and headed over to check out the scene.

Each of the twelve kiosks was now open, and throngs of townspeople clustered on the tiny porches eating and laughing. Dozens of families sat expectantly in the bleachers of a small pavilion surrounding a stage.

Asking around, we learned a live band was supposed to have been playing for the past half hour. Instead, an impromptu disc jockey had set up his personal stereo at center stage and was selecting random songs from a stack of CDs.

The music was loud and festive. We joined the adults in the stands, tapping our feet while half a dozen children danced on the stage. Fifteen minutes later, there was still no sign of a band, but nobody seemed to mind. Looking around at the pleasant faces of this highly blue-collar crowd, I was struck by how polite they were. Where were the hecklers? Why was no one scowling? Instead of razzing the poor DJ about the no-shows, the locals sat peacefully, smiles on their gentle faces as they soaked up the surroundings.

Tired from our trip, after a couple more songs we called it a day and returned to the boat. Long after crawling in bed, I could still hear the cheery folk tunes booming through the speakers. Music never failed to lift my spirits, and the concert was the perfect prescription after our stressful arrival.

I closed my eyes and tried to settle down, but sleep evaded me. We'd been going non-stop since tying up. Now that I was finally still, my brain insisted on rehashing the day's earlier events. Ty's sharp words still echoed in my mind, but I realized that for the past few weeks, I'd been ready to bark at him a time or two, myself. It bothered me that I'd been so irritable. I'd chalked it up to the enforced togetherness of being on a small boat, but after the incident with the sails, the cause of my crabbiness was suddenly obvious.

We were supposed to be co-captains, but I didn't feel like one.

It was mostly my own doing. Twenty years as an officer had instilled in me an instinctual deference to those senior to me. Retired or not, husband or not, Ty would always be the captain. When he went out on deck in big seas, leaving me in the safety of the cockpit, I let him go instead of pushing the issue. During thunderstorms, he insisted on taking the wheel, and I chose not to argue. Even though we made all major decisions together, when it came to the boat, he had the final say.

We both knew that in an emergency, there could only be one captain. There was no doubt that if things went to hell, it wasn't going to be *me* giving the orders, nor did I want it to be. Sure, if we were about to do something that didn't seem right, I'd voice my concerns, but it only made sense that the one with the most experience was the one in charge.

Now that I'd thought it through, it was clear what I had to do to stop my inner turmoil. I had to demote myself. There was nothing wrong with being the mate, I reasoned. On commercial ships, it was a respected position. Even Ty had served as a relief mate on an Alaskan cruise ship when I was stationed in Seattle.

Glad that I'd figured out why I'd been so irritable, I rolled over to see if Ty was awake. The sound of his breathing told me he'd already drifted off. I decided to wait for an appropriate moment and broach the subject before we left port.

We were so busy the next day that the conversation got pushed to the side. After two loads of laundry and a trip to the grocery store, I still had one major item on my to-do list that I wasn't about to forego. I was going to get my hair cut, one way or the other.

I wasn't crazy about the salons we'd seen while walking around, but it didn't look like I had much choice. Port aux Basques was small, but it was the largest city we were likely to visit the rest of our time in Newfoundland. Unwilling to put up with scraggly hair for another month, I decided to take my chances and go for it now.

Ah, that old 20/20 hindsight…

Following the harbormaster's directions to the best salon in town, we walked two miles to the local shopping mall. Far from the modern complexes we were used to in the States, this was little more than a covered arcade. I found the salon wedged between a dollar store and a bookstore that sold only used paperbacks.

The large shop had only one customer, a burly man in a t-shirt that was too small for his bulging stomach. When I asked the young girl behind the counter if they took walk-ins, she motioned me to a chair.

I took a seat, and the stylist stepped up behind me. She asked how I wanted it cut, and I told her to keep the same style, but trim it half an inch. I recalled that back in Portland, when Beth cut my hair, she'd finished it off by thinning the layers with a razor. I liked the effect and asked this woman if she knew how to do a razor cut.

She looked puzzled, then said timidly, "Well, I could try…"

This was not the kind of confident answer I'd hoped for.

"No, no, that's ok," I said quickly.

In the chair next to me, the other stylist was conversing animatedly with her customer. Whatever they were talking about must have been interesting, but I couldn't understand a word they were saying. I'd been a language major in college, but nothing had prepared me for the Newfie accent!

So, perhaps it was a language problem that prevented my stylist from understanding my simple request to leave my hair resting along the tops of my ears. Taking a swatch of hair between her fingers, she chomped down with the shears.

Let me just say that "Uh oh," is not a phrase you want to hear in a beauty salon.

With one irreversible snip of the scissors, I was sentenced to a month of bad hair days. Staring at the glaring white patch of skin over my right ear, I grew instantly hot. There was no way to fix the gross blunder. She'd given me whitewalls as bad as any Marine. Worst of all, she'd have to do the same thing to the other side to even it out!

Nothing I could say could undo the damage, so I sat tight-lipped while she finished the trim. I'd joked before coming that they'd probably put a bowl on my head, and I wasn't far off. Even Ty could have done a better job than this girl.

Normally quite generous with compliments, Ty was short on words when I emerged from the salon.

"At least it'll grow," was the best he could do.

"This is the worst haircut I've ever had!" I moaned.

"I told you you should have let Joey cut it."

Resigned to hiding under a ball cap, we returned to the boat. Another townie was standing on the pier as we approached.

"Howdy," Ty said.

"Beautiful day!" the man replied, smiling broadly.

I looked at the sky. There wasn't a patch of blue to be seen.

Beautiful day?

"Nice yacht ya got, By."

This fellow's accent wasn't as thick as most, but by now there was no need to understand every word of the friendly folks who stopped by the boat. Their list of questions had become utterly predictable: Where were we from? Where were we going? Was this our first time in Newfoundland? How long were we staying?

When the lull in the conversation grew uncomfortably long, we excused ourselves and went below.

"He's still there," Ty said, peering through the port five minutes later.

Trapped in the boat, I figured this was as good a time as any to discuss what I'd decided the night before. When I told Ty I wanted to talk, he turned around, instantly wary.

"What'd I do?"

"Nothing," I insisted, patting the seat beside me. "It's just I've been thinking."

"That sounds dangerous," he said, joining me on the sofa. "Or expensive."

I snorted. "Neither, really. But it is kind of serious. It's just that I don't think this co-captain thing is working for me."

He frowned. "Hey, if this is about yesterday…"

I shook my head and put my hand over his. "No, it's a lot of things, really. I just feel that we both can't be calling the shots. In my mind, you're the Captain, and that's the way it should be."

Normally one to pump me up every chance he got, especially when it came to praising my skills, Ty was uncharacteristically quiet. I could see he couldn't deny that what I said was true.

"I'm happy to leave things the way they are," he said softly.

"But I'm not." I took a deep breath. "I've thought it over, and I think I'd be much happier if we just consider me the mate.

It took him a minute to digest this, then he slowly nodded his head.

"If you're sure..."

I was sure. I already felt less conflicted, knowing I didn't have to pretend to myself that I was on equal footing with my salty husband.

"So that's it then. From now on, I'm the mate. Not the "First Mate." Just the mate.

"What? No cheesy t-shirt?"

I picked up a pillow and threatened to clobber him.

The tension broken, he gave me a hug.

"What do you say I take you out for dinner in the ville?"

His offer sounded great, but from what we'd seen in our walk around town, the choices were slim: fried food, fried food, or pizza. Opting for the latter, we walked the short distance from the wharf to a pizzeria and settled into a booth. The server was in no hurry to wait on us, and by the time she finally appeared, we were ravenous. We'd had plenty of time to study the menu, and Ty got straight to our order.

"We'll take a large pepperoni, please."

The waitress scribbled on her pad, then looked up and asked, "You want cheese on that?"

Ty looked at me, and I looked at him, expressionless. With great effort, I swallowed a grin and looked away.

"Yes, cheese would be good," he said politely.

She disappeared into the kitchen and we broke out laughing.

"Look," Ty said, pointing outside, "It's raining again."

I turned and looked at the harbor through the large plate glass window. Droplets of water had begun to spatter against the pane. A few hundred yards away, our boat's mast towered above the row of flagpoles along the promenade. I noticed that a new group of Looky-Lou's had gathered by *Liberty*'s side. Undeterred by the raindrops, they stood, wordlessly, hands in pockets, and stared.

Things sure were different here.

Eighteen
WILDERNESS WOWS &
WILDERNESS WOES

Lots of places can claim to be God's Country, but most of them have been taken over by man. The southwest coast of Newfoundland remains much the same the way God created it: natural, unspoiled, and beautiful beyond words.

Under brilliant blue skies, we left Port aux Basques and sailed east. The farther we traveled, the higher and more rugged the coastline became. As much as we enjoyed Nova Scotia's scenery, this was splendor on a far greater scale. Thick, green bogs blanketed a treeless, yet magnificent landscape. Towering red cliffs, craggy and bold, held back the sea like a rocky fortress. Occasional clefts revealed the entrances to deep fjords, scoured out by glaciers that had long since melted.

This was a photographer's dream, a nature-lover's fantasy, yet we were the only ones around to appreciate it. Within half a day of leaving port, there wasn't another boat, another person, nor a man-made structure to be seen. We had a private viewing of this glorious masterpiece.

Newfoundland's awesome coastline

The area remained undeveloped for good reason. Forty miles east of Port aux Basques, the coastal road abruptly ended. Any buildings beyond that point could only be built one boat-load of lumber at a time.

If we didn't know better, we'd wonder why the government hadn't put in more highways. It was far warmer than we'd expected, and there wasn't any fog. This could be a vacation wonderland.

But we did know better. The season was abysmally short. This was early August. By the end of the month, strong gales would start blowing in from the sea. The first snow would fall in October, and by December, the smaller harbors could be completely iced in. The winter would seem endless, lasting far into Spring. Storms would lash the coast with relentless fury. Only the heartiest of souls could tolerate such brutal conditions.

And Newfoundland fishermen are about as hearty as they come.

The coast was sporadically dotted with small communities whose inhabitants' primary purpose was to fish the Cabot Strait and the Grand Banks. Over the years, the once-abundant supply of cod had seriously declined. But rather than restrict the foreign vessels that were decimating the supply on the Banks, the government put limits on their own fishermen's takes.

As a result, the Newfoundland "outports" are a dying breed. Their declining populations reflect the realities of their extremely harsh life. Most younger men have already left, gone to inland cities in search of jobs. Those who remain are there for the duration. Fishing is all they know and all their fathers knew.

Having never seen a town without roads, we excitedly plotted a course for our first outport. The tiny place, aptly named "Petites," lay at the head of a narrow inlet. Looking closely at the track Ty had marked, I couldn't believe what I was seeing. We were fast approaching a point of land called none other than "Butt Head!" I laughed, wondering who came up with some of the crazy names.

When I tried to share my discovery with Ty, he wasn't amused.

"Can we save the geographic commentaries until we're past the rocks, Suzanne?"

There was a good reason that he was the captain and I was the mate!

Reminded of my duties, I tried to compare what was on the chart with what I saw around us. According to the waypoints, our final leg called for a ninety-degree turn to the left. After that, the inlet would dead-end at the base of the town.

I moved to the bow for a better view. There was a smattering of houses around us already, but where was Petites? Surely, this wasn't all there was? And where was the sharp turn? The inlet seemed to end just ahead.

"I need you to keep a sharp eye on the depth up there," Ty shouted. "The turn's coming up soon."

His directions didn't make sense. The only opening in the rocks was a mere two feet wider than our boat. But now that we were closer, I could see a tighter cluster of houses beyond it, each with its own rickety dock.

My eyes widened in disbelief. "We're going in *there?*" I said, whipping around.

"That's what it looks like," Ty said, shaking his head.

We thought the authors of the cruising guide were kidding when they gave arrival instructions for Petites. They advised boats to "practically scrape the paint off the first wharf" to avoid a large ledge that stuck out from the opposite shore. Looking down into the translucent water, I could clearly see a huge boulder just to the right of our keel.

"Come left!" I shouted.

"I'm practically touching the wharf already!"

"Come left some more!"

We both held our breath as Ty threaded *Liberty* through the eye of that very sharp needle. Once clear, the harbor inside was little wider than our boat was long. A man standing on the public pier didn't seem to find anything unusual about this big fish in his small pond, and motioned us over. I tossed him a line and breathed a big sigh of relief when we were safely moored alongside.

Looking around, I noted that the countryside may have been incredibly beautiful, but the town was just a shade short of dilapidated. The wharf we tied up to was in the same poor condition as the abandoned fish plant beside it. While not the nicest backdrop for our night's stay, it was the only wharf big enough to hold us. And at least it was free.

Somber and soft-spoken, the man on the pier explained why things were so quiet. Petites used to be home to a hundred residents, but with the fishing industry in decline, the government could no longer afford to support the town. Sadly, he told us the power plant would be shut down within the next three months. Like pioneers on the frontier, a meager 14 diehards were holding onto the only home they'd ever known until the lights went out for good.

We left the boat and climbed an overgrown path to the crest of a hill. From here we could see the twenty-some buildings that made up the town. Other than the power plant and a church, the rest were homes -- small, square, and plain, just like in Port aux Basques. There was no school, no store, and no library. The Post Office took up a corner of the postmaster's house. The nearest groceries were an hour's boat-ride away.

At least half the homes were closed up and empty, but they were still neat and tidy. As we walked along the cracked cement walkways, no one came out to greet us, but I could sense life behind some of the windows. It was fascinating, but spooky to witness a town that was taking its last breaths.

The small, one-room church stood on a rise, overlooking the sea. It looked strangely out of place. Then I realized what was missing. There was no parking lot. Without roads, there were no cars. Without cars, there was no need for a place to park them. Instead, the church was set among rocks and weeds in the middle of a field.

A sign proclaimed this was the oldest wooden church in Newfoundland. In contrast to its neglected neighbors, the building maintained its dignity. The white paint was bright, the red trim cheery, proof that the townspeople still cared.

We hiked beyond the church, lured by the vast expanse of lushly carpeted countryside, dappled with ponds and shrubs. A small sign indicated a hiking trail, and we followed it along the coast.

There, dotting the hillside in no apparent design, were a dozen small family cemeteries. Each was surrounded by a neat, white picket fence . The view from the plots was stunning -- nothing but sea, sky, and rocky shores as far as the eye could see. It saddened me to think that some of the residents of Petites would remain here for eternity, while their descendants had no choice but to leave this little slice of Heaven.

We left at sunrise the next morning. As much as I enjoyed seeing the outport and the incredible surroundings, Petites was a little too eerie. I was more than ready to leave the ghosts behind.

Pulling away from the pier, Ty steered the boat forward a hundred yards to the widest part of the harbor. Backing and filling, he twisted the boat around her pivot point until we were aimed at that narrow exit. Having done it once, the second time was slightly less hairy, and we glided through with *Liberty's* paint and our nerves intact.

That evening we anchored in a small bay forty miles farther along where we'd been told to look for clams. Armed with a bucket and trowels, we dinghied to a sandy spot half a mile from where we'd dropped the hook. Walking along the shore, I kept an eye on a streambed that emerged from the trees nearby. If I were a thirsty caribou, this was the perfect spot to stop for a drink.

Unfortunately, it wasn't the perfect spot for clams. Digging at the little holes in the beach turned up nothing but sand. Resigned to spaghetti and meatballs for dinner, we started heading back to the boat.

"Wait a minute!" Ty said, walking toward one of the rocks. Suddenly, his eyes lit up. Sticking his hand into the water, he pulled it back with three, large blue-black mussels. The clams may not have panned out, but we'd struck shellfish gold.

The rocks were blooming with keepers, three layers thick. I was a novice at mussel picking, but once I learned they were neither sharp nor slimy, I jumped right in. Oblivious to the cold water, we stood knee deep, tossing shells by the handful into our bucket. Only when the handle threatened to break under the strain did we stop.

Basking in the scenery and the solitude, dinner was a feast for the senses. Wine-garlic steam scented the air as we swallowed the succulent morsels by the dozens. Washed down with mugs of cold beer, the taste was all that much sweeter because we'd harvested the meal ourselves.

Like the people of Petites, we didn't need a grocery store. We were hunter-gatherers! Our boat was our island, and we swung smugly on our anchor, reveling in our self-sufficiency.

The next day our track took us past Burgeo. Connected to the main highway by a two-lane road, the town offered more amenities than the isolated outports. But Burgeo sounded no different than Port aux Basques. We had all the fuel, water, and groceries we needed. Knowing we'd have more chances to meet the locals later, we decided to press on.

It was the right call. Along the way, curious seals and playful porpoises cavorted in our wake while sheerwaters and kittiwakes provided an aerial escort. Sighting our first pair of puffins with their bright orange beaks rounded out a day of close encounters with nature unlike any we'd ever experienced.

Our destination was Grey River, the first of the spectacular fjords that make cruising Newfoundland so unique. Long, narrow, and hundreds of feet deep, the only anchorage was at the far end. The guidebook noted that the entrance to the river was easily missed unless you really looked for it. With the next fjord miles beyond and the sky growing darker by the minute, believe me, we looked hard!

From three miles offshore, the cleft carved by the river was nothing but a shadow on the wall. Up close, it was easy to see why. The fjord's entrance was a mere two hundred yards from side to side. We'd been warned when we bought the charts that some of them could differ from GPS by as much as half a mile. At the time, the information had merely raised my eyebrows. Now, it raised the hair on the back of my neck.

With a clear view of the opening, Ty centered the boat between the cliffs and headed in. Out of curiosity, I ducked below and took a look at our electronic chart. The computer automatically plotted our position, based on GPS input, and showed us as a green boat at the center of a moving map. Looking at the display, my jaw dropped. The river was shown in blue, the land was shown in brown, and there was *Liberty*, well inside the brown, traveling along the hillside!

Looking out the ports, I could clearly see that we were a hundred yards from the cliffs on either side. The GPS position was accurate, but the charts were off. *Dangerously* off. Had we entered Grey River in the dark or fog, trusting only our GPS, we would have sailed right into the wall.

"You have to see this," I said to Ty.

I took the wheel and he stepped below. He came back shaking his head. "That's why we don't use electronic charts as our primary navigation tool."

It was a valuable lesson, and one I was glad we didn't have to learn the hard way.

Grey River was home to an outport of the same name. Half a mile inside the fjord, the town came into view. Thirty or so buildings lay nestled in a triangular space at the base of a cliff. Built as far up the ledge as gravity allowed, there was no room for further construction. Just like Petites, the way in or out was only by boat or helicopter.

Looking forward to spending a night at anchor at the end of a fjord, we kept on going. The absence of roads kept further construction in check, and once past the outport, we were on our own. If we wanted to get away from it all, we'd come to the right place.

It was three miles to water shallow enough to anchor for the night. After setting our 66-pound Bruce in the muddy bottom, we sat side by side in the cockpit, soaking up the silence. Surrounded by thousand-foot-high walls, we found ourselves whispering, almost reverently, in the cathedral-like atmosphere.

Nightfall came quickly once the sun dipped behind the cliffs. In this perfectly sheltered anchorage, we got ready for bed, looking forward to a good night's sleep with no noise and no rolling. Before turning the lights out, I went topside for a last look around and blinked, astonished at the all-encompassing darkness. It was a moonless, starless night, so black I couldn't distinguish water from rock, or rock from sky.

This was not the place to be if you had to leave in a hurry.

A few hours later, I awakened. I was physically uncomfortable, like something wasn't quite right, but I couldn't identify the feeling. I checked the clock by my pillow and saw that it was only a little after midnight. Rolling over, I bunched the covers around my neck and tried to go back to sleep.

Minutes later, an urgent rumble deep in my belly told me I needed to hurry to the head. Trying not to wake Ty, I slipped out of bed as quietly as possible. Pulling the door to the bathroom closed behind me, I cursed my bad luck. It must have been the mussels... and they'd been so good! Even though it was twenty-four hours since our shellfish feast, I could think of no other reason for what I was sure was about to happen.

The mild discomfort that first awoke me abruptly turned to intense pain. Within minutes I was bearing down against knife-like cramps, gripping the hand-rails to keep from crying out. Half an hour of trying to expel whatever was making me miserable produced no results, only more agony.

Frightened and frustrated, I needed to find a more comfortable position, but when I tried to stand, my trembling legs wouldn't support me. Discarding my dignity, I cracked open the door and called for Ty. Strained and high-pitched, I barely recognized my voice.

Instantly alarmed, he bolted out of bed and stood outside the head. "What's wrong? Are you okay?"

"I thought I had food poisoning, but nothing's happening," I said, grunting between words.

"What can I do?"

By now I was chilled and nauseous, and the pain was almost unbearable.

"Help me up," I said, pushing the door open.

Married or not, I was grateful the lights were out as Ty took my hands and gently pulled.

The settee in the salon was only two feet away, but even that short distance was too far to move. Groaning from spasms more intense than I'd ever experienced, I asked him to lower me right onto the floor.

Eyes wide, Ty stood over me with a helpless expression that made me feel even worse.

"What can I do?" he asked worriedly.

"Get the first aid book," I gasped. "It's on the shelf. Starboard side."

Years before, I'd been licensed as an Emergency Medical Technician. Ty had no stomach for hospitals, and was more than happy to let me be the ship's doctor. In preparation for eventually crossing an ocean, I'd put together an extensive medical kit and packed several advanced books.

Now he stood by the nav table light, fumbling through the index for "abdominal pains." I knew my moans were frightening him, but when I tried to stop, my whimpering scared him even more.

"How bad does it hurt?"

"9 ½."

Ty stiffened in alarm. On a scale of one to ten, neither of us had ever gone higher than an eight.

Turning the pages faster now, he found the right section and peppered me with questions. I lay in a ball on the floor, grunting my answers. According to the book, all kinds of nasty things could have been going on inside, but no one diagnosis matched exactly what I was going through. Before I could decide whether to use the narcotics or antibiotics we had aboard, I had to know what was wrong.

Clutching my stomach, I thought back to my training. As an EMT, I'd learned to splint fractures, bandage wounds, and perform CPR. But in the case of illness, the best we could do was "scoop and swoop" -- get the patient to the hospital as quickly as possible.

Now was not the time to feel smug about our self-sufficiency.

Things always seem worse in the dark, and at two in the morning, three miles down a dark fjord, the situation was grim. Surrounded by cliffs, our VHF was useless. If we were to go for help, Ty would have to do it single-handed. There were no navigation aids to show the way out of the black hole where we were anchored. The radar would certainly be beneficial, but the charts were more hazardous than helpful.

I willed myself to take deep breaths and assess the situation calmly. From the list of ailments Ty had read me, none of them was immediately life-threatening. No matter what I had, or how badly it hurt, I wasn't going to die by morning. The best option was to wait it out and try to find a doctor when the sun came up.

Ty joined me on the floor and stroked my hair, his face lined with worry. "Do you think it's your appendix?"

I pressed gently on my lower right side. "I'm not sure, but I don't think so."

The pain there did seem worse than on the left, but maybe it was my imagination. At least I didn't have a fever and I wasn't vomiting. Appendicitis was the diagnosis I feared the most. It was bad enough having my hair cut in Port aux Basques. The last thing I wanted was to have a Newfie cut on *me*!

I began to feel a little better, but the aft cabin was still too far to go on my shaky legs. With Ty's help, I moved to the settee. Trying to doze, the night dragged by ever so slowly, but with each hour the pain eased bit by bit. By the time the sun came up, the worst seemed to be over. I was able to move about, albeit bent over like an old lady.

I stayed below on the sofa while Ty pulled in the anchor and got underway. Our plan was to loiter off the town of Grey River and see if we could raise anyone on the VHF. The outport was small, but we crossed our fingers that they might have a clinic.

"We're coming up on the town," Ty called below.

Tired of being stuck below, I slowly climbed into the cockpit and sat on the seat, hugging my knees. Ty picked up the mike, already keyed to channel 16.

"Any station in Grey River, any station in Grey River, this is sailing vessel *Liberty*."

We stared at the houses pasted onto the hillside, willing someone to answer, but there was no sign of life in the empty streets. Granted, it was early, but this was a fishing village. Didn't they have to get up at sunrise to catch fish?

When we got no reply, Ty tried again, repeating the same call.

The town was worse than Petites -- dead quiet. Just as we were shaking our heads in a "what now" gesture, the radio came alive.

"Sailing vessel *Liberty*, this is Port aux Basques Coast Guard."

The female voice was that of an angel. Miraculously, we were seventy-five miles from Port aux Basques, half a mile inside a deep fjord, and the Coastie had copied our transmission.

"Port aux Basques Coast Guard, this is *Liberty*. We have a crew member on board with abdominal pains, and are trying to find out if there's a doctor in Grey River."

The woman told Ty to stand by. A long minute later she came back and informed us that there were no medical personnel in the town. Worse yet, the nearest nurse was two hours west, in Ramea. The closest doctor was in Burgeo, three hours back the way we'd come.

We opted for the doctor.

The Coast Guard asked if we wanted to be patched through to a physician in St. Johns, the provincial capital. I shrugged my shoulders. Why not? I knew there was little anyone could do for me over the radio, but frightened and isolated, I welcomed the reassurance of a professional.

The Coastguardsman asked us to switch to channel 26, then came back and said, "Go ahead, *Liberty*, the doctor's standing by."

I was acutely aware that using the VHF was the same as being on a party line. We often switched channels to listen in on other boats' conversations for sheer entertainment. Knowing that any number of people could be listening to my broadcast, I greeted the doctor, then described my symptoms exactly as I'd been trained in EMT school. I gave him a brief history of the problem, listed my vital signs, and described my abdomen clinically, in terms of quadrants.

"I'm having trouble hearing you," the doctor said, terse and impatient.

Taking a deep breath, I repeated the whole embarrassing story.

"You could have any number of problems," he said curtly. "I can't exactly diagnose you over the phone."

I was acutely aware of that fact and gritted my teeth. "Yes, Sir," I said, still hoping for the reassurance that a three-hour trip to Burgeo wasn't going to kill me.

"I understand you're on a boat?" the doctor asked.

I rolled my eyes. Why else would I be talking through this scratchy radio?

"Yes, Sir, that's correct."

"Well, then," the doctor said in a voice dripping with disdain, "I suggest you turn your little boat around and head for Burgeo."

Hearing his haughty tone, my nostrils flared and I growled like a bear. I'd been taught to be respectful of authority, but this arrogant bastard didn't deserve my respect. In a deliberately clipped voice, I replied, "That's exactly what we're already doing, doctor, thank you very much. This is *Liberty*. OUT."

From behind the wheel, Ty looked at me and shook his head in commiseration.

The Coast Guard stayed on and nicely asked if we needed an ambulance when we got to Burgeo. By now I was sure I could make it to the hospital on my own, and declined the offer.

Burgeo was a mere 18 miles away, but at 6 knots, the trip seemed endless. Luckily, the seas weren't too bad, and we arrived with no problems. The radioman had advised us to tie up by yet another abandoned fish plant. This one had once employed over six hundred people at its peak, and now the large structure made it easy to pick out our destination. Seeing it was a good half mile outside of town, I shook my head. I may not have needed an ambulance, but I wasn't up for a long walk to the hospital.

As we got closer, I made out the figure of a man in a blue uniform standing on the wharf.

"Looks like the local Coast Guard got a call from Port aux Basques," Ty said.

Sure enough, a young petty officer greeted us and helped Ty secure the boat. "Heard you're having some problems," he said. "My name's Shannon, and I'm here to give you a lift to the hospital if you'd like."

By now my pain was a tolerable six or seven. Embarrassed at all the attention, I thanked our escort and walked slowly to his pick up truck. Within minutes he dropped us off at the front door of a modern, blue building and told us to call if we needed anything else.

Inside the clinic, the hallways were empty. Lucky for me, it was a slow day in Burgeo, and I was immediately taken to an examining room. There a perky nurse my age took my vital signs and peppered me with as many personal questions as professional.

"You sailed here all the way from Washington?" she asked after learning of our trip.

"Yes, Ma'am."

"I've never been outside Burgeo."

We smiled at each other and laughed. I could no more imagine a life like hers, than she could mine.

She sent me down the hall with a specimen cup, and when I returned, a young man in blue jeans and a yellow polo shirt was looking over my chart. He had no name tag or white coat. The only thing that identified him as a doctor was the stethoscope around his neck.

Without introducing himself, the doctor asked me to lie down and began palpating my stomach.

"Have you been nauseous?"

When I answered yes, the nurse leaned over and whispered in my ear, "I'd be nauseous all the time if I lived on a boat!"

The doctor shot her a look of irritation, but she and I grinned at each other. After the hellish night I'd been through, it felt good to smile. It felt even better to be around people who could help me.

After telling the nurse to run a test on my urine sample, the doctor repeated the questions I was asked minutes earlier.

"Have you been using the bathroom a lot?"

"Maybe a little more than usual this morning, but not excessively."

"Mm hm. Has your diet changed?"

"No, Sir."

"But you're on vacation?"

"I'm not really on vacation. This is how I live. Other than some mussels two nights ago, my diet's the same as it always is."

"So you're eating more seafood now that you're on vacation."

I sighed. This guy just wasn't getting it.

"No more than usual." I said, wincing as he pressed on a tender spot.

"Mm hm. So you drove here today?" he asked.

"No, Sir, I don't own a car."

"You don't drive?"

"I drive, but we sold our cars to go cruising."

He stood back and crossed his arms. "How can I contact you if I need to?"

"You can't, really, unless you have a VHF radio. Our cell phone doesn't work here."

"What about your home phone?"

"My boat is my home."

He stared at me strangely. To the Newfies, a person from out of the country was "from away." To this doctor, I might as well have been from Mars.

Without a word, he joined the nurse at the counter and compared the color on a test strip with the color on a chart. Nodding his head, the doctor scribbled some words on a prescription pad. He tore off the page, handed it to me, and said, "All right, you can go now."

I stared at him dumbly. *I could go now?* Just like that? I was incredibly relieved that I didn't need surgery, but it would be nice to know what was wrong with me!

"Um, Doctor…," I said. "What's the diagnosis?"

He appeared put-out that I asked, and I wondered if doctors in Canada weren't used to being questioned. If not, that was too bad. It was my body, and I wasn't going back into the wilderness until I knew exactly what to expect.

His diagnosis was acute cystitis with renal colic. I'd never heard of a bladder infection causing the kind of intense pain I'd experienced the night before, nor did I have some of the other symptoms I associated with the ailment.[1] The doctor had only run one little test, and I'd heard the nurse tell him there was just a trace of blood in my urine. But then again, I hadn't been to medical school.

"So is this for antibiotics?" I asked, holding up the prescription.

"Yes. Do you have any allergies?"

Nice of him to ask! Luckily, I didn't, but I had to question him still further to find out if it was okay to take something for my discomfort. I wasn't feeling warm and fuzzy about the whole situation, but there didn't seem to be much else I could do. This was the only show in town, and the only town for miles.

I thanked both of them, took the prescription, and walked to the waiting room where Ty was reading a magazine. Seeing me, he sprang to his feet. When I told him the diagnosis, and that I'd hopefully be cured with a course of antibiotics, his face relaxed for the first time all day.

Canadians don't pay for their medical care, except through high taxes. The receptionist shuffled through her desk, trying to find the paperwork to bill people "from away." When all was in order, she gave us directions to the nearest pharmacy, which was on the road back to the boat. Ty

---

[1] Author's note: two cruising physicians who subsequently heard this account told me that I had the "textbook" symptoms of a kidney stone.

offered to call the Coast Guard for a lift, but I was feeling good enough to walk, if a bit slower than usual.

The pharmacy was a pleasant mom-and-pop establishment, with friendly folks behind the counter. After exchanging comments about the beautiful day, I handed my prescription to the pharmacist. He looked at the paper and said, "You're from away, aren't ya?"

"That's right. We 're on a sailboat."

He nodded in recognition. "Saw ya come in."

"Me, too," said his female assistant, smiling. The cashier also nodded enthusiastically.

I looked around the windowless pharmacy. Burgeo was a small town all right.

Antibiotics in hand, I thanked them, paid the cashier and walked outside. Once out of earshot of the locals, Ty leaned over.

"Did you see the rack of reading material?" he asked.

"No."

"There were ten different quilting magazines, but not one news magazine."

I raised my eyebrows. "Supply and demand, huh?"

He shook his head in amazement.

On the way back to the boat, we stopped at a snack stand so I could get a glass of water and start the pills right away. Knowing the best medicine of all, Ty bought me a chocolate ice cream cone. The treat raised my spirits, but by the time we got to *Liberty*, I was beat. I'd had more than enough excitement for one day, and Ty could tell.

"You want to just stay here for the night?" he asked as I plopped wearily onto the seat.

I had to admit, the thought was appealing. I'd been worrying ever since we left the hospital. What if the doctor was wrong and I got worse? What if I had a reaction to the pills? What if, what if.

But I was feeling okay. Definitely better than the night before. And this fish plant was really ugly...

"Is there some place prettier we could go where we could get back quickly if we needed to?"

Ty picked up the cruising guide and turned to the pages after Burgeo. A small cove called "Doctor's Harbour" was less than six miles away.

"Secluded, peaceful, beautiful," Doctor's Harbour sounded like the best prescription of all.

That evening, as we rested at anchor, Doctor Ty cooked dinner and catered to me royally. After clearing the table and handing me my book so I wouldn't have to get up, he sat down beside me on the cockpit cushion.

"Did I tell you about the article I was reading at the hospital while you were in with the doctor?"

"No," I said, resting my book on my lap.

"It was written by some wacko Canadian environmentalist. He said that Newfoundland is having problems with urban sprawl, and wrote that the populated areas have grown to a worrisome *three percent* of the province."

I pictured tiny Petites with its fourteen residents and the miles of empty coastline we'd sailed past since then. Even now, we were only six miles from the largest town around, yet it might as well have been six hundred.

"Three percent," I repeated.

"Yep."

Our laughter faded away, leaving nothing but hushed silence.

Urban sprawl, indeed.

Nineteen

FRIENDLY FOLKS & FRIENDLY FIRE

We may not have had a schedule, but we did have a weather window. I wasn't about to let a sore stomach keep me from enjoying what few good days remained of the short Newfoundland cruising season.

After a peaceful night in Doctor's Harbour, I felt confident enough of my condition to head back out to the boonies. Our destination was Francois, an outport that was supposed to have the friendliest people on the southwest seaboard.

Leaving the calm waters of the anchorage behind, we plotted a course to keep us two to three miles off the coast. The seas this day were larger than normal, six to eight feet. They were hitting us on the starboard quarter. After strapping down and securing anything that might take a tumble below, I climbed into the cockpit, then gasped.

"Ty! Look at the dinghy!"

Our excessive rocking and rolling was making the little boat swing wildly from the davits. With each wave, the red gas tank slid from one end to the other. Several times it looked like the tank would keep right on going over the dinghy's gray tubes and into the sea. Cursing that we hadn't lashed the boat on deck, Ty ran aft to snug it in while I took the helm.

Sitting behind the wheel, I could almost feel my organs sloshing back and forth just like the gas tank. The motion was too much for my tender tummy, but I found that standing made it bearable. For the next six jarring hours, I either stood at the wheel, or under the dodger. Bracing myself like a large "X," with legs apart and a wide grip of the grab rail overhead, I ticked off each disagreeable mile. If cruising meant taking the good with the bad, there were surely good days ahead.

Like many places in Newfoundland, Francois wasn't pronounced the way it looked. People knew immediately if you were from away if you didn't say the name like the locals. No hoity-toity French accent would do for these down-to-earth folks. Their town was "France-way," plain and simple.

The harbor was in a large bowl, surrounded by mountains. A hundred yards after passing through the narrow neck at the entrance, the seas magically flattened. Right away, we could see that Francois was unique. Even from the water we could make out white railings along neat, paved paths that followed the contours of the hillside. Festive banners in green, blue, red, and yellow lined the main walkway.

The friendly outport of Francois, Newfoundland

"I think there's something going on." I said. "Look at all the people on the shore over there!"

Unlike the ghost towns of Petites and Grey River, there must have been a hundred people on a small beach at one end of the village.

"Looks like some kind of race," Ty said.

Peering through the binoculars, I watched as a man and woman in a single dory rowed furiously around two orange floats. The crowd ashore cheered wildly as the boat completed the short course. As soon as the couple got out, another replaced them and the clock started again.

"This is great," I said sarcastically. "The whole town's going to watch us dock."

Going pierside in a new port always held an element of stress. Add to that the knowledge that if there are other sailors around, they're sure to be watching to see how well you do. It's a boat thing, and we're just as guilty of it as the next guy.

"That might not be a problem," Ty said. "because it doesn't look like there's anywhere to tie up anyway."

Looking around, I saw he was right. Every wharf was full of fishing boats. Ours was the only pleasure craft in the whole harbor. A few orange mooring balls bobbed around us, but they were smaller than we'd need. Anchoring wasn't desirable, as we'd seen nothing less than 60 feet under our keel, and the bottom was rocky. Looking back at the waves beyond the entrance, I felt a growing dread that we'd have no choice but to go back out in search of another port.

"Calling the Morgan 46 in the harbor, come in please."

I looked at Ty in surprise. Not only was someone hailing us on the VHF, but they even knew our boat's model!

"This is *Liberty*." I said into the mike.

"*Liberty*, the harbor's a little crowded, but go ahead and tie up alongside Thelma Louise, that blue fishing boat off your starboard bow. Her owner's not around today, but I know he won't mind."

I thanked the man, relieved that our problem was solved. Then, to satisfy my curiosity, I asked how he knew we were a Morgan 46.

"Because I own one," he replied, "but it's in Burgeo for repairs."

Ty and I gaped at each other. We had yet to see a boat like ours anywhere, yet another Morgan owner was right here, in tiny Francois! Suddenly, a distant memory excited my brain cells.

I asked, "You wouldn't happen to be the American who sailed to Newfoundland and liked it so much he stayed, would you?"

There was a pause. "That would be me."

"Did you know you're a legend?"

The man laughed. "Well, that's a dubious honor."

He signed off, promising to stop by and see us as soon as the dory races were over. He told us we were lucky to be there for France-way Day. Hearing this, I clapped my hands like a kid. Until now, we'd met the Newfies in onesies and twosies. What better way to get a feel for the people than a good old small-town festival!

After putting out some extra fenders, Ty headed *Liberty* into the strong breeze and eased us next to the high-sided steel trawler. Docklines in hand, I scanned the other deck for cleats, then tensed when I saw there was nothing to tie off to. In a do-or-die scramble energized by adrenaline, I ended up aboard the other boat. Scurrying aft, I looped a line around a pole fixed to the trawler's stern while Ty found an attachment up forward for our bow line.

Within the hour we were enjoying France-way's talent show on the school yard basketball court. Sitting on the grass, sipping beer, we chatted with our new friends, the legendary Americans, Ralph and Deb Shields. A jovial and huggable couple, it was obvious from watching their interactions with the crowd that they were as much a part of the community as those who'd lived there all their lives. On the stage, two women in matching T-shirts struggled through the lyrics to a folk song as they sang and laughed at the same time.

Just as Ralph and Deb must have been adopted when they'd sailed into the harbor five years earlier, we were invited to partake in the pot-luck supper after the show. When I asked what I could bring, my offer was cheerfully brushed aside.

We followed the path to the community center at the appointed time. Surrounded by ruddy faces crisscrossed with laugh lines, we filled our plates and grabbed a seat at one of twenty long tables. In between mouthfuls of stewed moose and caribou sausage, Ralph filled us in on life in an outport. All the men around us were fishermen, save for a couple of teachers, shopkeepers, and two who kept the power plant running. Trash collection and other duties normally performed by civil servants were handled by the residents themselves, according to a rotating schedule. When the harbor got iced in, people shared what food they had. Doors were never locked in this town of 104, and neighbors walked in and out of each others' houses unannounced.

Pointing at a row of colorful, round targets on the wall, Ralph explained that in the winter, darts were serious business in Francois. Men's and women's tournaments lured folks from their warm houses several nights a week for some healthy but stiff competition.

"This is a great place to live." Ralph said. "If you're interested, there's a house near mine that's up for sale. I'm sure it'll go for less than ten thousand."

I gawked. Ten thousand dollars for a house?! Yes, they were modest, but for that price, it was almost a shame to say no!

Nearby, Deb sat in a circle of women, chatting animatedly. Two fellows gave Ralph a friendly slap on the back as they went back to the food table for seconds. It was easy to see why they'd chosen to live here. Life in Francois wasn't about cars, or shopping malls, or movie theaters. It was all about community -- sharing, helping, and loving thy neighbor.

But Deb and Ralph were from Michigan. They were used to harsh weather. With visions of turquoise water and white, sandy beaches, we politely declined the deal on the house.

Once the supper ended, everyone took their dishes and went home to rest. But France-way Day wasn't over yet. At ten o'clock, with the kids put to bed, the older folks returned to the community center dressed to the nines. I felt shabby in my blue jeans and deck shoes, never expecting these fishermen's wives to show up in slinky dresses and strappy sandals.

The entertainment was a talented one-man-band. I quickly sensed he must have played a gig or two in the hall before this particular evening. Strumming his guitar and singing to the accompaniment of a synthesized piano and drums, the whole crowd sang along with every song. They swooped onto the dance floor when he struck up a new tune, and returned to their seats en masse between numbers.

"Aren't you going to dance?" Deb asked as another snappy song started up.

I shook my head. "It looks like fun, but I'm not quite up to snuff tonight. I don't think I could handle jumping around."

With a look of concern, she asked what was wrong. I told her about the abdominal attack I'd suffered just two nights earlier in Grey River.

Her face lit up. "Oh! You're the one!"

I smiled weakly, knowing what was coming.

"We all heard about you on the radio!" she said excitedly. "The whole town was worried."

Suspicions confirmed. The party line was alive and well. I assured Deb that I was doing much better, and she went off to spread the news. I shook my head and laughed. There were always two sides to life in a small town.

When we said goodnight, well after midnight, the dance was still going strong. Deb and Ralph apologized that they wouldn't be around to see us off the next day. One of the coastal ferry captains lived in Francois, and they were leaving with him early in the morning to bring back their boat from Burgeo.

Understanding the needs of sailors, they kindly offered us the use of their home to do our laundry and take showers. We happily accepted. The next morning, after breakfast, we followed the path to their cheery, freshly-painted red house. As expected, the door was unlocked. Not used to just walking into people's houses, we tentatively pushed it open. As we did, a waist-high bundle of fur trundled over to greet us.

The Shields truly had gone native, right down to their Newfoundland dog.

"You must be Bear," Ty said, reaching down to pet the gentle giant.

Seeing the huge dog, I chuckled and shared with Ty a story Deb told me about the time he slipped his lead in a public park. It was no wonder people got out of the way quickly when Deb ran after the big, brown animal yelling, "Bear! Bear!"

With our clothes in the washer, we settled into two comfortable easy chairs in the living room. It felt strange to be in a house for the first time in months. Noticing a television across the room, we realized it had also been that long since we'd seen TV news. Excited to catch up on all we'd been missing, I waited expectantly while Ty tuned in CNN.

We sat back and watched the lead story with amazement. The same celebrity trial that was making headlines when we left Washington was still being rehashed and dissected ad nauseum. Ty got up from his chair, huffed across the room, and flicked the TV off in disgust.

"Let's go sailing," he said.

And sail we did! As soon as our laundry was done, we slipped the lines from Thelma Louise. We were on the open ocean minutes later. The seas were down, and the wind blew a steady fifteen knots from the south. Off went the motor and up went the sails. No longer in trawler mode, we reached along at 7 knots under full main and jib.

Only when we came abeam of Hare Bay did we reluctantly lower the sails and start the iron genny. The entrance to this fjord was an easy one, wider than the last. We merely had to motor down the center until we came to the place on the chart that Ty had marked with a hand-drawn anchor. Deb had recommended this spot for its choice of scenic waterfalls, excellent hiking, and wild blueberries by the handful.

As we neared the end of the route, Ty asked, "Is that a mast up there?"

I peered ahead and excitedly agreed. Through a stand of trees on a narrow spit of land, I could just make out a tall white pole that was clearly man-made. Rounding the point, a blue-hulled ketch the same length as *Liberty* came into view. A red, white, and blue flag waved a friendly welcome from the backstay.

"They're from New Hampshire," I said, reading the homeport on their transom.

"It's about time we had some company!" Ty said.

"Yeah, and if they came all this way, they must really be..." I paused, waiting for Ty to fill in the blank. He knew what I was up to, and joined me in shouting: "INTREPID!"

Unsure if our neighbors wanted privacy or company, Ty passed deliberately close and slowed down. The sound of our engine had the desired effect. Within seconds, two blond heads popped out of the cabin. The couple, in their mid-fifties, smiled and waved a cheerful greeting.

"Good to see some other cruisers!" The woman said.

Ty answered back, "That's what we were just saying!"

"How about getting together for a sundowner?" the man asked.

"Great!" I shouted. "Why don't you come over to our boat after we get settled?"

Within half an hour we were helping Marc and Terry from "Joyous" climb the ladder on our transom. We stood on the aft deck and exchanged boat cards, then Marc presented me a striking photo of *Liberty* at anchor, the background nothing but rock wall.

I turned around and looked at the cliff behind us. It was the same scene. "You must have just taken this!"

He smiled proudly. "Yeah, I'm really into digital photography."

"Me, too! There's nothing like instant gratification, huh?"

"Marc's a professional photographer," Terry informed us.

I asked about her interests, and learned she was a mental health counselor. Both had the kind of enviable jobs that allowed them to leave work for months at a time to cruise. Like us, they'd been in Newfoundland for a little over a week, but they'd arrived at the town of Fortune and were working their way west to Port aux Basques.

As we led them below to the cabin, Ty answered their questions about our own backgrounds and how we came to be cruising. While Terry looked around the galley, Marc immediately gravitated to a framed photo on the wall over the settee.

"Is that a battleship?" he asked.

"Yep. That's IOWA," Ty answered.

"This is incredible," Marc said. "Look at the shock waves in the water from the guns going off!"

The photo was one of my favorites – a real attention-grabber. It showed the battleship firing a broadside -- all nine of its 16-inch guns going off only a tenth of a second apart. A mushroom of orange and yellow flame bloomed outward no less than a hundred yards along the warship's 900-foot length from each of the three turrets -- forward, amidships, and aft.

"Ty was Operations Officer on that ship," I said proudly.

"No kidding!" said Marc, turning around with heightened interest.

"What does that entail?" Terry asked.

"A lot of things," Ty said as he poured drinks. The Ops Boss was responsible for the planning and execution of all the ship's operations, he explained, from short underway training, to major fleet exercises and deployments. He supervised the ship's communications, signaling, Combat Information Center, TOMAHAWK and HARPOON missile firing, intelligence collection, navigation, electronics, and radars.

"Wow. Sounds like some job," Marc said, whistling under his breath.

"Next to command, best in the world."

"Ty was on exchange with the Royal Navy in England when the assignment came up," I told them. "He wanted to serve on a battleship so badly that he bought his own plane ticket to fly back to Washington and lobby for the job."

"There's nothing like a battleship," Ty said wistfully, his eyes a thousand miles away.

Marc shook his head. "I don't know. I'm having enough trouble as it is with just my own little vessel."

"What's the matter?" Ty asked, snapping back to the present.

Marc's expression took on that of a frustrated boat owner, one I'd seen a time or two myself. He told us his engine hadn't been responding to the throttle the same way it used to. He'd spent the whole day in this beautiful cove cooped up below trying to troubleshoot the problem.

"I can't pin it down to any one thing," he said, "but when I put the engine in idle and give it some gas, it just doesn't seem right."

On hearing those familiar words, I looked at Ty and said in a leading tone, "If it doesn't seem right…"

He nodded conspiratorially and replied, "It probably isn't."

Terry cocked her head. "Sounds like there's a story there."

"Sure is," I said. "And it has to do with the battleship, in fact."

The three of us turned to Ty, who shrugged his shoulders modestly.

"Come on, Honey. Tell them!"

It only took a little encouragement, but once he got started, our guests listened, raptly, engrossed in his story.

IOWA was in the Caribbean, Ty told them. The ship was preparing to conduct a live firing exercise with a destroyer, two aircraft, a submarine, and USS SOUTH CAROLINA, a nuclear powered guided missile cruiser. The target was an old merchant ship that had been cleaned environmentally and was sanctioned for sinking.

As called for in the exercise plan, a tug boat towed the large, unmanned ship to a designated spot in open water, then set the hulk adrift. The tug captain didn't want to be anywhere near the area when the Navy started unloading live missiles on it, and as soon as he cut loose his tow, he beat feet. Still, it took him five or six hours to clear the firing area. Meanwhile, the shooters moved to their assigned positions fifty to sixty miles from the hulk, well out of sight of the target and each other.

As the senior ship in the exercise, IOWA had the lead. As IOWA's Ops Boss, Ty was calling the shots. Literally. Once he got word that the tug was clear of the firing area, he sent an E2C Hawkeye to fly over the target and confirm its position. An early warning and reconnaissance aircraft, the Hawkeye spotted the ship and radioed back the hulk's position as a bearing and range from IOWA.

Standing in the battleship's Combat Direction Center, Ty watched as his sailors plotted the target's latitude and longitude on a plotting table and marked it on a computer screen with a "hostile" symbol. When he saw the position the Hawkeye had reported, Ty was puzzled. It just wasn't where the target was supposed to be.

Sensing that the information was off, he told his air controller to have the pilot fly over the target a second time and give him a visual identification that it was indeed the unmanned merchant ship. The message was delivered, the pilot complied, and reported back positively, that yes, it was the hulk.

In the dark room, surrounded by the dim glow of radar screens and computers, Ty shook his head. The target was thirty miles from where it should have been. Unfortunately, the tug was too far away to ask where, specifically, he'd dropped it.

Ty turned to his senior enlisted Operations Specialist. He asked the master chief to call the F-14 Tomcat that was on Combat Air Patrol during the exercise, and have the fighter jet do a visual ID of the target at the latitude and longitude given by the E2C – a second opinion, if you will.

The Tomcat did as ordered and reported back that the vessel at the designated position was, indeed, the target ship.

Ty scratched his head. It just didn't seem right. In the Caribbean, the trade winds blew from the east. If the tug had dropped off the target where it was supposed to, the hulk would have had to drift 30 miles *upwind* to be where it was reported to be.

They now had two Navy aircraft, an E2C and an F-14, reporting the target in the same position. Both had visually identified it. The battleship's captain was standing over Ty, wondering what the delay was all about. IOWA's HARPOON missile, with its live 700 pound warhead, was armed and ready to be fired, as were HARPOON missiles on the other ships and aircraft, and the captain was under pressure to launch all of them on time.

With every eye in the room watching him, Ty stood his ground. His training as a Surface Warrior had shown him that if something didn't seem right, it probably wasn't. Lucky for him, the battleship's commanding officer had gone to the same school. Taking his Ops Boss' advice, the Captain told Ty to do whatever he thought best. Safety came first.

At this point, Ty ordered a *third* look, this time sending an aircraft that knew ship identification better than any other – an SH3 Sea King helicopter. E2Cs fly high, and F-14s fly high and fast. He knew they weren't really trained to identify ships, other than the carriers on which they land.

The helo flew to the position given by the previous two aircraft as Ty stared at the plotting table and the Captain drummed his fingers. Minutes later, the helicopter radioed back to the battleship, "IOWA, we are at the position reported. Be advised, the vessel at this location is the USS SOUTH CAROLINA."

You could have heard a pin drop in IOWA's Combat Direction Center... and in *Liberty's* salon as Ty finished the story.

"You mean, if you'd listened to the first report, or even the second, you would have fired your missiles at another Navy ship?" Marc asked, incredulously.

"That's right."

"What would that have done?" Terry asked, gaping.

"Well, the HARPOON missile can break a ship in half... kill hundreds of people. That's what it's designed to do," Ty said matter-of-factly.

"Where was the hulk?" Marc asked, still stunned.

"Right where it was supposed to be – within one mile of where the tug dropped him."

"So it was just gut instinct that told you to go back for a third look?"

Ty shrugged his shoulders.

I knew my husband wasn't about to blow his own horn, and finished the story for him. "It's human nature to assume things are ok, especially when people repeatedly tell you they are. But in this case, it all came down to that one fundamental lesson: If something doesn't seem right, it probably isn't."

There was a long silence as the four of us stared at each other, lost in frightening possibilities. Then, without warning, Marc stood up and smiled sheepishly.

"I'd love to stay for another drink, but you know, I think I'd better go have another look at my engine!"

Twenty

LA VIE EN FRANCE

We spent the next week alternating between secluded coves and tiny outports. By mid-month we'd gone as far east as time allowed if we were to get back to Nova Scotia by September.

Our turn-around point was the French island group of St. Pierre and Miquelon, just thirty-five miles from Newfoundland's southeast shore. Until we'd decided to cruise this far north, I hadn't known there was French territory here. But once we started poring over the charts, we learned about the two islands and realized how easy it would be to spend some time in a little piece of France.

Thinking ahead, we tried to buy a courtesy flag to hoist when we crossed into sovereign French territory, but the chandleries in neighboring Newfoundland carried only their own red maple leaf design. I knew no one was going to deny us entry if we didn't fly the tricolor flag, but we wanted to look like we had our act together. So, a few days before our arrival, I dug out my sewing machine and sewed strips of blue, white, and red cloth into a flag that would make Napoleon proud.

We arrived in Miquelon and made a bee-line for a pale green building marked "*Adouane*." It was disconcerting yet exciting to walk into the Customs office and find ourselves surrounded by men in crisp blue uniforms speaking a foreign language. In Canada, everything from beer bottles to butter was labeled in both English and French. But here, there were no concessions to the neighboring country's language. The signs over the doors, the posters on the wall, and the conversations around us were one hundred percent *en francais.*

I don't know if it was their flag flying from *Liberty's* halyard, or my rusty college French, but the officials cleared us with only a cursory glance at our documentation. They never set foot on the boat. Within minutes of our arrival, we each had a new stamp in our passport and were free to roam the island.

The tiny harbor where we tied up was industrial and not very attractive. We hoped some interaction with the locals would make up for the lack of charm. The pier came alive when the ferry from St. Pierre arrived, but not a soul stopped by to chat. It was a radical change from the greetings we'd grown accustomed to in Newfoundland, and we felt a let-down at being ignored.

Twenty-five miles long, Miquelon was five times larger than St. Pierre, but it had only one-tenth the people. Most of the island was windswept and unpopulated, with the bulk of the buildings clustered just beyond the harbor. Figuring if the locals wouldn't come to us, we'd go to them, we went for a walk after dinner.

The streets were strangely deserted. The weather was fine, but people seemed to be hiding inside. Passing tightly closed-up homes, I sensed curious stares from behind the curtained windows.

We arose the next morning and went for a run along the shoreside road. When the occupants in passing cars failed to return our waves of greeting, we decided we'd had enough of Miquelon. Returning to the boat, we showered and got underway. Others had told us St. Pierre was the more cosmopolitan of the two islands, and we hoped the city-folk would prove to be more cordial.

The crossing from Miquelon to St. Pierre was short, but well worth the trip. Ever since Maine, we'd been on the lookout for puffins, but had seen only a handful. Rounding the rocky northeast corner of St. Pierre, we sailed past an entire colony of the funny little birds. Those bobbing in the water flapped their black wings franticly as we approached, looking like over-loaded helicopters without enough lift.

As we approached St. Pierre's harbor, the wind piped up to a brisk 26 knots. Just like in Newfoundland, there was no one to call on the VHF to help us tie up. Instead, Ty did his best to maneuver the boat close enough for me to lasso a piling. I tossed the breast line into the air, only to have it fly back in my face.

Not twenty yards away was St. Pierre's Club à Voile, a center supposedly dedicated to promoting seamanship. Several sailors stood around chatting idly, studiously ignoring our travails. I watched them incredulously as Ty took the boat around for a second pass.

With no thanks to the men on the dock, we got *Liberty* secured in her slip and headed to the office to sign in. Our reception there was no warmer, consisting of a cheerless exchange of paperwork and money, and a stern warning to heed the schedule posted on the restroom doors.

So far the only good thing about this little side trip was the wildlife. Wandering the city's streets, I thought back to the trip across the strait the day before. As we'd crossed into French territory, two enormous finback whales had swum right up to our boat, but the people of St. Pierre and Miquelon were avoiding us like bad cheese.

Disheartened, we headed for a grocery store where our spirits were instantly raised. For the past three weeks, we'd survived on iceberg lettuce and Wonder Bread. If a Newfie store had tomatoes in stock, it was a good day. Cucumbers were cause for celebration. Now, here before us lay a selection of produce and pastries as good as any in downtown Paris. The cheese counter contained no less than seventy varieties, and nearby shelves overflowed with fine French wines.

Returning to the boat with arms full of booty, we stowed the provisions and looked at each other glumly. Now that we'd stocked up, there didn't seem to be much reason to stick around. Climbing into the cockpit, Ty opened a bottle of Côtes du Rhône, and we sipped the wine over a chart, planning an early get-away for the following morning.

I looked up and was startled to see a man on the pier. We'd been in St. Pierre nearly a day and this was our first visitor. Since we were at the end of the dock, he had to have gone out of his way to check us out.

"We have company," I said quietly. He was tall and thin, in his mid-forties, and had an unruly mass of curly brown hair. His striped polo shirt hung casually outside a pair of faded blue jeans.

Tired of speaking French to people who failed to return my pleasantries, I merely nodded at the man. It was Ty who spoke up and asked in English, "Are you a sailor?"

Looking back, it's amazing how that one little question changed our whole impression of St. Pierre. If Ty had merely nodded as I had, the stranger would most likely have returned to the street. We would have sailed away from St. Pierre the next day disappointed and disgruntled.

Instead, the man stopped, gave a very Gallic shrug of his shoulders, and answered Ty's question in a heavy accent.

"I used to be."

Constrained by the language barrier, the three of us nodded and smiled some more, until I thought the man was simply going to walk away. Then Ty surprised me by inviting the man to join us for a glass of wine.

Shrugging again, our visitor stepped aboard and introduced himself as Jean-Pierre Latinie, a long-time resident of St. Pierre and the owner of a computer repair shop in town. In English that improved with every sentence, he told us that he'd sold his wooden boat some years back, but still enjoyed wandering the docks. I could relate to that. Once boats get in your blood, they become an addiction.

Taking the last sip of wine, Jean-Pierre set down his glass and asked if we'd like to have a tour of the island. Delighted at the chance to see more than what we'd explored on foot, we happily accepted.

His green van was parked at the head of the pier. Opening the passenger door, I immediately noticed there was no back seat. The rear of the vehicle held nothing but a green carpet, covered with white dog hair. Climbing behind the wheel, our host apologized and indicated that Ty and I were to sit together. With one cheek on the seat and the other on the emergency brake, we took off. I held onto Ty with a death grip to keep from impaling myself.

Five minutes into the tour, my quadriceps were screaming from the awkward angle. Suddenly, Jean-Pierre made a sharp turn down a narrow street and abruptly pulled onto the sidewalk.

"I come right back," he called over his shoulder as he hopped out of the van and disappeared into a nearby house.

"Let me out!" I said to Ty, trying not to fall over as he stood up.

I was still rubbing my legs when Jean-Pierre returned and got back in the van.

"I tell my wife you eat with us this evening."

I glanced at Ty in surprised delight. Things were definitely looking up. First a tour of the island, no matter how uncomfortable, and now a chance to experience the French culture close up and personal!

"That's very kind of you," I said, climbing back onto my precarious perch. "Are you sure your wife doesn't mind?"

Jean-Pierre waved his hand in the air and whistled a dismissive "pffft."

"Eez no problem. We return last night from five weeks in France. She must go to ze store in any case, so I tell Jacqueline to buy food for four peoples, not two."

I winced, knowing how I'd feel if Ty dragged in two strangers off the street the day after we got home from a five week trip abroad.

Taking his cue from our host, Ty responded to my alarmed reaction with a dismissive wave and "pfft" of his own.

The hour-long tour took us past all the major highlights. With five thousand residents, St. Pierre was more big town than small city. The look was totally different from any place we'd visited in the last several months. Many of the houses and shops were painted in chartreuse, orange, pink, and other bright colors not usually applied to exterior walls. Boxy Peugeots and Renaults zipped up and down the narrow streets. Old men in berets clustered on a dirt court, tossing silver balls in a game of *boules*, the French version of shuffleboard.

With the tour complete, we returned to Jean-Pierre's house. Passing though the first-floor workshop on numb legs, I struggled up the stairs. We emerged into second-story living room that smelled faintly as if it had been closed up for some time. Jacqueline emerged from the kitchen to greet us, apologizing that she hadn't had a chance to air out the house.

Tall and thin like her husband, she had long, jet-black hair, and wore a pair of flattering European jeans and a tight knit top. If she was upset about the impromptu dinner, she gave no indication.

We settled onto a couch on the sun porch and were treated to a glass of "tea punch," a sugary rum drink with a powerful kick. Jacqueline brought out a tray with toast points, butter, and a pale pink spread in a tiny bowl.

My parents taught me to try everything once, and I discovered to my relief that cod liver paté tastes far better than it sounds.

The conversation was easy, aided by our hosts' excellent grasp of English. Jacqueline and Jean-Pierre were happy to practice and to educate us about the finer points of French culture in a way we never could have learned from a book.

The source of the dog hair in the van turned out to be "Hi Fi," a rambunctious retriever named after the little white dog on the old RCA record labels. "Eefie," as Jean-Pierre pronounced the name, was overjoyed to have his owners home, and bounded around the sun room while we tried to converse.

"*Hi Fi! Asseyez vous la bas! Ne bougez pas!*" Jacqueline scolded him sternly.

As the dog skulked off to a corner, I looked at Ty and said, "Gee, Honey, the dog understands French better than you!"

My husband was not amused.

Over a light meal of grilled sausages, cheese, pickles, tomatoes, and two kinds of bread, we sampled several bottles of wine, both red and white. The hands on the clock revealed it was well past midnight, yet our hosts showed no signs of fatigue. We were pikers, used to going to bed early, and finally had to call it a night.

Thinking we were leaving in the morning, we said our farewells at the door. Jean-Pierre had other plans.

"Tomorrow I must fly my plane. You will go with me."

It wasn't a question. It was a statement of fact. I was stunned. He'd mentioned earlier that he had a private pilot's license, but I didn't realize he owned his own plane! In a way, I was excited at the thought of an aerial tour, but at the same time, I was hesitant. I'd flown on a lot of aircraft in my military career, but always with highly trained professionals at the controls. Jean-Pierre was a nice guy, but he was a computer technician!

Ty appeared far more eager than I, and instantly accepted for both of us. Not wanting to look like a wuss, I kept my concerns to myself. At least if we stuck around for a mid-day flight, I figured it would give us a chance to reciprocate their hospitality.

After conferring quickly with Ty, we invited them to enjoy an American meal aboard *Liberty* the following evening. Kissing our hosts on both cheeks, we said *bon soir* and walked back to the marina.

The next day, Jean-Pierre picked us up at the yacht club and drove us to the airport. His plane was one of only two in a small hangar near the commercial terminal. I had to admit the aircraft looked sturdier than I'd expected. A four-seat Grumman Tiger, it appeared to be well cared for. It was a bit of a shock, however, to watch Jean-Pierre hook a tow-bar to the front of the plane and manually pull it from the hangar onto the tarmac. The small bird looked mighty light to carry the three of us high above the clouds.

Like a prisoner heading to the firing squad, I climbed onto the plane's wing and folded myself into the back seat. Cinching my seat belt as tight as it would go, I watched as Jean-Pierre went through his pre-flight checklist in the front seat. I knew the plane hadn't been touched in at least five weeks, and noted with dismay that neither of the fuel tanks was full. I forced myself to relax. Surely he knew how much fuel we needed for the flight he had planned.

Our pilot flipped some switches, pushed a button, and suddenly the propeller gave a mighty lurch. Another push and another less powerful lurch followed, but it was soon obvious even to me that there wasn't enough juice to get the thing going. Each subsequent push of the button produced diminishing whirs and clunks until there was only a light clicking sound in the cabin.

"Sheet," Jean-Pierre said, banging his hand on the controls. "Sheet, sheet, sheet."

I bit my lip to keep from laughing – not just that he was cursing in English, but from relief at not having to fly after all. I felt sorry for Jean-Pierre, who was obviously disappointed and embarrassed, but I felt like I'd been given a new lease on life. The dead battery was a sign. We were just not meant to fly that day.

Ty seemed as disappointed as our host, so I kept my mouth shut as I happily gathered my camera and scrambled out of the back seat into the fresh air.

Jean-Pierre glumly dragged the plane back into the hangar. I started heading for the van, already planning what to do with the rest of the day, when he held up his finger.

"Wait! I try one more sing."

I watched, incredulous, as he carted a small battery over to the plane, lifted the engine cover and hooked up a few wires. He was going to jump start the engine? And then expect me to get back in there?

He left the battery connected for a mere twenty minutes. Not half an hour later, like a bad case of déjà vu, I found myself strapped back in my seat, resigned to the fact that if Ty and I went down, we'd go down together.

This time the propeller coughed, then caught. With a smile of triumph, Jean-Pierre slid the glass canopy closed. The air was instantly stuffy. I found it hard to breathe as I realized we were really going through with this. Hoping my mechanical knowledge translated to aircraft as well as boats, I prayed that once the battery got the engine started, the alternator would provide enough juice to keep it going.

I have to give credit where it's due. Jean-Pierre knew what he was doing. Through the headset he'd given me, I listened as he communicated crisply with the tower, then taxied to the end of the runway. The little plane rattled and jiggled as we picked up speed, then smoothly lifted into the air.

Admittedly, the view was fantastic. The high cliffs that dropped to the sea below us were post-card material. Within seconds we were crossing the blue water and looking down on the hour-glass shape of Miquelon. I could clearly see the roads we'd jogged on and the pier we'd stayed at two days before, as well as the large mid-island lagoon that connected what used to be two separate islands. Jean-Pierre swooped down low so we could get a better view of a colony of sea lions sunbathing on a sandbar.

The problem with small planes is you feel every little bump. Sitting in the back seat, the Tiger felt like a puppet, with someone above playfully jerking the strings. I'd been known to embarrass myself on flights in the past when we hit excessive turbulence. Curse words would pop out of my mouth completely uncontrolled, no matter who was sitting near me. Now I kept my lips tightly sealed and silently repeated my mantra: *This is fun! I'm having a great time!*

I carefully watched Jean-Pierre's profile for signs of concern as we bobbed and weaved, but he was the picture of serenity. Taking my cues from him, I forced myself to smile. I snapped photo after photo, as much for a distraction as for the memories.

After an hour of flying, we circled back over St. Pierre. Having had enough, I was relieved to see the runway lined up before us in the distance. I remembered that my camera allowed me to film short segments of video and decided to record our landing. I turned the dial to the symbol of a movie camera and raised the camera to my eye as the plane wiggled and waggled toward the airstrip.

Looking through the viewfinder, I gasped in horror. Moments before, the propeller was spinning so fast it was transparent. Now, without warning, the prop had slowed to the point where I could see the individual blades moving in a jerking motion around the nose cone. My heart threatened to pound its way out of my chest as I realized this was just like in the movies, when the plane's one and only engine is about to give up the ghost.

So much for my theory on alternators, I thought with the sickening realization that we'd lost power and the runway was still out of range. It was only moments until we dropped like a pot-bellied puffin into the cold ocean below.

Lowering the camera to my lap, I wondered why Jean-Pierre and Ty weren't reacting to the emergency. Wasn't there a checklist for this sort of thing? How could they be sitting there so calmly?

I looked through the window and noticed I could no longer see the blades. The prop hadn't fallen off, it was spinning normally again. Relieved, yet confused, I fought to make sense of what just happened. My earlier thoughts ran through my mind.

Just like in the movies…

Moving pictures were made of individual frames. Videos filmed with a digital camera would be a succession of individual frames, too, wouldn't they? With dawning comprehension, I raised my camera and peered through the viewfinder again. Sure enough, there was the propeller, jerking past the window, frame by frame by frame.

The only way I was going to die on this flight was from embarrassment.

Lucky for me, I was in the back seat and no one heard my gasp. By the time we were safely on the ground, the color had returned to my face. Seconds later, we were at the hangar. When Jean-Pierre slid back the canopy, I greedily sucked in the fresh air and hopped off the wing onto terra firma. I refrained from kissing the tarmac, but instead posed with Ty by the plane and thanked our host.

"That was fun!" I said, "I had a great time!"

If they only knew.

Back on the boat, I patted the coach top fondly. Here, I was in my element. Here, I felt safe. When people heard I was going cruising, they'd used words like "brave" and "courageous," and I'd laughed. I joked about being intrepid, but it was always in fun. I wasn't intrepid! Truth be told, I was a chicken at heart! Ty was the warrior, not me. But I constantly worked to overcome my fears through knowledge and experience.

What frightened me on airplanes was fear of the unknown. Sitting in the back seat, with no understanding of airplane controls, I felt helpless. If anything happened to the pilot, I'd be as useless as a life ring in the desert.

Standing at the helm of my boat, I knew what to expect. I understood how everything worked and what to do in an emergency. Mother Nature would always be in charge, but at least I had plans if she threw me a curveball.

There would always be an element of the unknown in cruising, but my confidence was growing with each new adventure. Already on this trip I'd survived discomfort, fear, and illness, and I was stronger for it. Boredom was just too high a price to pay to sit at home in safety.

Jean-Pierre and Jacqueline enjoyed the dinner we served that evening onboard *Liberty*. They ate every drop of the fried chicken, buttered noodles, and apple pie I'd prepared. It was particularly nice being tied securely to a pier where our dishes didn't slide off the table.

Now that we'd made friends, we could have stayed in St. Pierre much longer, enjoying the comfort and conveniences. But it was time to start retracing our steps and head south. Winter gales were just around the corner.

I knew about gales. I knew about the ferocious winds and dangerous waves they could bring. And I knew enough to make tracks before they got here. With our new friends shouting *au revoir* from the pier, we slipped the lines and headed back into the unknown.

Twenty-One
LATE IN THE SEASON

More than a couple of people told us not to miss McCallum. While outwardly just another roadless fishing village, it was purported to be nattier than most, with some mighty friendly people. Sure enough, Herman Fudge, McCallum's one-man welcoming committee, was on the pier to take our lines and add our name to his address book. The boat was barely secured before Herman took us on a guided tour of the well-kept town.

Upon our return, we were greeted by Terry MacDonald, a fisherman by trade, and the outport's reluctant harbormaster. Hanging his head, he informed us there was a six dollar fee for tying up to the public wharf. When he saw we didn't hold the exorbitant charge against him, he smiled and pulled out a colorful guest book. We invited him to join us in the cockpit while we signed the book, and he clambered down the wooden ladder on the side of the wharf.

Opening to the first page of the guest book, I was surprised to see only a dozen signatures.

"Is this every boat that's visited McCallum this year?" I asked.

"That's right," Terry said, happily accepting a glass of rum and coke from Ty. "I don't expect we'll see any more after you, either. Fact is, I was pretty surprised to see you comin' in. It's a little late in the season to be up here, don't you think?"

Ty gave a start of surprise, and shot me a wary glance. We'd spent the last three days sheltered deep in the next fjord to the west while the winds blew steadily over twenty-five knots. He assured Terry we were working our way back to Port aux Basques as quickly as possible.

Picturesque McCallum, Newfoundland

Above us on the pier, two fishermen tossed their day's catch into plastic packing boxes filled with ice. While they worked, a man in gray cover-alls washed down the wharf with a thick black hose. When some of the goo sloshed onto *Liberty's* foredeck, he directed the spray onto our boat.

"Thanks for the freshwater washdown!" Ty called forward, happy to have the corrosive seawater from our trip rinsed off the stainless steel rails and lexan hatches.

"Ain't fresh," the hose man answered as he continued dousing our deck.

I shot Ty an "oh, boy" look. I could tell he wanted to throttle the guy, but instead, he swallowed his shock and smiled with resignation. "How 'bout another drink?" he asked, turning to Terry.

We'd heard outport men would jump at the chance to have a drink or two away from the watchful eyes of their wives, so we'd bought an extra bottle of rum for just this kind of encounter. With no bars in McCallum, the harbormaster was only too happy to accept this fringe benefit of his part-time job.

When he got up to leave, Terry asked if we'd think about sticking around longer than the one night we'd paid for. He invited us to his home the following evening, when his wife planned to make Jigg's dinner, the traditional Newfoundland meal of salt beef and vegetables.

My heart sank. I'd been looking forward to trying the dish, and it would be especially nice in the company of new friends. But the clock was ticking. We had only four days before the end of August. After Terry's comment about it being late in the season for recreational boaters, we were getting a bit anxious. Nova Scotia was still a long way off at our six knot pace.

We awoke the following morning to fog. Our Newfoundland travels had been blessed so far with surprisingly good visibility. Now, we had yet another omen that we might have overstayed our welcome. Staring through the mist toward the invisible harbor entrance, we were severely tempted to take Terry up on his offer and stay an extra day, but the specter of gale force winds held more sway.

Fog or no fog, we decided to get underway. The inside cover of our cruising guide showed a sailboat anchored at the base of a cascading waterfall. The caption claimed the shot was taken in LaHune Bay. When I'd first seen the dramatic photo, I knew we had to go there. Today we would.

Waving goodbye to Terry and Herman, we powered up the radar and headed out.

According to our chart, LaHune Bay was yet another long fjord. The topographic lines down both sides were more tightly bunched than most, with the annotated heights averaging a thousand feet. The entrance was narrow -- not the sort of place that gives you warm and fuzzies when entering in the fog.

We'd already learned our lesson with the GPS. We weren't about to trust the position it gave us to within a few hundred yards. Ty plotted a position that was in open water, one mile off the entrance. When we reached that spot, we took the sails down and turned on the motor. Altering course ninety degrees to starboard, we pointed the bow to where the fjord's entrance was supposed to be. Now it was the radar's chance to shine.

From this far out, the coast showed up as a thick horizontal line across the screen. The cleft between the cliffs was clearly visible, if only electronically. Tuning the range close-in to 1 ½ miles, the opening became even more apparent, and we steered straight for it. Neither of us spoke much. The air was thick with tension as we pictured the waves crashing against the rocks at the side of the inlet. There was little room for error.

We heard the surf before we saw it. The radar showed the cliffs were just off the bow. Suddenly, the fog cleared, revealing walls that towered above us on either side. While somewhat intimidating, I breathed easier at the sight. We were exactly where we were supposed to be, motoring right down the center of LaHune Bay.

"Gee, that was fun," I said, half sarcastic, half serious. Once the danger was past, I had to admit that I actually enjoyed the challenge.

No outports graced this glorious region, for there was nowhere to build. Everything went straight up. On a lark, Ty turned the boat toward the cliff off our starboard beam and motored ahead until our bow nearly touched the wall. Only one yard off the cliff, the depth sounder read one hundred fifty feet.

Seven miles farther along we anchored in a cove where the land sloped down to a sandy beach. There we found mussels buried in a stream bed and greedily filled a bucket. With full bellies, we went for an after-dinner hike that had us scrambling through spongy, knee-high brush. Large cloven prints in the mud were the only signs of life around us. Within half an hour we were a thousand feet up the side of a hill, looking down on the bay and the tiny white dot that was our boat

The next morning, per our daily routine, we listened to the weather broadcast before raising anchor. The fog off the coast was gone, but winds were brisk at twenty to twenty-five knots. Fortunately, they were forecast to decrease throughout the day to a more reasonable ten to fifteen, and we decided to make tracks.

With high walls on both sides, LaHune Bay was deceptively calm. I worried what would happen once we cleared the entrance. I could see surfer-sized waves rolling in between the cliffs. I reminded myself that this kind of bottleneck often caused high waves, but once you punched through them, things moderated.

Not this time.

Doing a perfect imitation of the opening scene of "Victory at Sea," *Liberty* pounded up and over rollers that were easily eight feet high. We'd been through plenty of waves this size before, but going from dead calm to these rough and tumble waters turned my legs instantly to rubber. At the wheel, Ty struggled to keep the boat headed away from the rock walls.

After going a hundred yards, it was clear the waves weren't getting any smaller. I shot Ty a questioning glance. My wide eyes mirrored his.

"What do you want to do?" he asked tensely.

I gawked. I knew he was trying to be considerate, but he wanted *me* to make the call?

"*You're* the captain!" I said, enjoying immensely my new position as the mate. I knew if I said I wanted to go back, we'd turn around, but I didn't want my personal fears to delay our trip. If I kept my mouth shut, Ty would base his decision on rational judgment.

"Well," he said, looking around at the roiling ocean, "The wind's supposed to start decreasing any time now."

I nodded, remembering the forecast. These conditions were miserable, but I could handle them if it was going to get better.

"I say we press on," he said, and I agreed. This kind of weather was exactly why we were hurrying to get back to Nova Scotia. Another day's delay in LaHune Bay would only put us more behind.

Until now, Environment Canada's forecasts were surprisingly reliable.

Today, they must have had a new guy on watch. The winds were, in fact, twenty to twenty five when we headed out, but instead of decreasing, they slowly built the farther we got from land.

We'd picked a destination that was forty miles west along the coast. Once we got far enough offshore to settle onto our desired course, we saw that the waves would be hitting us broad on the port side. The thought of rolling back and forth in seas this size was unacceptable. Looking at the chart for alternatives, we decided to head for the island group of Ramea, a few miles south of Burgeo. That way, we could continue on our present course, cutting through the waves instead of being rolled by them. Once we got to Ramea, the islands would offer good protection from the winds.

Over the next few hours, we watched the gusts increase into the mid-thirties as we lurched into waves that slowed our progress to a pathetic three knots. Half our normal speed meant dragging out our misery twice as long. The tension and constant pounding left me struggling with queasiness.

I ran below and strapped a Relief Band onto my wrist. The battery powered device served me well the few times I'd needed it in the past, and now I cranked it up to the highest setting. The red light blinked on the dial, and the tingling sensation through my fingers told me it was working. If all went well, the jolt would interrupt the circuit between my brain and my stomach, keeping me from losing my breakfast.

While I didn't barf, I sure didn't feel so hot, either. Staring out at the whitecaps as we plodded onward, I was listless and depressed, sure symptoms of seasickness. Trying to gauge the severity of my condition, I gave myself a little self-test: If a whale suddenly surfaced beside the boat, would I be excited? As the boat shuddered into yet another huge wave, I knew that Moby Dick, himself, could pay us a visit and I wouldn't give a damn.

Thankfully, the Relief Band did its job, and soon I was better able to function. Ty, however, was the one who now looked depressed.

"What's the matter?" I asked, sliding next to him and bracing myself at the wheel.

"Those weather-guessers sure called this one wrong. It's only getting worse out here." He shook his head while he stared at the wind speed indicator. "That last gust was forty-two knots!"

So, this is what a gale feels like. It was rough and uncomfortable, but *Liberty* was handling the conditions well. I was hanging in there, too. I'd learned on previous trips that if I sang to myself or smiled, I instantly felt better. I started singing the Star Spangled Banner under my breath, the first song that came to mind. I grinned like an idiot and pretended I was having the time of my life.

Ty looked at me and shook his head. "I can't tell if you're happy or scared to death!"

"Oh, I'm happy now," I said, pointing ahead. "Look! You can just make out the islands!"

Ramea was nothing more than a smudge on the horizon. At this rate, it would be another couple of hours before we got there, but at least relief was in sight. I thought Ty would share my excitement, but instead, he grew more solemn.

I'd seen this before. When we first started cruising, I was often exasperated with how somber he was. Sailing was supposed to be *fun*, but more often than not, his brows were knitted together in serious thought. Now, I knew what was going on in there.

"You're doing what-if drills again, aren't you?"

Focused as he was, he merely nodded in response. Instead of blotting out the unpleasantness, like I did, he was thinking up everything that could possibly go wrong and what he would do if it did. What if the engine dies when we come alongside the rocks? What if one of us falls overboard?

I planned for contingencies, too, but I saved my what-if drills for calm days, when my mind was free to wander. I was stressed out enough, and was happy to leave the worrying to the captain until I was needed.

Luckily, forty-two knots was as bad as it got. With steady winds in the thirties, however, things were still dicey when we turned to make our approach to the islands. With the waves now on the beam, the boat took on my least favorite motion. The first time the inclinometer pegged out at forty-five degrees, I said a few choice words. Once I saw the boat recovered just fine, I merely sang a little louder the next time we rolled.

When I get nervous, my kidneys kick into high gear. Today, they were working overtime. Giving in to the call of nature, I reluctantly went below. The lateral motion was going to make things exceedingly difficult in the small head.

Cursing my lack of a Y chromosome, I struggled to pull my pants down. Why did going to the bathroom have to be such a chore? A lurch of the boat threw me back against the bulkhead. Luckily, my heels hit the lip of the door frame and kept me from falling over. Suddenly, I realized I was in the perfect position to adjust my clothes! With my feet wedged in the doorway and my shoulders braced against the bulkhead behind me, I was no longer banging around and my hands were free!

Within seconds, I was safely undressed, and I lowered myself in a controlled manner onto the toilet. Laughing at how ocean sailing turns even the simplest tasks into major achievements, I smugly congratulated myself. Bit by bit I was learning to adjust to this new life we'd chosen.

I can handle gales! I thought with pride. We didn't stay too late in the season, after all!

I may have learned a thing or two in the few months we'd been out, but I obviously hadn't learned Lesson Number One: *never get cocky*. Before I had a chance to finish my business, the boat took a roll, and the toilet seat abruptly broke loose from its hinges. In one smooth motion, I slid right off the toilet, an unwilling passenger on my oval flying saucer.

Somewhere up above, Mother Nature looked down on me and laughed. She was still in charge.

Twenty-Two
REALITY CHECK

It was hard to believe the Bras d'Or Lake was originally our ultimate destination. After Newfoundland's fjords, Cape Breton's rolling hills seemed less than spectacular. Had we turned around here instead of going farther north, we would have missed the most stunning scenery of the whole cruise. And the most interesting towns. And the whales.

While it was a relief to be back inside the lake's protected waters, I had to admit, it was also a little, well, dull. It's not that I liked being constantly tossed around, my home's contents strewn across the floor. Hardly! It's just that we'd already seen all this stuff once. You know: been there, done that.

My whole life I'd been extremely goal-oriented. No matter what the objective, I thrived on new challenges. Give me something to work toward, and I'd throw myself into it with intense focus. Once I met the goal, I had to have a new one. Right away.

Until now, I hadn't realized that for me, Newfoundland was more than just a destination, it was a goal. I loved the experiences we had there, but now that we'd met the challenge, I needed a new one.

Our plan all along was to cruise to Canada for the summer, then head for the Bahamas. So there it was: my new goal. The only problem was, the islands were a long, long way from Bras d'Or Lake.

Newfoundland spoiled me. It was one exciting experience after another. There was always something new, even after we turned around and worked our way back along the coast.

I'd enjoyed Nova Scotia, Maine, and the rest of New England, but we'd hit all the highlights on the way north. I didn't tell Ty, but I wasn't thrilled with the prospect of spending the next three months retracing our steps. Knowing that every day couldn't be filled with excitement, I resigned myself to more mundane cruising until we reached new waters.

So here we were, back in Baddeck. Having spent a full week in the town on the way to Newfoundland, we would have sailed right by the second time around. But we had some mail waiting for us. At least, I hoped we did.

Dropping the hook in our familiar old spot, it felt like déjà vu all over again. As familiar as I was with the town, however, I was unprepared for the shocking difference between Baddeck and those we'd spent the last month exploring on the far side of Cabot Strait.

Like a newly arrived immigrant, I wandered the streets with a sense of wonder. Unlike pale Port aux Basques, Baddeck's buildings were a rainbow of primary colors. Vibrant yellows, bright reds, and cheery greens flooded my senses with color. Dormer windows, angled roofs, and gingerbread accents seemed an eye-catching extravagance after the outports' boxy buildings. The two provinces were less than a hundred miles apart, but we'd returned to a different world.

Like an old friend, Gregor greeted us happily when we walked into Baddeck Marine. "So, yer back, eh? How'd ya like Newfoundland?"

We described our impressions of the trip with great animation, and he gave us an I-told-you-so smile.

"Yup. Not a sailor goes up there doesn't want to go back," he said. Then, before we could ask, he held up a finger. "And yer package finally arrived!"

He disappeared into a back room and came out carrying a large box. I instantly recognized my mother's familiar writing and clapped my hands with excitement.

Thanking Gregor, Ty took the care package, and we hurried back to *Liberty*. Once aboard, it was Christmas in September as I tore off the brown paper and dug in to the box. Out came crinkly packages of oriental noodles we'd been unable to find. I laughed at my excitement over such a mundane item, but their unavailability made them all the more desirable.

I reached in and handed Ty two pounds of flavored coffee.

"Your parents really came through for us," he said, opening a bag and sticking his nose in.

"They sure did! Look at this!"

I pulled out a *Time* magazine and dangled it in front of him. Nostrils flaring, Ty snatched it from my fingers and whipped it open like an adolescent boy with a centerfold.

"There's a whole bunch of back-issues in here!" I said, digging to the bottom of the box. Soon, two months of *Time*, *Newsweek*, and *US News and World Report* were scattered across the table, and we pawed through them hungrily. The food was nice, but it was news we craved more than anything.

Now that we'd retrieved our mail, there was only one other pressing piece of business: fixing my hair. While it had finally grown over my ears after the disastrous cut in Port aux Basques, the rest of it was nothing but a thick, shapeless mess.

We dinghied back ashore and parted ways at the town's main street. While Ty went to the library to use the Internet, I crossed the street to a classy salon. The place had a nice feel to it when I'd tried to get an appointment a month earlier. Now that the summer rush was over, I opened the door and hoped for the best. The owner recognized me immediately.

"I see you found a place to get your hair cut," she said.

I ran a hand over my head. "Yeah, and that's the problem. Now I need someone to undo the damage. Do you have any openings?"

I held my breath while she glanced at her book.

"My last appointment cancelled. I think I can still squeeze you in before my next one, but give me five minutes."

I pumped my fist in victory and grinned. While she bustled about in a back room, my eyes wandered idly around the reception area. I noticed a stack of business cards next to the cash register. Walking over to pick one up, I was cheered even more. Not only was this woman the owner, she was a "Certified Master Stylist" -- and an instructor, to boot! I was guaranteed a month of good hair days.

Once in the chair, the stylist asked me the standard "how do you like your hair?"

I rolled my eyes, "Not like this, that's for sure."

She laughed as I described my experience at the salon in Port aux Basques. Then, she got down to business. Working at twice the speed as the last so-called stylist, she confidently snipped and chopped at my unruly mop.

I thought I might have been exaggerating how bad the last cut was, until I watched the woman in the mirror. Grabbing a swatch of hair between two outstretched fingers, she pulled it straight up from my scalp. She stared at the hair, then squinted as if she needed glasses. The hair that should have loosely followed the shape of her fingers, stuck out above them in a wildly jagged line.

Tilting her head to one side, the stylist looked in the mirror, locked eyes with mine, and asked, "Did this woman go to the Newfoundland School of Hairdressing for the *Blind*?"

Suspicions confirmed.

Twenty minutes later, I walked out to the street, my step far bouncier than when I went in. Meeting Ty on the corner, I made a peppy pirouette to show off my new locks.

"Now *that's* a haircut!" he said, showing far more enthusiastic than he had a month earlier.

With all our business taken care of, there was nothing keeping us in Baddeck. If Frank and Dee were here, we would have stayed longer, but without *Vagabond Tiger*, the anchorage seemed empty. We decided to head out the next morning.

I was ready to scoot for the Bahamas, but Hurricane Fabian was headed our way. The only smart thing to do was to stick around the lake until the storm was well clear.

Most sailors would be thrilled to spend more a few more days in these sought-after cruising waters, but I'd had enough. We'd already seen the lake's two towns. Other than that, there was nothing here but pretty anchorages. Natural beauty is great, but I was ready to meet other cruisers. I longed for nice restaurants... maybe a little Thai food or sushi... something other than fried fish and pizza. I dreamed of mega-bookstores and cozy coffee shops where we could sip cappuccino and read the Sunday paper.

But I didn't share these thoughts with Ty. It was useless to complain. We had to cover a lot of miles before we got back to my idea of civilization. And as always, we could only do it as the weather allowed.

The next day, we chose a five-star cove on the lake's western shore as our destination. Nothing was far on the Bras d'Or, so we were in no particular hurry. Passing over a spot marked "Cod Shoals," Ty decided to have a go at catching dinner.

I killed the engine and let the boat drift. While Ty went aft with his rod and reel, I picked up a copy of *Newsweek* and sat back on a cushion. The magazine was full of stories about our soldiers in Iraq, and I soaked up the news like a thirsty sponge. It felt strange to read about the Pentagon, the White House, and the Capitol when we were so far away.

I wanted to shout, "I've been to all those places! I know these people!" but I doubted anyone would care. When you live in Washington, you think it's the center of the universe. Once you leave, you realize how little attention most people pay to what goes on there. One Canadian we met wasn't even sure which coast our capital was on!

As I read, unfamiliar pangs of homesickness settled into the pit of my stomach. I had to admit, I really missed this stuff. As I listlessly turned the page, my eyes fell on a full-page photo of a man who looked strangely familiar. I blinked, shook my head to make sure I was seeing right, then jumped to my feet.

"Holy mackerel, Ty! I don't believe this!"

He looked up, surprised at my excited outburst as I ran to him, waving the magazine.

"Look at this! It's Ranger Jones!"

"You're kidding!"

"No! Right here, in full color, in *Newsweek!*"

I held the magazine open and we leaned in for a closer look. There was no need for a microscope. It was Ranger, all right, as big as life, looking as handsome and squared away as ever. He was posed behind a large, executive desk, surrounded by photos of himself with assorted world leaders. He wore a perfectly tailored business suit with his green

Army uniform rank insignia and ribbons cleverly morphed over his left chest and shoulder.

The ad touted the sense of mission one gets from serving in the military. With hard-hitting words it told how Marc "Ranger" Jones had risen from Army cook to senior enlisted aide to the fourteenth Chairman of the Joint Chiefs of Staff.

I was aide to the fourteenth Chairman, too, I thought, pushing down a twinge of envy.

I'd heard that Ranger left the Army for bigger things. It was definitely the Army's loss. Reading on, we learned he was now the CEO of his own company.

"Good for him!" Ty said.

"No kidding! This is fantastic!" I said, genuinely happy and proud of my former sidekick's success.

Returning to the cockpit, I stared at the photo as waves of nostalgia washed over me. Ranger may have been wearing a suit in the picture, but in my mind I saw him in PT gear, racing me to the top of a mountain in Santiago, Chile... and in his uniform, helping me carry gifts to the Minister of Defense in Delhi, India... making sure I got my photo taken with the King of Jordan... flying with me in helicopters over Kosovo, Korea, and Kuwait.

I was thousands of miles away, but Ty's voice snapped me abruptly back to the present as he stepped back into the cockpit.

"Ain't no stinkin' fish out here."

I laid the magazine by my side. "Wanna try somewhere else?"

"Nah, let's just go to anchor."

"Okay. I'll drive."

There wasn't any wind, so I started up the engine and took a seat behind the wheel. Ty picked up the magazine I'd left on the seat and immediately became engrossed in an article. In the silence, I had lots of time to think.

So, Ranger was out there movin' and shakin' with the big boys. He was making things happen, getting things done -- just like the good old days. There was no doubt he was still telling anybody who asked him that he was "livin' a dream."

The back of my throat tightened and my eyes teared unexpectedly.

I was living a dream, too, wasn't I? I might not be a CEO, but I was captain of my own vessel. Or, at least, I used to be. I wasn't moving in the same circles as Ranger, but I was meeting lots of new people. Granted, fishermen were a far cry from defense ministers and generals, but they were a lot more down to earth than most politicians I'd met.

I sniffed and rubbed at my nose. My emotional reaction surprised me. Then I nodded my head. This must be the post-retirement let-down everybody talked about. Mine was just delayed a few months. This would pass. I'd get over it. I was happy out here, wasn't I?

I put on a pair of sunglasses, afraid Ty would see my red-rimmed eyes. Every now and then he looked up and commented on a news story, unaware of my turmoil. I answered him as normally as I could, but inside I grew ever more heavy-hearted. I fought an insane urge to run below and throw myself on the bed. But there was no way Ty wouldn't notice *that*.

When you share the same small space with someone twenty-four hours a day for months on end, it doesn't take long to notice something's wrong. Despite my best efforts, Ty soon picked up on my melancholy mood.

"What's the matter? You seem kind of down."

"Umm. Yeah. I guess seeing Ranger in that ad kind of got to me."

"Made you remember all the excitement, huh?"

I sniffed. "Uh huh. After reading that magazine, I'm kind of feeling like a nobody."

My comment gave Ty a start. "Suzanne. How can you say that!" He paused, then asked, "Do you want to go back to work?"

My instantaneous "No!" sounded just a little too quick, even to me. He cocked his head.

"I'll get over this," I said. "Don't worry about it."

"Are you sure?"

I waved off his concern and turned to stare at the water. Out of the corner of my eye, I watched him shake his head, then go back to the magazine.

I was glad he let the subject die so quickly. I didn't have any desire to go back to work! Neither one of us had so much as mentioned the "W" word since the day we left, other than to gloat that we weren't doing any. Getting back into the rat race was the last thing we wanted, even if it did offer mental stimulation and challenge, conversations with like-minded colleagues, and enough money to go out to dinner whenever we wanted…

I wondered if maybe we'd made a mistake going to such a remote area right off the bat.

But Ty hadn't dropped the subject, after all. He'd merely let it marinate. Later that afternoon, he poured us each a glass of Merlot and sat down beside me. We chatted for a while about his bad luck at fishing, the hurricane, and what was for dinner. Then, when he was sure I was nice and mellow, he popped the question again as if he hadn't heard my answer the first time.

"So, Suzanne, do you want to go back to work?"

This time I was a little slower to answer "no," and my reply didn't hold the same conviction that it did earlier.

"Are you sure?" he asked.

I was surprised he'd raised the question a second time. Now, he didn't seem to want to let it go.

"Why?" I asked. "Do you?"

He tilted his head. "I don't know. I feel kind of lazy out here."

I stared at him, letting his unexpected answer soak in for a moment. If he was at all unhappy with this cruising life, it was news to me. But then again, it shouldn't surprise me that he was feeling unchallenged. Ty was one of the smartest, hardest workers I knew. I'd been to hundreds of farewell parties in my career, but when his office mates gave him a send-off, they'd heaped praise on him unlike any I'd ever heard.

I thought back to my tour in Seattle when he'd given up his job to transfer with me. He'd gone with me willingly, but it didn't take long before I sensed his growing dissatisfaction. He needed to be challenged as much as I did, if not more.

"I had no idea you were dissatisfied," I said. "You haven't said a word!"

He shrugged. It wasn't his nature to discuss feelings.

"If you feel lazy now," I said, "what's it going to be like when we get to the Bahamas? There's only so much snorkeling and fishing you can do!"

He nodded his head knowingly, as if this wasn't the first time the thought had occurred to him. Now he was on a roll. "Know what else? I miss being around other ducks."

I could certainly understand that.

"And I miss variety."

I agreed enthusiastically.

Even though we were seeing new places all the time, in between, the days were pretty much the same. We raised anchor, traveled forty or fifty miles, then anchored somewhere else. It wasn't so bad when we could sail, but if the wind wasn't strong enough, or blowing from the right direction, the motor droned on and on for hours.

Before our cruising life, sailing was our main focus, but we spiced it up with other activities like biking, hiking, and backpacking. Now, I recalled that not two days earlier Ty suggested we leave the boat every few months and do something totally different. I realized that the lack of diversity must have been getting to him, too.

Getting into the spirit of things, I added my own complaint to the list. "I miss girl talk!"

Ty made an aren't-I-good-enough face, and I held up a hand. "Don't get me wrong, Honey. I enjoy your company, but there really is a difference."

"Thank God for that!" he said, laughing.

I couldn't believe we'd both been thinking these things, but hadn't talked about them aloud. Now that we'd opened the flood gates, our thoughts bounced back and forth like the volley in a tennis match.

"I miss people, in general," Ty said.

I knew what he meant. The Canadians were friendly enough, but we rarely got to socialize with them. The cruisers we met were few and far between. When we did get together, the conversation was always the same: "Where are you from? What are your plans? What did you do before cruising?" I used to cringe when Ty would get into a good, rousing argument about politics and religion, but now a spicy debate was downright appealing!

"I miss being in charge of things," I said. I'd spent twenty years in leadership positions, and now it was just the two of us. The only thing I was in charge of was taking care of myself and the boat. I was content to be the mate, but it was an adjustment, just the same.

"You know," Ty said. "I'll bet they still haven't filled that job my company offered you."

I stared at him, owl-like. The company he'd worked for had over three hundred employees. Part of Washington's booming defense industry, they handled mostly Navy contracts. Dolly, their Director of Administration had been there for years and was looking to retire. She had her own office and over twenty people working for her. They didn't want just anyone to replace her, and the president of the company, himself, had called to offer me the position.

I was greatly flattered, but at the time, I didn't want anything to do with the job. Now, after the conversation we'd just had, I had to admit, it held a certain appeal. I'd be back in the real world, making things happen. Yes, I'd be back behind a desk, but maybe I could make a difference in other people's lives. It meant moving back to Washington, but that wasn't all bad, was it? The city had an incredible variety of ethnic restaurants, endless opportunities for cultural events, entertainment, socializing...

I looked around us at the anchorage. All I could see were trees.

"What about you?" I asked. "You wouldn't want to go back to the same job?"

He gave that one some thought. "I don't know. I miss the guys, and the work was interesting."

"We'd be bringing home more money than we ever dreamed of."

"And we could charter boats wherever we wanted."

"Kind of like the best of both worlds..."

It felt like we were walking on coals, both of us afraid to put our full weight down-- scared we'd get burnt—but energized, all the same.

I wasn't sure where to go next with the conversation, when Ty took the bull by the horns. He leaned over, picked up our Pocketmail email composer, and started typing.

"What are you doing?" I asked, puzzled.

"I'm writing to Dave back at the office to see if Dolly's job is still available and if there's a chance they'd take me back."

My eyebrows shot up in surprise. This kind of impetuous act was something I would do, not him! I started to ask if he was sure he wanted to do that, but a niggling desire to know what the answer would be kept me from doing so.

Running my fingers over my lips, I watched silently while he typed out the message. When he finished, he read the note aloud. It was exactly what I would have written, and I gave him a nod. I watched, holding my breath, as he held the device to our cell phone and pressed "send."

After that, there didn't seem to be much else to say. Suddenly the ball was out of our hands. Maybe the Bahamas wasn't our next destination, after all. Maybe I had a totally different goal to work towards.

We ate dinner and chatted about a variety of things, but the earlier discussion was never far from my thoughts. It hung in the air, hovering over my head like a cloud that was neither black nor white.

We went to bed, and I stared at the ceiling, my thoughts bouncing around in my head like an errant ping pong ball. If they wanted me for the job, I'd have a million things to do. The three months of retracing our track would be filled with plans of a different sort. But was this really what I wanted? Was it what Ty wanted? We hadn't discussed our discontent until today, and just like that, we were considering giving up our new life.

The email Ty sent would show the folks back home that we were interested. After that, this thing might take on a life of its own.

Tossing and turning, I tried every trick up my sleeve to stop thinking and calm my racing mind. But sleep wouldn't come. I'd had restless nights on our cruise before, but always it was due to outside forces, like the howling wind or a rolly anchorage.

This time, for the first time since we'd left Washington, it was job worries that kept me awake.

Twenty-Three
DECISION TIME

Hurricane Fabian brought eighteen foot seas to Nova Scotia's east coast. We made the right call to stay in the lake. Once the storm passed, however, Canso Strait quickly calmed down. It was safe for us to leave Cape Breton.

But first, we had to pass through the locks at St. Peter's.

We hadn't seen another boat since we left Baddeck three days earlier. Rounding an island at the end of St. Peter's Canal, suddenly there were two other sailboats in front of us. Both flew the American flag and I could see one couple on each boat. I didn't know where they'd come from, but I looked forward to chatting with them once we were tied up to the sea wall inside the lock.

Our three boats backed and filled to maintain our position while waiting for the gate to open. There was an unspoken rule in this kind of situation that you went through in the order you arrived. Many times, when waiting for bridge openings, we'd seen power boats charge to the front of the line, but for the most part, sailors were a pretty polite group.

The lock master announced on the radio that the gate would open in five more minutes. While I kept the boat in place, Ty readied docklines and fenders. The cruising guide clearly stated that southbound boats should tie up to the west wall, so he rigged everything on the starboard side.

Five minutes came and went, but there was no sign of the gate opening. Finally, after ten minutes of bobbing about smartly, the red light on shore turned green. Following the two boats in front of me, I slowly moved forward.

There was enough room inside the lock for four boats on each side. The west side had the small cleats we were used to tying off to. The east side was reserved for larger vessels, and had giant bollards instead of cleats.

The first boat pulled over to the wall, and the second slowed. I put the engine in neutral, then had to back down when he came to a full stop before the entrance to the lock.

"What's he doing?" I asked impatiently. I wasn't in a hurry, but the channel leading to the lock was narrow, with little room for maneuvering. Once the wind and current got us, things could get interesting.

Looking ahead, I saw the problem. Rather than pulling all the way to the end of the lock, the first boat had stopped two boat lengths back from the gate.

"I hope he's not going to tie up right there!" I groused.

"No, look," Ty said, "They got off the boat and are pulling it forward by hand."

"Good."

There was plenty of room now for the second boat to pull in, but he was slow to get going. I huffed and growled, making a conscious effort to relax my grip on the wheel. This should have been a very simple drill. It was no different than if three cars were pulling into three consecutive parking spaces on a one-lane street. After the first guy pulled up to the front, the next two would pull in neatly behind him, one-two-three. Nothing to it!

But, no. Instead of moving to the far end, the first boat cleated off her lines three-quarters of a boat length from the gate. I waited for the second boat to pull up and noticed the currents were getting squirrelly. Liberty's stern was starting to slew around. Deciding this was not the time to practice my boat handling, I turned the wheel over to Ty.

Now standing amidships with a breast line in hand, I watched the boat in front of us finally start to move. Ty put the engine in gear and inched up behind him.

Once through the gate, the second boat's captain decided to be different. He unexpectedly pulled over to the side and stopped.

"What the hell is he doing?!" Ty asked, slipping the throttle back into neutral.

I gawked, incredulous, as the mate started to cleat off her lines.

"Are you stopping right there?" I called over.

"Yeah."

I glanced ahead of her. There should have easily been room for four boats to fit along the wall. Because the first boat hadn't pulled all the way forward, and the second boat stopped where it did, there was now barely enough room for one boat in between them. Had the second boat pulled up behind the first, in a polite and seamanly manner, we could have easily tucked in behind. Instead, we were now faced with a tricky parallel parking situation inside the swirling waters of the lock.

"We have everything rigged to starboard," I shouted across to the woman. "Just like the cruising guide says!"

"Well, you shouldn't have rigged anything until you got inside," she replied nastily. "There's plenty of room on the other side."

I turned and gaped at Ty. Rigging lines and fenders was not something you saved for the last minute. It took at least five minutes to get everything set. Proper seamanship called for careful preparation in anticipation of docking. Switching everything to the port side under pressure would be a royal pain, but I was ready to jump to it if Ty gave me the nod.

"Screw it," Ty said. "I'm going in."

My eyes widened and I glanced again at the space between the two boats. I certainly wouldn't attempt it, but if anyone could do it, Ty could. Suddenly, my trepidation turned to orneriness. He'd show 'em how it was done!

When Ty pulled Liberty forward, passing closely abeam of the second boat, it was the woman's turn to gawk.

"Where are you going?" she sputtered.

I struck a defiant pose and jabbed my index finger in front of her bow.

"Right there."

She stiffened in alarm and stared. I deliberately relaxed and let the dock line hang limply at my side while I waited for Ty to work his magic.

Lacking the luxury of twin screws and a bow thruster to crab sideways, Ty expertly used his single screw and rudder to ease our forty-six foot boat into the forty-eight foot space. Just like Cinderella's foot in the glass slipper, Liberty slipped right in.

I turned and shot a smile that was half smug and half smart-ass to the woman on the boat behind us. She scowled and pivoted sharply on her heel. I was so proud of my husband, I could have burst.

"That was some nice boat handling," The lock master said from the wall as I casually handed him a line.

I stepped up beside him and turned to look at Ty. "Thanks," I said, then added matter-of-factly, "He used to drive destroyers for a living."

Needless to say, we didn't get out and chat amiably on the pier with our fellow Americans while the water in the lock went down. Instead, I sat on the deck and did some deep-breathing to get my pulse back to normal. I'd naively thought that all sailors were alike, but this drill showed me the jerks weren't just limited to the highways.

As we slid lower in the lock, a passing foursome of tourists stopped to chat.

"Where ya from?" the oldest man asked.

It was the same conversation as always when people stopped by the boat, but this time, a few of our answers were different. In response to his question of where we were headed, Ty and I looked at each other sheepishly.

"We might be going back to Washington," Ty said. "To work. We're not sure yet."

The words sounded strange. A few days ago, I liked the idea of a career change. But after the display of teamwork and describing our exciting trip to the two couples, I wasn't quite sure.

The gates in front of us started to open. Saying goodbye to our visitors, I scurried to take in the lines while Ty started the engine. Once the channel was clear, the three vessels motored out in a nice, single file. The boat behind us behaved themselves this time.

At the recommendation of a couple in Baddeck, we tied up that evening on Isle Madame, just a short hop from Cape Breton. As soon as we were secured, I pulled out the Pocketmail composer and checked email.

Ty had written to his colleague Dave about the jobs, but I half expected an answer from Dolly, his wife. She was the woman I might be replacing. When I first met the pleasant couple, I found it interesting that they both worked for the same company. The thought that Ty and I might replace them as they retired intrigued me.

When there was no email waiting for us, I suggested we give Dolly a call. I knew I seemed schizophrenic – one minute wanting the job, the next minute not, but the lure of knowing if my skills were wanted tugged at my ego.

I thought by now that Ty might have cooled to the work idea. Instead, he encouraged me to make the call.

I got straight through to Dolly, who was happy to hear from us. She explained that Dave hadn't answered Ty's email because she wanted to discuss our interest with the company's president first.

I held my hand over the mouthpiece and passed this news to Ty. He raised his eyebrows at mention of the president. Already this had gone farther than we wanted.

Dolly quickly informed me that both jobs were still quite available. While surprised at our change of heart about cruising, all were thrilled at the thought of having us join their team. I couldn't help but feel a burst of pleasure.

Feeling I owed her more of an explanation than what was in Ty's email, I gave Dolly the reasoning behind our interest in coming back. With her own retirement looming large, she wasn't happy to hear about the lack of mental stimulation we'd found being unemployed.

In answer to my questions, Dolly filled me in on the specifics of her duties. I listened with growing excitement as she rattled off responsibilities with which I was well familiar. I had to admit, the job sounded perfect for me. It required a mix of all the things I'd done in my twenty year Navy career. Before I knew it, we were talking resumes and timelines.

I was right. This thing had taken on a life of its own.

When I hung up the phone, Ty and I pored over the notes I'd scribbled.

"Looks pretty good," I said.

"From the sound of your conversation, if we want the jobs, they're ours."

I nodded, amazed. Then I tilted my head. "I can get exited about Dolly's job, but are you really sure you want to go back and do the same thing you were doing before?"

"Well, at this point, we can't say no."

I looked at him, startled. "What do you mean?"

"She's already talked to the president."

I chewed my lip. I knew Ty thought we'd look like fools if we started fishing around, then blithely said, "no thanks." Personally, I could still back out at this point without a problem. But it was hard to say no when two very good offers were dangling enticingly in front of our faces.

Before leaving the Navy, I'd attended a pre-retirement seminar. All week long they stressed how hard it was to find a job. They'd made job hunting sound scary and stressful. This was all so easy. I wouldn't even need to sit through an interview.

I'd told Dolly that even if we hurried, it would still take us at least six weeks to get back to Washington. Looking at the map, it was clear why we couldn't get back any faster. We'd come a good distance from Newfoundland already, but we were still way the heck up north.

I'd had enough fishing villages to last a while, but even those were few and far between up here. Before us still lay miles of the remote and rugged coastline the Nova Scotia cruising guide warned about. The thought of days on end of more rocking and rolling before we even got to New England made me all the more anxious for a drastic change.

Never one to drag my feet, I spent the evening putting together a resume. Ty already had several versions of his work history, but until now I'd never needed one.

Sitting at the computer, I listed my qualifications. Laid out before me on the screen, I realized that the administrative duties I'd looked down on as a Fleet Support Officer would be valued by a civilian organization. Now that I no longer had to compete with warriors, I could see myself actually taking pride in being an administrator.

I pushed "print" on the keyboard and sat back. While the pages fed through the printer, I thought about the ramifications of what I was doing. Yes, we'd be giving up a lot, but this would be an exciting change. It would be a whole new image for me. I'd be a *corporate executive*.

There was no doubt that I enjoyed the constant change our current lifestyle offered, but I was tired of being brave. A little stability and security wouldn't be all bad. Nor would the money. And Ty would feel challenged again, not lazy...

Picking up my resume, I folded it neatly and slid it into the envelope next to his. Licking the gummy strip, I hesitated. We still had to discuss salaries, then wait for actual offers in writing. But once these resumes went in the mail, Ty was right. We couldn't say no and still save face.

Staring at the envelope, I took a deep breath. Then I pressed the edges together and sealed our fate.

Twenty-Four
COMMITTED

If you want to tie up in downtown Beantown, you'd better be ready to pay for it. On the way north, we weren't. $2.25 a foot was Boston's going rate, and that was just a little too rich for our wallet. For our forty-six foot boat, the pricey sum worked out to over a hundred bucks. And for what? A finger pier and a couple of pilings to throw a rope around? People pay a lot less than that at Motel 6, and they get fresh linens and free HBO!

But on the way north, we were cruisers on a budget. On the way south, we were corporate executives in the waiting. We had the signed letters of offer in a drawer to prove it. If we were going to start raking in the dough in just a few weeks, we figured we might as well splurge.

From the water, the entire downtown sparkled in the distance. The towering office buildings with their solid walls of windows were just a taste of what was to come. Beyond the waterfront lay Little Italy, Quincy Market and the USS CONSTITUTION. Not rich yet, we'd only reserved one night at the marina, but I was determined to fit in as much sightseeing as time allowed.

The harbor entrance was crowded. Magenta lines criss-crossed the chart, showing the best tracks to follow. Many of them converged on the deep-water access at President Roads. Our guide book cautioned small boats to stay clear of big commercial traffic, a warning I found quite unnecessary. An enormous supertanker chugged past us, heading to sea, and I instinctively pulled to the far right of the channel.

While Ty studied the electronic chart at the nav table below, I verified our position on the paper chart by my side. We were approaching the southern tip of Deer Island. A light to the south of the point marked a shoal I'd be wise to avoid. On my chart, the navigation aid stood out from others nearby. Squiggly gray lines in a circle around the red symbol indicated rip rap. Sure enough, I could make out a circular pile of rocks around a towering light just off the starboard bow.

Ty popped his head up through the companionway. "Don't come too close to that light up ahead."

"Roger that," I replied. "I got it."

I'd already seen why he was warning me. If I cut the corner too closely, the fathometer would go from fifty feet to four in a mere boat length.

The navigable channel was half a mile wide just opposite the light. Normally, I'd come left and run directly down the center. But a tug towing a large barge was headed for the same spot I was, just off my port beam. Technically, I had the right of way, but I could maneuver a lot easier than him. Looking at the chart, I figured I was on a good course to comfortably clear the shoal and still give the tug plenty of room.

Just as I rounded the light, Ty popped his head up again. He looked over the starboard side, blinked, then did a double-take.

"What are you doing?" he shouted, then ducked back below.

I looked at the fathometer. As far as I could see, everything was under control. But something told me told me I might want to come left hard. Now.

I maneuvered more toward the center of the channel. I was closer to the tug than I would have liked, but the water was definitely deeper here.

"What's your depth?" Ty asked, scrambling back into the cockpit.

"Fifty-three."

Ty looked at the rocky light, then did a 360-degree scan. When his eyes came back to rest on mine, they were stony.

"Suzanne," he said ominously, from a mere two feet away, "I want to ask you something."

My stomach clenched. Suddenly, I was Seaman Schmuckatelli, standing before the Captain as he prepared to read me my rights. I pulled my neck into my chin and uttered a meek, "Okay."

In a voice devoid of any humor, enunciating each word like a foreign language professor saying a new phrase for the first time, he asked, "What part of 'don't-come-too-close-to-the-light' didn't you understand?"

Blood rushed to my face, and I stared at him, pie eyed.

He stared back, awaiting my answer. I quickly discerned this was not a rhetorical question.

I glanced away, as much to gather my wits as to make sure I wasn't wandering from the channel. As an officer candidate, the correct response in a situation like this was a crisp, "No excuse, Sir!" But I wasn't a midshipman, for God's sake! And I *did* have an excuse, darn it!

Looking back at him I said softly, "I didn't think I was too close, and I didn't want to come too far left with that tug there."

He stepped back and waved dismissively at the tug and tow. "He's not a problem. He would have stayed out of your way."

In spite of the cool fall air, I was hot as a mixture of fear, anger, embarrassment, and shame duked it out in my head. What had gone wrong? Nothing, as far as I could see! I'd done exactly as he said. I didn't think I'd come too close to the light, but Ty sure thought I did. He thought I'd ignored his order and endangered the boat.

I would have been happy to escape below, but I was pleased he still trusted me to bring us in. I was trembling as I steered down President Roads and struggled to make sense of the situation. Ty had snapped at me before, but the tone he'd used this time was a new one altogether. It was one I didn't care to ever hear again.

A 757 lifted off the runway at Logan Airport and temporarily distracted me. It flew right over our mast, its engines drowning out my thoughts. I was glad when the huge jet banked and headed away from the city. I hated loud noises. Thank God Ty wasn't a screamer. But after the way he'd looked at me, I didn't know what was worse: him yelling or him thinking I'd "disobeyed an order."

Then, suddenly, I realized what the problem was. It was a classic example of he-thought-she-thought. This was Leadership 101. We'd both taught this stuff! When you give an order, the person on the receiving end doesn't necessarily interpret it the same way you intend it to come across. It all depends on how it's worded.

Ty had told me not to come too close to the light. But what exactly did that mean? It was obvious to me now that "too close" meant something different to him than it did to me. I realized how many times one of us had looked at the chart and told the helmsman to "come right a little bit." To me, that meant one or two degrees. Now, I wondered how Ty interpreted "a little bit."

Having figured out what caused the incident, I was instantly energized.

"Ty," I said, finding my voice again. "You know what happened back there?"

"What?" he asked, looking up from the chart. He was still on edge.

"'Too close' doesn't mean the same thing to me as it does to you!"

He gave me a what-are-you-talking-about look, but I jabbered on.

"If you'd said, 'Don't come within a hundred yards of that light,' I would have known *exactly* how far off you wanted me to stay."

He stuck out his lower lip, then nodded slowly.

"From now on," I said excitedly, "we need to *quantify* things!"

"Well, we don't have much farther to go, at this point, but it's a good lesson."

His comment instantly brought me back down to earth. He was right, we wouldn't be out here much longer. Ever since we'd accepted the jobs our focus had changed from thoughts of future cruises to our future in the office. It still took a little getting used to.

I had my new goal after all. I was going to have a whole new image. I should have been more excited, but neither one of us was overly enthusiastic.

I knew what the problem was. When we'd first discussed going back to work, we'd been through months of large ocean waves, with more to follow. We were miles from the nearest city. It had been weeks since we'd been shopping or eaten out. Longer still since we'd seen a movie. Since then, we'd been to bookstores in Halifax. Eaten out in Bar Harbor. Saw "Seabiscuit" in Portland.

If we'd sat on the decision just a bit longer, at least until we got back to civilization, we might not have ended up where we were – committed to new jobs. But a deal was a deal. If we were going back to work, then by God, I was going to make the most of it!

* * *

When we decided to go cruising, it became the center of my life. I threw myself into planning for it with a frenzy. Everything I did was focused on that goal.

Some things never change.

Now that we were returning to Washington, I made a list of all the things we needed to do. We needed work clothes. We needed transportation. We needed a place to live. And we needed to take care of the things on the list before we started working. After all, there'd be little time for personal errands once our time was no longer our own.

I really wanted to continue living on the boat, but none of the marinas near the office had any more liveaboard slips. Both Ty and I agreed we weren't willing to commute more than half an hour. That put *Liberty* off limits during the week. I knew we'd end up going to the boat every weekend, just like we had before we'd moved aboard. It was a pain then, packing clothes and food on Fridays, then hurrying home on Sundays in time to unpack and do laundry. What made me think it would be any different now?

Trying to make myself feel better, I pulled out my charge card when we sailed into New York City. Shopping was supposed to be therapeutic, and indeed, I had fun buying an entire wardrobe all at once. Seeing my reflection in the dressing room mirror, I hardly recognized myself. After six months of jeans and fleece jackets, the skirts and suits looked strangely out of place. The high heels were pretty, but they were awkward and uncomfortable. The pantyhose were downright suffocating.

But darn, I *looked* professional. And I loved how Ty's face lit up when I modeled the new clothes for him later on the boat. It really would be fun wearing a different outfit every day for the first two weeks. I tried not to think how quickly the newness would wear off.

We sailed back into the Chesapeake with ten days of freedom to spare. The waters of the Bay seemed amazingly calm after what the Atlantic had thrown at us. Even when the wind piped up to twenty-eight knots, the waves peaked out at a wimpy four feet. By now I knew better than to get cocky. Many a boat had come to grief in our home waters, and we certainly weren't immune. But after what we'd weathered on a daily basis over the last few months, I realized how far I'd come. And not just in miles.

We signed up for a week at a marina in Annapolis. Only an hour from DC, we could drive into the city to look for a house and buy our cars while still enjoying the bay. Then, when everything was set, we'd make the final four day sail up the Potomac. As transients, we could stay aboard the boat for the month it would take to close on a house.

Settled into our slip, we gave our friend, Jim, a call. He and *Beckoning* had long since returned from Portland and were now just up the creek. We'd kept in touch all summer, and looked forward to getting together. Within minutes, he bounded aboard, his friendly smile instantly lifting my spirits. Good friends like Jim would be much more accessible now that we wouldn't be gallivanting around any more.

"So you guys are really going to do it," he said, shaking his head.

I noticed even he couldn't bring himself to say the "W" word.

"Looks that way," Ty said, smiling sheepishly.

"I just can't figure it out. I'm counting the days 'til I can retire and go cruising."

"Well, we missed being around other people," I said, without looking at Ty.

"And the mental stimulation," Ty added, without looking at me.

Even to my ears, our words sounded lame. Jim looked more puzzled than before.

*   *   *

At first we were going to get by with just one car. Then we realized that wouldn't work. Our offices were miles apart, and surely one of us would have a meeting somewhere when the other had the car.

It's amazing how friendly car salesmen can be when they hear you want to buy *two* cars. It's also remarkable how two reasonably intelligent people lose all common sense when standing on a showroom floor. Must be something chemical in that new car scent.

Having driven no faster than 6 knots in the previous six months, within two days of returning I found myself zipping around town in a shiny new silver convertible. The top-down part was my concession to giving up all that fresh air out on the water. The 300 horsepower engine would get the blood flowing on my way to and from the office.

Ty got a nice macho SUV. The Honda Civic we sold to go cruising had served us well, but boat owners need *cargo capacity*. And comfortable seats to drive back and forth to the boat on weekends...

The cars were big ticket items, but they were a drop in the bucket compared to buying a house inside the Washington beltway. Supply and demand had sent costs rocketing. It killed us to think that for the price of a 1950s bungalow, we could buy a huge waterfront spread three hours down the bay. With a dock for our boat, even. But our offices were in the city, not on the water.

Back and forth we drove, from Annapolis to Washington, to meet with our realtor. After two days of looking, we found a place. Knowing we were committed, I allowed myself to get excited, picturing where each piece of furniture would go after we got it out of storage. But I was torn, too. I'd lived just fine for nearly a year without all that *stuff*.

Yes, it would be nice to sit in front of the fireplace on a cold, winter day, but I wouldn't need that fireplace if we'd kept going to the Bahamas!

The whole time we were looking for houses, I sensed that Ty was just going through the motions. We both agreed buying was the smart thing to do, financially, but emotionally, I wasn't so sure. We'd be tied down for years with mortgage payments. As he wrote out the deposit check, both of us were tense and snappy.

I was happy to get in our sports car and drive back to Annapolis. Fumbling through my new purse I pulled out the wrong key. One week earlier I hadn't needed a purse and I didn't own a single key. Now I had the keys to two cars and would soon be adding house keys to the collection.

"I need a key chain," I mumbled.

"Where do you want to go?" Ty asked.

"Let's stop by the Naval Academy. I want to get something with 'Navy' on it."

"Roger that."

He deliberately drove in the back gate, the farthest point from where we wanted to go. I knew what he was up to. This way, we'd have to drive along the sea wall that ran the whole perimeter of the Academy. It had always been one of our favorite running routes, allowing us to daydream as we looked out at all the boats bobbing in the harbor.

We parked outside the Visitor's Center. While I ran inside to the gift shop, Ty wandered over to the water's edge. When I came out, he was gesturing excitedly. He hadn't been smiling a whole lot lately, and I couldn't imagine what had suddenly made him so perky. I followed his pointing finger to a boat anchored in the harbor and instantly recognized the familiar twin hulls. It was *Vagabond Tiger*! The last time we'd seen her was on the Bras d'Or Lake. I could still picture Frank and Dee standing on deck, wishing us farewell as we headed for Newfoundland.

I broke into a trot and stopped beside Ty. "I don't believe it! They're here? This is fantastic!"

As excited as I was, I cringed at the thought of telling our first good cruising friends that we were going back to work. Frank and Dee had been living this life for fourteen years. We hadn't lasted half a year and were throwing in the towel.

"Look! There's Dee!" Ty said excitedly.

Our shouting and arm-waving caught her attention. Soon she was heading over to us in the dinghy. Seeing her standing up surfer-style brought back a wave of pleasant memories. I laughed, hearing Frank booming "yeehah" as he zipped around the anchorage. It would be great to see them again, no matter how embarrassing our news.

"Frank must be ashore," I said. I recalled the first time we invited them to dinner. He'd been running errands in Baddeck, and Dee wouldn't give us an answer until she'd consulted with him.

We waved excitedly as she pulled up to the sea wall.

"Hey, Dee! Great to see you!" I shouted.

"Same here," she said.

"I couldn't believe it when I looked out there and saw your boat," Ty said. "You guys have to join us for dinner so we can catch up on what you've been up to!"

"If you want to wait and check with Frank, you can call us later," I added.

"I guess you guys haven't heard the news," Dee answered, looking uncomfortable. Something in her manner made me tense. She seemed subdued. I suddenly remembered Frank mentioning a history of heart problems. Could he be sick?

"We haven't heard anything," Ty said warily. "Did something happen?"

Nothing could have prepared us for her answer.

"Frank passed away three weeks ago," Dee said. "He's buried at Arlington Cemetery."

Twenty-Five
CRYSTAL BALL

Frank's death hit both of us hard. We hadn't known him well, but our cruising lifestyle and similar backgrounds helped to forge a close bond in a short time. The fact that Frank was only a few years older than Ty didn't sit well with either of us. Most of all, we were heartbroken for Dee, and sorry that we'd never get to know Frank any better.

If news of our friend's passing put us in a funk, everything else on the final leg of our cruise conspired to make us truly miserable.

The weather was so doggone nice on the trip up the Potomac it was disgusting. It was unseasonably warm. Warm enough to take down the plastic panels around the cockpit for the first time in months. It was almost shocking to feel the fresh air on our skin. Worse yet, there was enough of a breeze to actually sail, and for once it wasn't on the nose.

With the sails up, engine off, and enclosure down, the serenity seemed to mock us. A blissful sail was the last thing we needed. Where was the cold, wet weather when we needed it? Why couldn't we be rolling back and forth a little more?

No longer able to bear the pleasant swooshing of the waves past the hull, I went below. Restless and punchy, I threw myself into organizing the aft cabin.

Bad choice.

Pulling my summer clothes from my drawers, I felt even more sorry for myself. There were the bathing suits I'd bought just for cruising. It had been so cool up north, I'd never even put them on. And there was my favorite tank top, still lying at the bottom of the pile. It was November already. Where had summer gone?

Feeling cheated, I shoved the skimpy clothes in a plastic grocery bag and tied it tightly closed. In their place, I stuffed some wool sweaters and a pair of purple long johns. I stared at them with a lump in my throat the size of a rock. They probably didn't even know what long underwear looked like down in the Bahamas!

With any number of good anchorages at the mouth of the Potomac, we chose the West Yeocomico River. We'd never been there before, and it sounded pretty.

In fact, it was too darned pretty.

We dropped the hook in a peaceful little cove. Along the shoreline, the leaves cast a red and orange reflection on the perfectly still water. We threw on some PT gear and dinghied ashore for a quick run. Rather than energize me, the exercise dragged me down. Jogging along quiet country roads, past ever-changing scenery, I pictured myself going back to the same old running trails we'd worn ruts in over the past few years.

Arriving back at the dinghy, we crossed paths with a white-haired man who was walking his dog.

"Beautiful day!" Ty said, in true Newfie fashion.

"Indeed it is," the man said, flashing a friendly smile. "That your boat out there?"

"Yes, Sir."

"Looks mighty pretty. You two heading south?"

Ty glanced at me. "In fact, we're heading up the river to Washington. Going back to work."

"That's too bad," the man said. "Used to live there, myself. Left three years ago."

Then he proceeded to tell us about the high-powered job he gave up when the fast-paced life in the city got to be too much. He raved about the stress-free days he now enjoyed and how much more easy-going the people were out here in the country.

If he wasn't such a pleasant old guy, I would have gladly strangled him.

As we dinghied back to the boat, I was glum. Nevertheless, I couldn't help but comment on the beautiful lighting. The setting sun shed a warm, soft glow on everything around us. Thomas Kinkaid couldn't have painted a more perfect picture.

Climbing into the cockpit, a flash of color caught my eye. I looked up, and there - I kid you not - was a *rainbow*. It stretched all the way across the sky, from north to south, as if taunting us. There was no doubt in my mind that the pot of gold was sitting somewhere down around Grand Bahama Island.

I closed my eyes and shook my head. *What is this, God? Some kind of conspiracy?!*

I couldn't keep my mouth shut any longer.

"Ty, I said, "we're making a terrible mistake."

He nodded gravely. "I know."

Suspicions confirmed. He felt the same way I did. Barely able to breathe, I decided to voice the niggling thought that had been taking shape in the back of my mind over the past week.

"It's not too late to tell them we've decided not to take the jobs."

He rolled his eyes. "Yes, it is. We signed a contract."

It was all I could do not to whine. "I know. But there was no time limit. The offer specifically said they wouldn't keep anyone who didn't want to be there."

Ty shook his head and stared out at the water glumly. "We can't back out now. People are counting on us."

That was it, then. End of discussion. Of course, I knew he was right. We would look like fools if we changed our minds at this point. We could never ask anything of his colleagues again.

Unfortunately, his answer was exactly what I'd expected. But now it was even worse. Now, I knew for sure he didn't want to go through with this any more than I did.

After dinner, we figured I'd better call Dolly and let her know things were on track. She'd been wonderful these past two months, keeping in touch as we worked our way south and asking if there was anything we needed. I got through to her at home and told her we'd see her in four days. When she asked if I was excited about the first day of work, I forced myself to find the enthusiasm to say yes.

When I hung up the phone, Ty raised his eyebrows. I gave him a sheepish shrug. What was I supposed to say to her? That I was dreading Monday morning? It would probably work out fine. I'd enjoy the challenge. And heck, I'd get to wear my new clothes.

From the Yeocomico River, the trip up the Potomac took two more days. Nothing more was said about our decision. We arrived outside the city Friday evening. The Washington beltway was all that lay between us and the end of our cruising days. Just like the day we departed, the Woodrow Wilson drawbridge that spanned the river only opened from midnight to six AM. We opted to anchor just south of the bridge and go through first thing Saturday morning.

When the alarm went off at 0430, I didn't want to move. It had been ages since I'd gotten up to an alarm. Starting Monday, it would be a daily occurrence.

Suddenly, I realized I could lie there and be miserable, or I could look at things differently. Attitude was everything, and I was tired of all this negativity. I hopped out of bed, pulled on my clothes, and started going through our underway checklist. I tried to be upbeat with Ty, but he merely grunted in response to my cheerful comments.

Chalking up his grumpiness to the early hour, I decided to maintain my positive attitude. Surely it would rub off.

Unfortunately, it didn't. It was soon clear that no amount of coffee was going to improve Ty's mood.

I gave up. Who was I kidding? I was as depressed as he was.

Other than calling the bridge tender to request an opening, once we raised the anchor, neither of us spoke. When we'd gone through the drawbridge on our first day of cruising, we'd been so excited. We had so much to look forward to. Neither one of us had expected to be back this way again, especially so soon.

Being a Saturday morning, traffic was light on the beltway. Even so, it backed up quickly. Ty goosed the engine and we hustled through. I turned around and watched as the twin spans closed behind us like the heavy metal doors of a prison.

I felt utterly trapped. We were right back in the very place I couldn't wait to get away from.

Suddenly, I could see the next few years as if they were playing on a screen before my eyes. I saw us coming home from the office, day after endless day. Ty's face would be as empty and lifeless as it looked right now. He'd spend his free time surfing cruising web sites, growing ever more withdrawn and depressed over what could have been. We'd go sailing on weekends, but what would we have to look forward to?

The future held nothing but regrets.

My heart was pounding, my palms sweaty. My survival instinct kicked in. We could not go through with this plan!

But Ty had already told me how he felt. He said we were committed.

I kept my emotions under control while we pulled into our slip at the downtown marina. I helped with the lines, but was incapable of doing more. Ty was still not talking. I couldn't have spoken if I wanted to.

I stumbled below and threw myself on the aft bunk, face down. I couldn't face being back in this city.

I'm not normally a crier. It takes a lot to get me going. The day I'd seen the photo of Ranger Jones that started all this mess, I'd merely sniffled a little. But now, the flood gates opened and I sobbed until the blanket below me was wet with tears.

When I was all cried out, I sat up and rubbed at my swollen face. I had to talk to Ty. That's all there was to it. We weren't just making a terrible mistake. It was the worst mistake of our lives!

I tromped to the companionway just as he was coming down the ladder. I hated for him to see me like this, but I was desperate.

"Ty! We can't go through with this!"

He only stared at me, his face haggard.

"I know we'll look like fools," I blustered, "but we'd be even more foolish to give up our dreams!"

"I need something to eat," he said, as if he hadn't heard me. "Grab your coat. Let's go get some breakfast."

Was he crazy? I stormed into the head and looked in the mirror. My face was blotchy, my eyes unrecognizable. "I can't go out looking like this!" I said, stepping back into the main salon. "You go without me."

He snorted. "I'm not going without you, Suzanne. I'll wait 'til you're ready."

He sat down and stared at a cruising guide that was lying on the table.

I sank down across from him. This was it. The final argument before the jury. We were down to the wire, and I had to plead my case with everything I had. He already knew the facts. This was pure emotion, and I trembled when I spoke.

"I know we made an offer on the house, but we didn't sign a contract yet. We can get our deposit back. We can put the cars in storage. I'll put my clothes in storage, too. But if we walk into that office on Monday, that's it. It's over. We may never go cruising again."

He nodded his head. Sensing a crack in the wall, I pushed.

"What are you thinking?"

He looked down at the floor. "I feel like I failed."

His words took my breath away. Worst of all, I couldn't argue with him.

All along I'd had the sneaking suspicion we'd come back because of me. Over and over I'd questioned if he really wanted to go back to the same job he'd left. Now I had to be sure.

"What about all those reasons you gave for wanting to go back to work, like feeling lazy? Were you just saying that to make me feel better?"

He chewed on his lip. "I guess I was rationalizing. When you said you felt like a nobody, you really threw me for a loop."

I sighed and closed my eyes. When I opened them, I looked straight at him and said, "I know I'm somebody. And I don't need a job to prove it."

He reached across the table. "Are you *sure* you'll be happy not working?"

I thought of Dee. Suddenly alone, she was forced to put *Vagabond Tiger* up for sale. She was moving ashore and going back to work, too. Unlike us, though, she had no choice.

I squeezed his hand. "I'm sure."

Ty shook his head. "I can't stop thinking about Frank. He was only five years older than me."

I was painfully aware of that. "At least he died doing what he loved."

"Exactly," Ty said, with an intensity that told me he'd been having the same thought. He looked down and slowly traced a finger over the cover of the cruising guide. "You know what I keep asking myself?"

"What?"

He looked back up at me. "If I knew I only had a few more years to live, would I want to spend them sitting in a cubicle or out here cruising?"

And there it was. The real reason we'd landed back in Washington. We'd lost sight of what our dream was all about: living life to the fullest, as if each day were our last.

Over bacon, eggs, toast and juice, we sat in a diner and discussed all the people we had to call. They wouldn't be easy conversations, especially with Dave, Dolly, and the company president. Some would understand, others wouldn't. But it was our life, no one else's. We had to live our dream while we had the chance, or we might never have it again.

We paid the check and headed for a phone.

I'm sure Frank would say we made the right call.

EPILOGUE

Once we made the decision to go, we didn't just take in the dock lines and head back out. It took a full week to undo everything we'd put in place for our return to the working world. We had to find a place to keep the cars. And cancel the deal on the house. And make all those phone calls.

That was the hard part. I felt like a kid who'd done something wrong. The guilt hung over my head like a dark cloud. But each day, the stress eased bit by bit. As we headed back under the Woodrow Wilson Bridge, the sun finally peeked out.

"Suzanne," Ty said, "I don't ever want to go under that bridge again."

We exchanged a knowing look.

"You've got a deal."

Neither of us promised we'd never go back to work. Indeed, with two new cars, our money wouldn't last forever. I might get to wear all those snazzy clothes some day after all. But when we did look for jobs, it would be some place warm. Somewhere we could continue to live on the boat.

As we headed down the Potomac, we tried something new. Instead of taking the helm for an hour at a time, we stood two hour watches. The difference was astounding. The person who wasn't driving could relax more and finish what they started while off watch. Two hours at the helm was no big deal.

Our new TV was another revelation. We'd been purists before, unwilling to bring a boob tube aboard. Now able to keep up with national news, we no longer felt isolated. Local weather forecasts with full-color graphics were a huge improvement over the National Weather Service's voice recordings.

We looked forward to joining the snowbirds as we sailed for warmer waters. That's where we'd find the cruising community. The ducks were down south! And if we got lonely, or needed a break from the boat, we vowed to take a different kind of trip every once in a while. We'd visit family or catch a space-available military flight some place exotic. We'd go backpacking in the mountains or hiking in the desert.

So, we made a few adjustments, but one thing didn't change. The incredible sense of freedom I felt every day while cruising was still there. Over time, I'd gradually taken it for granted. Now, I shuddered to think how close I'd come to giving it up.

Throughout our cruise, I'd maintained a web site for family and friends. The home page included a quote I liked: "It's not the destination, but the journey that matters."

When I first posted it, I considered that quote my cruising motto. Now, looking at my life anew, I realized the words hadn't applied at all. For me, our trip to Newfoundland had been all about the destination. Sure, I loved the people and places along the way. But once we got there, I'd immediately started looking toward the next destination.

As we began Part Two of our cruising life, I underwent a monumental shift. I no longer cared when, or even *if*, we got to the Bahamas. I was just happy to be on *Liberty*, with the man I loved, enjoying every day for what it brought.

Having almost given up our freedom, I finally understood what the journey was all about.

Suzanne and Ty in the Abacos, Bahamas

Follow Suzanne and Ty on Liberty at www.libertysails.com.

GLOSSARY

Abeam	Toward the beam
Aft	At the stern
Astern	Toward the stern or beyond the stern
Backstay	Wire that supports the mast from behind
Beam	The side of a boat
Bow	The front of a boat
Bulkhead	Wall
CJCS	The Chairman of the Joint Chiefs of Staff
Coasties	Affectionate term for members of the Coast Guard
Companionway	The ladder leading from the cabin to the cockpit
Davits	Metal arms used to hoist and store a dinghy
Dinghy	Small boat that can be hoisted aboard or towed behind a larger boat
Dodger	Canvas and plastic windshield that protects the cockpit from wind and spray
Dragger	Commercial vessel that catches fish by dragging nets
EPIRB	Emergency Position Indicating Radio Beacon. Handheld locator device used to indicate the position of a vessel in distress
Fairway	A channel, as in a harbor or between piers in a marina
Forestay	Wire that supports the mast from the front
Foulies	Foul weather gear. Water-proof outerwear
Galley	Kitchen

GPS	Global Positioning System. While the term describes an entire system of satellites, also refers to a handheld or permanently installed device that gives a latitude and longitude position
Halyard	Rope/line used to raise or lower a sail
Hatch	Overhead opening
Head	Bathroom
Heel	Lean or roll to the side
Inclinometer	Device that shows the level of heel
Iron Genny	The engine (genny = genoa, large foresail)
Isobars	Lines on a weather map of equal barometric pressure
Jack Lines	Webbing which runs down both sides of the boat, used for attaching harness tethers to keep crew aboard
Line	Rope
Newfies	Affectionate term for Newfoundlanders
O-6	Military officer's rank. Navy Captain or Colonel in the Army, Air Force, or Marines
Painter	A line that attaches a dinghy to the boat or a pier
Port	Left side of a vessel when facing forward. Also a vessel's window
Pulpit	Stainless steel railing
PT	Physical Training. Exercise
Quarter	Section of a boat between abeam and astern
Rigging	Wires that hold up the mast and ropes that control the sails
Rip Rap	Rocks surrounding a navigational aid
Settee	Couch
Sheet	Rope/line used to control the shape of the sails
Shroud	Wire that supports the mast from the side
Spinnaker	A large, billowing foresail used in light winds
SSB	Single sideband radio. Long range, high frequency radio used for communications over very long distances
Starboard	Right side of a vessel when facing forward
Stern	The back of the boat
Tender	Small boat that can be hoisted aboard or towed behind a larger boat

Toe Rail	Wood or stainless steel railing along the outer deck edge
VHF	Short range radio for ship-to-ship and ship-to-shore communications
Waypoint	An intermediate or ultimate destination given as a latitude and longitude

Printed in the United States
98115LV00001B/81/A